Designs in Fiction

DESIGNS IN FICTION

DESIGNS IN NONFICTION

DESIGNS IN POETRY

DESIGNS IN DRAMA

Designs in Fiction

ELIZABETH SCHELD

Formerly, Chairman, English Department
Los Angeles High School
Los Angeles, California

MACMILLAN PUBLISHING COMPANY
NEW YORK

COLLIER MACMILLAN PUBLISHERS
LONDON

ACKNOWLEDGMENTS

For permission to use material in this book, grateful acknowledgment is made to the following:

Isaac Asimov: For "The Feeling of Power," by Isaac Asimov. Copyright 1957, by Quinn Publishing Co., Inc.

Brandt & Brandt: For "The Sea Devil," by Arthur Gordon. First published in *The Saturday Evening Post*. Copyright 1953 by The Curtis Publishing Company. For "One Ordinary Day, with Peanuts," by Shirley Jackson. First published in *The Magazine of Fantasy and Science Fiction*. Copyright 1954 by Fantasy House, Inc. For "By the Waters of Babylon," by Stephen Vincent Benét, from *Selected Works of Stephen Vincent Benét*, Holt, Rinehart & Winston, Inc. Copyright 1937, by Stephen Vincent Benét.

Jonathan Cape, Ltd.: For "The Sniper," from *Spring Sowing*, by Liam O'Flaherty.

Borden Deal and Southern Methodist University Press: For "Antaeus," by Borden Deal, from *Southwest Review*, Spring 1961. © 1961 by Southern Methodist University Press. Reprinted by permission of the publisher and the author.

Doubleday & Company, Inc.: For "A Visit to Grandmother," from the book, *Dancers on the Shore*, by William Melvin Kelley. Copyright © 1964 by William Melvin Kelley. Reprinted by permission of Doubleday & Company, Inc.

Esquire, Inc.: For "The Tiger's Heart," by Jim Kjelgaard. Reprinted from *Esquire*, April 1951; © 1951 by Esquire, Inc.

Harcourt Brace Jovanovich: For "Road to the Isles," by Jessamyn West. Copyright, 1948, by Jessamyn West. Originally published in *The New Yorker* and now included in *Cress Delahanty* by Jessamyn West. For "The Parsley Garden," from *The Assyrian and Other Stories*, by William Saroyan. Copyright, 1949, by William Saroyan. For "The Sniper," from *Spring Sowing*, by Liam O'Flaherty. All reprinted by permission of Harcourt Brace Jovanovich.

A. M. Heath & Company, Ltd.: For "Road to the Isles," from *Cress Delahanty*, by Jessamyn West.

Cover design by Jacqui Morgan.

Macmillan Publishing Company
866 Third Avenue, New York, New York 10022
Collier Macmillan Canada, Inc.
Printed in the United States of America
ISBN 0-02-194050-9
23 24 25 26 27 28   98 97 96 95 94

ACKNOWLEDGMENTS (*continued*)

Alfred A. Knopf, Inc.: For "Camus at Stockholm," by Albert Camus, translated by Justin O'Brien. Copyright © 1958 by Alfred A. Knopf, Inc. For "The Guest" from *Exile and the Kingdom*, by Albert Camus, translated by Justin O'Brien. Copyright © 1957, 1958 by Alfred A. Knopf, Inc. Reprinted by permission of the publisher.

Littauer and Wilkinson: For "Hit and Run," by John D. MacDonald. Copyright © 1962, The Curtis Publishing Company.

Harold Matson Company, Inc.: For "Luke Baldwin's Vow," by Morley Callaghan. Copyright 1948 by Morley Callaghan. Reprinted by permission of the Harold Matson Company, Inc.

Harold Ober Associates, Inc.: For "Water Never Hurt a Man," by Walter D. Edmonds. Copyright © 1930 by Walter D. Edmonds. Renewed. Reprinted by permission of Harold Ober Associates, Inc.

Laurence Pollinger Limited: For "The Parsley Garden," from *The Assyrian and Other Stories*, by William Saroyan.

Jesse Stuart: For "Spring Victory," from *Tales From the Plum Grove Hills*, by Jesse Stuart.

Helen Thurber: For "The Secret Life of Walter Mitty" from *My World—and Welcome to It*, by James Thurber, published by Harcourt Brace Jovanovich. Copyright © 1942 James Thurber. Copyright © 1970 Helen Thurber. Originally printed in *The New Yorker*.

The Viking Press, Inc., and McIntosh and Otis, Inc.: For "Molly Morgan," from *The Pastures of Heaven*, by John Steinbeck. Copyright 1932 by John Steinbeck.

Contents

The Sum of the Parts   175

Designs in Fiction

Reading the Short Story

Within each of us there is a storyteller. From the time we are old enough to use language fluently, we create stories. Sometimes these stories remain secret, locked inside our minds and never shared. Sometimes we share these stories by presenting them orally or in written form. In this volume, you will read short stories that have been created by skilled literary artists specifically to be shared with you, the reader. You will find these stories enjoyable to read, but as you read them you should also examine them to see how they have been constructed and to understand what makes them worthwhile.

First and foremost, a good story should be entertaining. It should interest you and draw you so completely into its web that you shut out the real world around you—the story becomes reality. The stories in this book can do this if you give them a chance. Arrange to read them without interruption in reasonably quiet surroundings.

The entertainment you will enjoy from these stories requires a certain amount of participation on your part. You should not merely let the story happen to you. While you will react emotionally to the characters and to what happens to them, you should also react thoughtfully to them. You must remember that the characters do not say and do just anything that comes into their minds. The author very skillfully manipulates them and shapes them to the requirements of his or her story while, at the same time, he or she makes them seem real.

None of the stories in this book were put together haphazardly. In each story the writer is doing much more than merely describing a series of incidents. The author is carefully creating the events and building upon them so that he or she can make a point. Furthermore, the author is telling you, sometimes directly, but often in very subtle ways, what these occurrences signify. As each event leads to the next, the story inevitably has certain outcomes. These outcomes are also not a matter of chance. They are made reasonable and believable by clues and foreshadowing. Circumstances which at first seemed trivial, later assume major importance. The writer artfully weaves all these elements into the fabric of his or her story.

As you read the stories in this volume, you will discover that a good stort story should be read with both imagination and thought. Certainly, you will appreciate and enjoy these stories to a much greater extent if you take the time to recognize the craft of the writers.

WHAT
HAPPENS
IN A
STORY

What Happens in a Story

In reading a good short story, one of the most frequent questions a person asks is: "What's going to happen next?" What happens in a story is called the *plot*. It is one of the basic elements in all fiction.

The plot is the series of closely related events which happen to the main character, or *protagonist*. As the initial situation develops, the main character finds himself entangled in a series of circumstances which are distressing, even dangerous. A struggle or *conflict* of some kind arises between the main character and his *antagonist*. The antagonist may be another person or persons; it may be Nature; or it may be the main character's environment. These are called *external conflicts*. Or the conflict may be between warring elements within the main character's mind, such as the struggle between honesty and greed. This is called an *internal conflict*.

The main character struggles to resolve the conflict. This struggle creates *suspense*. At times, he seems to be winning; then he seems to be yielding to his foe. The suspense mounts as the story moves toward the *climax*. At this point the action reaches its greatest emotional impact. With the climax, the outcome of the conflict is determined. The reader knows whether the protagonist will be victorious or go down in defeat. The suspense subsides, and in a brief conclusion, or *denouement*, the conflict is resolved and the story ends.

The plot of each story in this section is distinctive in its originality and in the dramatic way it is presented. In "The Sea Devil" by Arthur Gordon, the conflict is between the swimmers—but only one of them is a human being! The resolution of the conflict hinges on "five seconds or less" and on some "twenty inches of frayed rope."

In "The Sniper" Liam O'Flaherty reveals life at its most turbulent. The main character, a citizen-soldier with "the face of a student," needs his wits as well as his weapons. What happens at the end is important not only for its shock value, but also for what it says about war.

In "The Tell-Tale Heart" Edgar Allan Poe shows his remarkable genius for telling a gripping and grisly story. The conflict is a furious struggle between good and evil within the protagonist, and it reaches a point of almost unbearable intensity.

In "Hit and Run" John D. MacDonald uses dialogue to propel action and to heighten interest in the dramatic story of a special investigator tracking down the guilty person in a hit-and-run case.

Plot, then, plays a predominant role in these stories. Each, in its own way, will have you asking: "What's going to happen next? How will it turn out?" Finding out is part of the pleasure of reading these stories.

The Sea Devil

ARTHUR GORDON

When a man casts a net into the sea, he must not be surprised at what he brings up.

THE man came out of the house and stood quite still, listening. Behind him, the lights glowed in the cheerful room, the books were neat and orderly in their cases, the radio talked importantly to itself. In front of him, the bay stretched dark and silent, one of the countless lagoons that border the coast where Florida thrusts its great green thumb deep into the tropics.

It was late in September. The night was breathless; summer's dead hand still lay heavy on the land. The man moved forward six paces and stood on the sea wall. He dropped his cigarette and noted where the tiny spark hissed and went out. The tide was beginning to ebb.

Somewhere out in the blackness a mullet jumped and fell back with a sullen splash. Heavy with roe, they were jumping less often, now. They would not take a hook, but a practiced eye could see the swirls they made in the glassy water. In the dark of the moon, a skilled man with a cast net might take half a dozen in an hour's work. And a big mullet makes a meal for a family.

The man turned abruptly and went into the garage, where his cast net hung. He was in his late twenties, wide-shouldered and strong. He did not have to fish for a living, or even for food. He was a man who worked with his head, not with his hands. But he liked to go casting alone at night.

He liked the loneliness and the labor of it. He liked the clean taste of salt when he gripped the edge of the net with his teeth as a cast netter must. He liked the arching flight of sixteen pounds of lead and linen against the starlight, and the weltering crash of the net into the unsuspecting water. He liked the harsh tug of the retrieving rope

5

around his wrist, and the way the net came alive when the cast was true, and the thud of captured fish on the floor boards of the skiff.

He liked all that because he found in it a reality that seemed to be missing from his twentieth-century job and from his daily life. He liked being the hunter, skilled and solitary and elemental. There was no conscious cruelty in the way he felt. It was the way things had been in the beginning.

The man lifted the net down carefully and lowered it into a bucket. He put a paddle beside the bucket. Then he went into the house. When he came out, he was wearing swimming trunks and a pair of old tennis shoes. Nothing else.

The skiff, flat-bottomed, was moored off the sea wall. He would not go far, he told himself. Just to the tumbledown dock half a mile away. Mullet had a way of feeding around old pilings after dark. If he moved quietly, he might pick up two or three in one cast close to the dock. And maybe a couple of others on the way down or back.

He shoved off and stood motionless for a moment, letting his eyes grow accustomed to the dark. Somewhere out in the channel a porpoise blew with a sound like steam escaping. The man smiled a little; porpoises were his friends. Once, fishing in the Gulf he had seen the charter-boat captain reach overside and gaff a baby porpoise through the sinewy part of the tail. He had hoisted it aboard, had dropped it into the bait well, where it thrashed around, puzzled and unhappy. And the mother had swum alongside the boat and under the boat and around the boat, nudging the stout planking with her back, slapping it with her tail, until the man felt sorry for her and made the captain let the baby porpoise go.

He took the net from the bucket, slipped the noose in the retrieving rope over his wrist, pulled the slipknot tight. It was an old net, but still serviceable; he had rewoven the rents made by underwater snags. He coiled the thirty-foot rope carefully, making sure there were no kinks. A tangled rope, he knew, would spoil any cast.

The basic design of the net had not changed in three thousand years. It was a mesh circle with a diameter of fourteen feet. It measured close to fifteen yards around the circumference and could, if thrown perfectly, blanket a hundred and fifty square feet of sea water. In the center of this radial trap was a small iron collar where the retrieving rope met the twenty-three separate drawstrings leading to the outer rim of the net. Along this rim, spaced an inch and a half apart, were the heavy lead sinkers.

The man raised the iron collar until it was a foot above his head. The net hung soft and pliant and deadly. He shook it gently, making sure that the drawstrings were not tangled, that the sinkers were hanging true. Then he eased it down and picked up the paddle.

The night was black as a witch's cat; the stars looked fuzzy and dim. Down to the southward, the lights of a causeway made a yellow necklace across the sky. To the man's left were the tangled roots of a mangrove swamp; to his right, the open waters of the bay. Most of it was fairly shallow, but there were channels eight feet deep. The man could not see the old dock, but he knew where it was. He pulled the paddle quietly through the water, and the phosphorescence glowed and died.

For five minutes he paddled. Then, twenty feet ahead of the skiff, a mullet jumped. A big fish, close to three pounds. For a moment it hung in the still air, gleaming dully. Then it vanished. But the ripples marked the spot, and where there was one there were often others.

The man stood up quickly. He picked up the coiled rope, and with the same hand grasped the net at a point four feet below the iron collar. He raised the skirt to his mouth, gripped it strongly with his teeth. He slid his free hand as far as it would go down the circumference of the net so that he had three points of contact with the mass of cordage and metal. He made sure his feet were planted solidly. Then he waited, feeling the tension that is older than the human race, the fierce exhilaration of the hunter at the moment of ambush, the atavistic desire to capture and kill and ultimately consume.

A mullet swirled, ahead and to the left. The man swung the heavy net back, twisting his body and bending his knees so as to get more upward thrust. He shot it forward, letting go simultaneously with rope hand and with teeth, holding a fraction of a second longer with the other hand so as to give the net the necessary spin, impart the centrifugal force that would make it flare into a circle. The skiff ducked sideways, but he kept his balance. The net fell with a splash.

The man waited for five seconds. Then he began to retrieve it, pulling in a series of sharp jerks so that the drawstrings would gather the net inward, like a giant fist closing on this segment of the teeming sea. He felt the net quiver, and knew it was not empty. He swung it, dripping, over the gunwhale, saw the broad silver side of the mullet quivering, saw too the gleam of a smaller fish. He looked closely to make sure no sting ray was hidden in the mesh, then raised the iron collar and shook the net out. The mullet fell with a thud and flapped wildly. The other victim was an angel fish, beautifully marked, but too small to keep. The man picked it up gently and dropped it overboard. He coiled the rope, took up the paddle. He would cast no more until he came to the dock.

The skiff moved on. At last, ten feet apart, a pair of stakes rose up gauntly out of the night. Barnacle encrusted, they once had marked the approach from the main channel. The man guided the skiff between them, then put the paddle down softly. He stood up, reached for the net, tightened the noose around his wrist. From here he could drift down upon the dock. He could see it now, a ruined skeleton in the starshine. Beyond it a mullet jumped and fell back with a flat, liquid sound. The man raised the edge of the net, put it between his teeth. He would not cast at a single swirl, he decided; he would wait until he saw two or three close together. The skiff was barely moving. He felt his muscles tense themselves, awaiting the signal from the brain.

Behind him in the channel he heard the porpoise blow again, nearer now. He frowned in the darkness. If the porpoise chose to fish this area, the mullet would scatter and vanish. There was no time to lose.

A school of sardines surfaced suddenly, skittering along like drops of mercury. Something, perhaps the shadow of the skiff, had frightened them. The old dock loomed very close. A mullet broke water just too far away; then another, nearer. The man marked the spreading ripples and decided to wait no longer.

He swung back the net, heavier now that it was wet. He had to turn his head, but out of the corner of his eye he saw two swirls in the back water just off the starboard bow. They were about eight feet apart, and they had the sluggish oily look that marks the presence of something big just below the surface. His conscious mind had no time to function, but instinct told him that the net was wide enough to cover both swirls if he could alter the direction of his cast. He could not halt the swing, but he shifted his feet slightly and made the cast off balance. He saw the net shoot forward, flare into an oval, and drop just where he wanted it.

Then the sea exploded in his face. In a frenzy of spray, a great horned thing shot like a huge bat out of the water. The man saw the mesh of his net etched against the mottled blackness of its body and he knew, in the split second in which thought was still possible, that those twin swirls had been made not by two mullet, but by the wing tips of the giant ray of the Gulf Coast, *Manta birostris,* also known as clam cracker, devil ray, sea devil.

The man gave a hoarse cry. He tried to claw the slipknot off his wrist, but there was no time. The quarter-inch line snapped taut. He shot over the side of the skiff as if he had roped a runaway locomotive. He hit the water head first and seemed to bounce once. He plowed a blinding furrow for perhaps ten yards. Then the line went slack as the sea devil jumped again. It was not the full-grown manta of the deep Gulf, but it was close to nine feet from tip to tip and it weighed over a thousand pounds. Up into the air it went, pearl-colored underbelly gleaming as it twisted in a frantic effort to dislodge the clinging thing that had fallen upon it. Up into the starlight, a monstrous survival from the dawn of time.

The water was less than four feet deep. Sobbing and choking, the man struggled for a foothold on the slimy bottom. Sucking in great gulps of air, he fought to free himself from the rope. But the slipknot was jammed deep into his wrist; he might as well have tried to loosen a circle of steel.

The ray came down with a thunderous splash and drove forward again. The flexible net followed every movement, impeding it hardly at all. The man weighed a hundred and seventy-five pounds, and he was braced for the shock, and he had the desperate strength that comes from looking into the blank eyes of death. It was useless. His arm straightened out with a jerk that seemed to dislocate his shoulder; his feet shot out from under him; his head went under again. Now at last he knew how the fish must feel when the line tightens and drags him toward the alien element that is his doom. Now he knew.

Desperately he dug the fingers of his free hand into the ooze, felt them dredge a futile channel through broken shells and the ribbon-like sea grasses. He tried to raise his head, but could not get it clear. Torrents of spray choked him as the ray plunged toward deep water.

His eyes were of no use to him in the foam-streaked blackness. He closed them tight, and at once an insane sequence of pictures flashed through his mind. He saw his wife sitting in their living room, reading, waiting calmly for his return. He saw the mullet he had just caught, gasping its life away on the floor boards of the skiff. He saw the cigarette he had flung from the sea wall touch the water and expire with a tiny hiss. He saw all these things and many others simultaneously in his mind as his body fought silently and tenaciously for its existence. His hand touched something hard and closed on it in a death grip, but it was only the sharp-edged helmet of a horseshoe crab, and after an instant he let it go.

He had been under the water perhaps fifteen seconds now, and something in his brain told him quite calmly that he could last another forty or fifty and then the red flashes behind his eyes would merge into darkness, and the water would pour into his lungs in one sharp painful shock, and he would be finished.

This thought spurred him to a desperate effort. He reached up and caught his pinioned wrist with his free hand. He doubled up his knees to create more drag. He thrashed his body madly, like a fighting fish, from side to side. This did not disturb the ray, but now one of the great wings tore through the mesh, and the net slipped lower over the fins projecting like horns from below the nightmare head, and the sea devil jumped again.

And once more the man was able to get his feet on the bottom and his head above water, and he saw ahead of him the pair of ancient stakes that marked the approach to the channel. He knew that if he was dragged much beyond those stakes he would be in eight feet of water, and the ray would go down to hug the bottom as rays always do, and then no power on earth could save him. So in the moment of respite that was granted him, he flung himself toward them. For a moment he thought his captor yielded a bit. Then the ray moved off again, but more slowly now, and for a few yards the man was able to keep his feet on the bottom. Twice he hurled himself back against the rope with all his strength, hoping that something would break. But nothing broke. The mesh of the net was ripped and torn, þut the draw lines were strong, and the stout perimeter cord threaded through the sinkers was even stronger.

The man could feel nothing now in his trapped hand, it was numb; but the ray could feel the powerful lunges of the unknown thing that was trying to restrain it. It drove its great wings against the unyielding water and forged ahead, dragging the man and pushing a sullen wave in front of it.

The man had swung as far as he could toward the stakes. He plunged toward one and missed it by inches. His feet slipped and he went down on his knees. Then the ray swerved sharply and the second stake came right at him. He reached out with his free hand and caught it.

He caught it just above the surface, six or eight inches below high-water mark. He felt the razor-sharp barnacles bite into his hand, collapse under the pressure, drive their tiny slime-covered shell splinters deep into his flesh. He felt the pain, and he welcomed it, and he made his fingers into an iron claw that would hold until the tendons were severed or the skin was shredded from the bone. The ray felt the pressure increase with a jerk that stopped it dead in the water. For a moment all was still as the tremendous forces came into equilibrium.

Then the net slipped again, and the perimeter cord came down over the sea devil's eyes, blinding it momentarily. The great ray settled to the bottom and braced its wings against the mud and hurled itself forward and upward.

The stake was only a four-by-four of creosoted pine, and it was old. Ten thousand tides had swirled around it. Worms had bored; parasites had clung. Under the crust of barnacles it still had some heart left, but not enough. The man's grip was five feet above the floor of the bay; the leverage was too great. The stake snapped off at its base.

The ray lunged forward, dragging the man and the useless timber. The man had his lungs full of air, but when the stake snapped he thought of expelling the air and inhaling the water so as to have it finished quickly. He thought of this, but he did not do it. And then, just at the channel's edge, the ray met the porpoise coming in.

The porpoise had fed well this night and was in no hurry, but it was a methodical creature and it intended to make a sweep around the old dock before the tide dropped too low. It had no quarrel with any ray, but it feared no fish in the sea, and when the great black shadow came rushing blindly and unavoidably, it rolled fast and struck once with its massive horizontal tail.

The blow descended on the ray's flat body with a sound like a pistol shot. It would have broken a buffalo's back, and even the sea devil was half stunned. It veered wildly and turned back toward shallow water. It passed within ten feet of the man, face down in the water. It slowed and almost stopped, wing tips moving faintly, gathering strength for another rush.

The man had heard the tremendous slap of the great mammal's tail and the snorting gasp as it plunged away. He felt the line go slack again, and he raised his dripping face, and he reached for the bottom with his feet. He found it, but now the water was up to his neck. He plucked at the noose once more with his lacerated hand, but there was no strength in his fingers. He felt the tension come back into the line as the ray began to move again, and for half a second he was tempted to throw himself backward and fight as he had been doing, pitting his strength against the vastly superior strength of the brute.

But the acceptance of imminent death had done something to his brain. It had driven out the fear, and with the fear had gone the panic. He could think now, and he knew with absolute certainty that if he was to make any use of this last chance that had been given him, it would have to be based on the one faculty that had carried man to his pre-eminence above all beasts, the faculty of reason. Only by using his brain could he possibly survive, and he called on his brain for a solution, and his brain responded. It offered him one.

He did not know whether his body still had the strength to carry out the brain's commands, but he began to swim forward, toward the ray that was still moving hesitantly away from the channel. He swam forward, feeling the rope go slack as he gained on the creature.

Ahead of him he saw the one remaining stake, and he made himself swim faster until he was parallel with the ray and the rope trailed behind both of them in a deep U. He swam with a surge of desperate energy that came from nowhere so that he was slightly in the lead as they came to the stake. He passed on one side of it; the ray was on the other.

Then the man took one last deep breath, and he went down under the black water until he was sitting on the bottom of the bay. He put one foot over the line so that it passed under his bent knee. He drove both his heels into the mud, and he clutched the slimy grass with his bleeding hand, and he waited for the tension to come again.

The ray passed on the other side of the stake, moving faster now. The rope grew taut again, and it began to drag the man back toward the stake. He held his prisoned wrist close to the bottom, under his knee, and he prayed that the stake would not break. He felt the rope vibrate as the barnacles bit into it. He did not know whether the rope would crush the barnacles or whether the barnacles would cut the rope. All he knew was that in five seconds or less he would be dragged into the stake and cut to ribbons if he tried to hold on; or drowned if he didn't.

He felt himself sliding slowly, and then faster, and suddenly the ray made a great leap forward, and the rope burned around the base of the stake, and the man's foot hit it hard. He kicked himself backward with his remaining strength, and the rope parted and he was free.

He came slowly to the surface.

Thirty feet away the sea devil made one tremendous leap and disappeared into the darkness. The man raised his wrist and looked at the frayed length of rope dangling from it. Twenty inches, perhaps. He lifted his other hand and felt the hot blood start instantly, but he didn't care. He put this hand on the stake above the barnacles and held on to the good, rough, honest wood. He heard a strange noise, and realized that it was himself, sobbing.

High above, there was a droning sound, and looking up he saw the nightly plane from New Orleans inbound for Tampa. Calm and serene, it sailed, symbol of man's proud mastery over nature. Its lights winked red and green for a moment; then it was gone.

Slowly, painfully, the man began to move through the placid water. He came to the skiff at last and climbed into it. The mullet, still alive, slapped convulsively with its tail. The man reached down with his torn hand, picked up the mullet, let it go.

He began to work on the slip-knot doggedly with his teeth. His mind was almost a blank, but not quite. He knew one thing. He knew he would do no more casting alone at night. Not in the dark of the moon. No, not he.

Questions for discussion

1. How did the man in the story get into trouble? Was it by making mistakes? By breaking the law? By being careless? Was it something else?

2. Did the porpoise save the man's life? Support your answer by referring to the story.

3. What was the man struggling to do? What was the giant ray strug-

gling to do? Were the man and the ray fighting each other? If so, who do you believe won the fight?

4. "But the acceptance of imminent death had done something to his brain." What does this sentence mean? What has happened to the man's brain?

5. "The man raised his wrist and looked at the frayed length of rope . . . Twenty inches, perhaps." What is the significance of "Twenty inches, perhaps"?

6. How did the man react to his release from danger? Why did he put his hand on the stake (p. 13)? Why does the writer refer to the stake as "the good, rough, honest wood"?

7. Why did the man throw the mullet back into the water at the close of the story? Has he decided not to do any more fishing in the future?

8. Why does the writer introduce the paragraph about the airplane at the close of the story? Earlier, at the bottom of page 9, there is a paragraph about an "insane sequence of pictures" that flashed through the man's mind. What is the effect of this paragraph?

9. There is a kind of justice in the help that is given to the man by the porpoise. Why? What other experience had the man had with porpoises?

10. COINCIDENCE OR CHANCE. The struggle in a story, if the story is successful, must be settled in terms that you find satisfying and believable. If coincidence or chance settles the struggle, the story is hard to believe and not satisfying. In "The Sea Devil," is the action of the porpoise believable? Is its appearance a matter of chance? How has the author prepared you for the appearance of the porpoise?

11. POINT OF VIEW. A writer's *point of view* is the standpoint from which he tells his story. He may tell it through the eyes of an *outside observer*, putting down only those things that an observer would see or experience in the situation. Or, a writer may tell his story through an *all-knowing observer* who can move from place to place and can see into the hearts and minds of all the characters. (This is called the *omniscient* point of view.) A third way a writer may tell a story is from the point of view of one of the characters in the story; this character then serves as the narrator and talks *in the first person*. Which point of view does the author of "The Sea Devil" use? Support your answer by referring to the story.

12. What is the theme, or main idea, of "The Sea Devil"? How does the plot illustrate the theme? Why do you think the main character is nameless?

Vocabulary growth

VARIANT MEANINGS. Many words in common use have special and unusual meanings. One such word is *ray*, which in "The Sea Devil" refers to a fish. Another is the word *true*. On pages 5-6 you read, "He liked the harsh tug of the retrieving rope around his wrist, and the way the net came alive when the cast was *true* . . ." Can you figure out from the context of the sentence what the word *true* means as it is used here?

IMAGES. Words that appeal to the senses arouse pictures or images in the reader's mind. "The Sea Devil" is rich in its use of such words. For example, in the first page of the story the writer speaks of "*glassy* water," "*clean taste* of salt," "*harsh* tug of the retrieving rope." Look through the story again and pick out other examples of image-words.

FIGURES OF SPEECH. A figure of speech is a way of making a comparison. In some figures of speech, "like" and "as" appear. For example, ". . . a porpoise blew with a sound *like* steam escaping." In other figures, *like* does not appear, and one thing is spoken of as if it were another: ". . . Florida thrusts *its great green thumb* into the tropics." Florida does not have a thumb, but on the map it looks like a thumb. There is another example on the first page of the story: ". . . summer's *dead hand* still lay heavy on the land." Find other figures of speech in the story.

For composition

1. Write a brief account of the man's arrival at the house. Write it from the wife's point of view, and use dialogue. You might begin:

    "My husband had been out longer than usual, but it did not occur to me to worry, because he is very skillful with boats and fishing equipment. I had just turned off the radio, when I heard a strange noise, like someone crying . . ."

2. Assume that a newspaper reporter called the next morning. Write an account of the interview. If you prefer, write the news story that the reporter turned in. Your headline:

    "Local Man Cheats Death in Battle with Giant Ray"

3. The man in the story is very skillfully portrayed even though he is given no name. Make a list of his personality traits and characteristics. Give him a name and write a character sketch of him.

The Sniper

LIAM O'FLAHERTY

In the 1920's, civil war broke out in Ireland. The question was whether the country should be a Free State within the British Commonwealth, or a completely independent nation. Families were divided, and friend was set against friend. Property was destroyed and blood was shed.

The story below is set in these dark and troubled times. To the solitary sniper on the roof top it was all an exciting game until—

THE long June twilight faded into night. Dublin lay enveloped in darkness, but for the dim light of the moon, that shone through fleecy clouds, casting a pale light as of approaching dawn over the streets and the dark waters of the Liffey. Around the beleaguered Four Courts the heavy guns roared. Here and there through the city machine guns and rifles broke the silence of the night, spasmodically, like dogs barking on lone farms. Republicans and Free Staters were waging civil war.

On a rooftop near O'Connell Bridge, a Republican sniper lay watching. Beside him lay his rifle and over his shoulders were slung a pair of field-glasses. His face was the face of a student—thin and ascetic, but his eyes had the cold gleam of the fanatic. They were deep and thoughtful, the eyes of a man, who is used to look at death.

He was eating a sandwich hungrily. He had eaten nothing since morning. He had been too excited to eat. He finished the sandwich, and taking a flask of whiskey from his pocket, he took a short draught. Then he returned the flask to his pocket. He paused for a moment, considering whether he should risk a smoke. It was dangerous. The flash might be seen in the darkness and there were enemies watching. He decided to take the risk. Placing a cigarette between his lips, he struck a match, inhaled the smoke hurriedly and put out the light. Almost immediately, a bullet flattened itself against the parapet

16

of the roof. The sniper took another whiff and put out the cigarette. Then he swore softly and crawled away to the left.

Cautiously he raised himself and peered over the parapet. There was a flash and a bullet whizzed over his head. He dropped immediately. He had seen the flash. It came from the opposite side of the street.

He rolled over the roof to a chimney stack in the rear, and slowly drew himself up behind it, until his eyes were level with the top of the parapet. There was nothing to be seen—just the dim outline of the opposite housetop against the blue sky. His enemy was under cover.

Just then an armoured car came across the bridge and advanced slowly up the street. It stopped on the opposite side of the street fifty yards ahead. The sniper could hear the dull panting of the motor. His heart beat faster. It was an enemy car. He wanted to fire, but he knew it was useless. His bullets would never pierce the steel that covered the grey monster.

Then round the corner of a side street came an old woman, her head covered by a tattered shawl. She began to talk to the man in the turret of the car. She was pointing to the roof where the sniper lay. An informer.

The turret opened. A man's head and shoulders appeared, looking towards the sniper. The sniper raised his rifle and fired. The head fell heavily on the turret wall. The woman darted toward the side street. The sniper fired again. The woman whirled round and fell with a shriek into the gutter.

Suddenly from the opposite roof a shot rang out and the sniper dropped his rifle with a curse. The rifle clattered to the roof. The sniper thought the noise would wake the dead. He stooped to pick the rifle up. He couldn't lift it. His forearm was dead. "I'm hit," he muttered.

Dropping flat on to the roof, he crawled back to the parapet. With his left hand he felt the injured right forearm. The blood was oozing through the sleeve of his coat. There was no pain—just a deadened sensation, as if the arm had been cut off.

Quickly he drew his knife from his pocket, opened it on the breastwork of the parapet and ripped open the sleeve. There was a small hole where the bullet had entered. On the other side there was no hole. The bullet had lodged in the bone. It must have fractured it. He bent the arm below the wound. The arm bent back easily. He ground his teeth to overcome the pain.

Then, taking out his field dressing, he ripped open the packet with his knife. He broke the neck of the iodine bottle and let the bitter fluid drip into the wound. A paroxysm of pain swept through him. He placed the cotton wadding over the wound and wrapped the dressing over it. He tied the end with his teeth.

Then he lay still against the parapet, and closing his eyes, he made an effort of will to overcome the pain.

In the street beneath all was still. The armoured car had retired speedily over the bridge, with the machine gunner's head hanging lifeless over the turret. The woman's corpse lay still in the gutter.

The sniper lay for a long time nursing his wounded arm and planning escape. Morning must not find him wounded on the roof. The enemy on the opposite roof covered his escape. He must kill that enemy and he could not use his rifle. He had only a revolver to do it. Then he thought of a plan.

Taking off his cap, he placed it over the muzzle of his rifle. Then he pushed the rifle slowly upwards over the parapet, until the cap was visible from the opposite side of the street. Almost immediately there was a report, and a bullet pierced the center of the cap. The sniper slanted the rifle forward. The cap slipped down into the street. Then, catching the rifle in the middle, the sniper dropped his left hand over the roof and let it hang, lifelessly. After a few moments he let the rifle drop to the street. Then he sank to the roof, dragging his hand with him.

Crawling quickly to the left, he peered up at the corner of the roof. His ruse had succeeded. The other sniper, seeing the cap and rifle fall, thought that he had killed his man. He was now standing before a row of chimney pots, looking across, with his head clearly silhouetted against the western sky.

The Republican sniper smiled and lifted his revolver above the edge of the parapet. The distance was about fifty yards—a hard shot in the dim light, and his right arm was paining him like a thousand devils. He took a steady aim. His hand trembled with eagerness. Pressing his lips together, he took a deep breath through his nostrils and fired. He was almost deafened with the report and his arm shook with the recoil.

Then, when the smoke cleared, he peered across and uttered a cry of joy. His enemy had been hit. He was reeling over the parapet in his death agony. He struggled to keep his feet, but he was slowly falling forward, as if in a dream. The rifle fell from his grasp, hit the parapet, fell over, bounded off the pole of a barber's shop beneath and then cluttered on to the pavement.

Then the dying man on the roof crumpled up and fell forward. The body turned over and over in space and hit the ground with a dull thud. Then it lay still.

The sniper looked at his enemy falling and he shuddered. The lust of battle died in him. He became bitten by remorse. The sweat stood out in beads on his forehead. Weakened by his wound and the long summer day of fasting and watching on the roof, he revolted from the sight of the shattered mass of his dead enemy. His teeth chattered. He began to gibber to himself, cursing the war, cursing himself, cursing everybody.

He looked at the smoking revolver in his hand and with an oath he hurled it to the roof at his feet. The revolver went off with the concussion, and the bullet whizzed past the sniper's head. He was frightened back to his senses by the shock. His nerves steadied. The cloud of fear scattered from his mind and he laughed.

Taking the whiskey flask from his pocket, he emptied it at a draught. He felt reckless under the influence of the spirits. He decided to leave the roof and look for his company commander to report. Everywhere around was quiet. There was not much danger in going through the streets. He picked up his revolver and put it in his pocket. Then he crawled down through the skylight to the house underneath.

When the sniper reached the laneway on the street level, he felt a sudden curiosity as to the identity of the enemy sniper whom he had killed. He decided that he was a good shot whoever he was. He wondered if he knew him. Perhaps he had been in his own company before the split in the army. He decided to risk going over to have a look at him. He peered around the corner into O'Connell Street. In the upper part of the street there was heavy firing, but around here all was quiet.

The sniper darted across the street. A machine gun tore up the ground around him with a hail of bullets, but he escaped. He threw himself face downwards beside the corpse. The machine gun stopped.

Then the sniper turned over the dead body and looked into his brother's face.

Questions for discussion

1. There is a sharp contrast between the killing of the sniper's first two victims and the killing of the "enemy" on the roof top across the way. Did you see it? What is the difference between the duel with this "enemy" and the killing of the old woman in the street? What is there about a sniper's job that seems revolting?

2. What sort of man was the sniper at the start of the story? Reread the paragraphs down to, "Then he thought of a plan." What do these items disclose:

    a. The look in his eyes.

    b. Killing an old woman in cold blood.

    c. The dressing of his wounded arm.

3. What was the effect upon the sniper of his success in killing the enemy across the roof tops? He suddenly began hating something. What was it?

4. The sniper's reaction after his victory showed the kinds of psychological effects war can have on a man. Describe his reaction.

5. The sniper did not give a second thought to the old woman, or to the man in the armored car. Why was he so curious about the other sniper? Why did he go out into the street to look at him? Does this suggest a reason for his earlier remorse for having killed the man?

6. RESOLUTION OF THE PLOT. Notice how the author resolves the plot in a final, single sentence. In writing a story with a surprise ending, an author must prepare the reader in advance; otherwise, the ending can seem unreasonable and unconvincing. Do you think the author of "The Sniper" prepared you for the ending? Does the end of the story seem reasonable? Why or why not?

7. IRONY. Irony may be defined as a combination of circumstances that is the opposite of what is appropriate or expected. For example, it would be ironical if a fire engine were destroyed by fire. What is the irony of this story? What do you think the author is trying to say through this ironical ending?

Vocabulary growth

WORDS ARE INTERESTING. It is interesting to speculate about the history of some words. A word such as *ascetic*, for instance, has an interesting background. It means "self-denying" or "austere," and it comes from a Greek word meaning "to exercise, or to train as an athlete does." Today people think of an *ascetic* as one who denies himself pleasures and comforts for religious reasons. Athletes in training have to deny themselves certain things in order to stay in condition. Ascetics and athletes thus have something in common.

A *beleaguered* city is one that is surrounded by enemy forces. The *league* part of the word comes from a Latin word meaning "camp." In short, when a military force camps around a city to prevent anyone from entering or leaving, that city is *beleaguered*.

WORD PARTS. The prefix *para-* has many different meanings, one of which is "to guard" or "protect." It has this meaning in *parapet*. The *pet* part of the word comes from an Italian word *petto*, meaning "breast." In military affairs a parapet is a structure that protects the soldier's breast from enemy fire. What other meaning does parapet have? Consult your dictionary. Find two other common words in which *para-* also means "protect."

For composition

1. What happened to the sniper? Did he go back to report to his company commander? Did he leave the army? Write two paragraphs in the same style as the story to describe what finally happens to the sniper.

2. Assume that the sniper has quit the war. He is writing a letter of explanation to his former company commander. He begins, "I make no apology. I have had enough of war. No man has given more to the cause . . ." Write the rest of the report.

The Tell-Tale Heart

EDGAR ALLAN POE

The man denies that he is insane. He offers proof. Can you believe
him?

TRUE! nervous—very, very dreadfully nervous I had been and am;
but why *will* you say that I am mad? The disease had sharpened my
senses—not destroyed—not dulled them. Above all was the sense of
hearing acute. I heard all things in the heaven and in the earth.
I heard many things in hell. How, then, am I mad? Hearken! and
observe how healthily—how calmly I can tell you the whole story.

It is impossible to say how first the idea entered my brain; but
once conceived, it haunted me day and night. Object there was none.
Passion there was none. I loved the old man. He had never wronged
me. He had never given me insult. For his gold I had no desire.
I think it was his eye! yes, it was this! He had the eye of a vulture
—a pale blue eye, with a film over it. Whenever it fell upon me, my
blood ran cold; and so by degrees—very gradually—I made up my
mind to take the life of the old man, and thus rid myself of the eye
forever.

Now this is the point. You fancy me mad. Madmen know nothing. But you should have seen *me*. You should have seen how wisely
I proceeded—with what caution—with what foresight—with what
dissimulation I went to work! I was never kinder to the old man than
during the whole week before I killed him. And every night, about
midnight, I turned the latch of his door and opened it—ah, so gently!
And then, when I had made an opening sufficient for my head, I put
in a dark lantern, all closed, closed, so that no light shone out, and
then I thrust in my head. Oh, you would have laughed to see how
cunningly I thrust it in! I moved it slowly—very, very slowly, so that
I might not disturb the old man's sleep. It took me an hour to place

my whole head within the opening so far that I could see him as he lay upon his bed. Ha!—would a madman have been so wise as this? And then, when my head was well in the room, I undid the lantern cautiously—oh, so cautiously—cautiously (for the hinges creaked) —I undid it just so much that a single thin ray fell upon the vulture eye. And this I did for seven long nights—every night just at midnight—but I found the eye always closed; and so it was impossible to do the work; for it was not the old man who vexed me, but his Evil Eye. And every morning, when the day broke, I went boldly into the chamber, and spoke courageously to him, calling him by name in a hearty tone, and inquiring how he had passed the night. So you see he would have been a very profound old man, indeed, to suspect that every night, just at twelve, I looked in upon him while he slept.

Upon the eighth night I was more than usually cautious in opening the door. A watch's minute hand moves more quickly than did mine. Never, before that night, had I *felt* the extent of my own powers—of my sagacity. I could scarcely contain my feelings of triumph. To think that there I was, opening the door, little by little, and he not even to dream of my secret deeds or thoughts. I fairly chuckled at the idea; and perhaps he heard me; for he moved on the bed suddenly, as if startled. Now you may think that I drew back —but no. His room was as black as pitch with the thick darkness (for the shutters were close fastened, through fear of robbers), and so I knew that he could not see the opening of the door, and I kept pushing it on steadily, steadily.

I had my head in, and was about to open the lantern, when my thumb slipped upon the tin fastening, and the old man sprang up in bed, crying out, "Who's there?"

I kept quite still and said nothing. For a whole hour I did not move a muscle, and in the meantime I did not hear him lie down. He was still sitting up in the bed listening—just as I have done, night after night, hearkening to the death watches in the wall.

Presently I heard a slight groan, and I knew it was the groan of mortal terror. It was not a groan of pain or of grief—oh, no!—it was the low stifled sound that arises from the bottom of the soul when overcharged with awe. I knew the sound well. Many a night, just at midnight, when all the world slept, it has welled up from my own bosom, deepening, with its dreadful echo, the terrors that distracted me. I say I knew it well. I knew what the old man felt, and pitied him, although I chuckled at heart. I knew that he had been lying awake ever since the first slight noise, when he had turned in his bed. His fears had been ever since growing upon him. He had been trying to fancy them causeless, but could not. He had been saying to himself—"It is nothing but the wind in the chimney—it is only a mouse crossing the floor," or "It is merely a cricket which has made a single chirp." Yes, he had been trying to comfort himself with these suppositions: but he had found all in vain. *All in vain*; because Death, in approaching him, had stalked with his black shadow before him, and enveloped the victim. And it was the mournful influence of the unperceived shadow that caused him to feel—although he neither saw nor heard—to *feel* the presence of my head within the room.

When I had waited a long time, very patiently, without hearing him lie down, I resolved to open a little—a very, very little crevice in the lantern. So I opened it—you cannot imagine how stealthily, stealthily—until at length a single dim ray, like the thread of the spider, shot from out the crevice and fell upon the vulture eye.

It was open—wide, wide open—and I grew furious as I gazed upon it. I saw it with perfect distinctiveness—all a dull blue, with a hideous veil over it that chilled the very marrow in my bones; but I could see nothing else of the old man's face or person; for I had directed the ray as if by instinct, precisely upon the damned spot.

And have I not told you that what you mistake for madness is but overacuteness of the senses?—Now, I say, there came to my ears a low, dull, quick sound, such as a watch makes when enveloped in cotton. I knew *that* sound well, too. It was the beating of the old man's heart. It increased my fury, as the beating of a drum stimulates the soldier into courage.

But even yet I refrained and kept still. I scarcely breathed. I held the lantern motionless. I tried how steadily I could maintain the ray upon the eye. Meantime the hellish tattoo of the heart increased. It grew quicker and quicker, and louder and louder every instant. The old man's terror *must* have been extreme! It grew louder, I say, louder every moment!—do you mark me well? I have told you that I am nervous: so I am. And now at the dead hour of the night, amid the dreadful silence of that old house, so strange a noise as this excited me to uncontrollable terror. Yet, for some minutes longer I refrained and stood still. But the beating grew louder, louder!

I thought the heart must burst. And now a new anxiety seized me —the sound would be heard by a neighbor! The old man's hour had come! With a loud yell, I threw open the lantern and leaped into the room. He shrieked once—once only. In an instant I dragged him to the floor, and pulled the heavy bed over him. I then smiled gaily, to find the deed so far done. But, for many minutes, the heart beat on with a muffled sound. This, however, did not vex me; it would not be heard through the wall. At length it ceased. The old man was dead. I removed the bed and examined the corpse. Yes, he was stone, stone dead. I placed my hand upon the heart and held it there many minutes. There was no pulsation. He was stone dead. His eye would trouble me no more.

If still you think me mad, you will think so no longer when I describe the wise precautions I took for the concealment of the body. The night waned, and I worked hastily, but in silence. First of all I dismembered the corpse. I cut off the head and the arms and the legs.

I then took up three planks from the flooring of the chamber, and deposited all between the scantlings. I then replaced the boards so cleverly, so cunningly, that no human eye—not even *his*—could have detected anything wrong. There was nothing to wash out—no stain of any kind—no blood spot whatever. I had been too wary for that. A tub had caught all—ha! ha!

When I had made an end of these labors, it was four o'clock— still dark as midnight. As the bell sounded the hour, there came a knocking at the street door. I went down to open it with a light heart —for what had I *now* to fear? There entered three men, who introduced themselves, with perfect suavity, as officers of the police. A shriek had been heard by a neighbor during the night; suspicion of foul play had been aroused; information had been lodged at the police office, and they (the officers) had been deputed to search the premises.

I smiled—for *what* had I to fear? I bade the gentlemen welcome. The shriek, I said, was my own in a dream. The old man, I mentioned, was absent in the country. I took my visitors all over the house. I bade them search—search *well*. I led them, at length, to *his* chamber. I showed them his treasures, secure, undisturbed. In the enthusiasm of my confidence, I brought chairs into the room, and desired them *here* to rest from their fatigues, while I myself, in the wild audacity of my perfect triumph, placed my own seat upon the very spot beneath which reposed the corpse of the victim.

The officers were satisfied. My *manner* had convinced them. I was singularly at ease. They sat, and while I answered cheerily, they chatted of familiar things. But, erelong, I felt myself getting pale and wished them gone. My head ached, and I fancied a ringing in my ears: but still they sat and still chatted. The ringing became more distinct—it continued and became more distinct; I talked more freely to get rid of the feeling; but it continued and gained definiteness—until, at length, I found that the noise was *not* within my ears.

No doubt I now grew *very* pale—but I talked more fluently, and with a heightened voice. Yet the sound increased—and what could I do? It was *a low, dull, quick sound—much such a sound as a watch makes when enveloped in cotton.* I gasped for breath—and yet the officers heard it not. I talked more quickly—more vehemently; but the noise steadily increased. I arose and argued about trifles, in a high key and with violent gesticulations; but the noise steadily increased. Why *would* they not be gone? I paced the floor to and fro with heavy strides, as if excited to fury by the observations of the men—but the noise steadily increased. Oh, God! what *could* I do? I foamed—I raved—I swore! I swung the chair upon which I had been sitting, and grated it upon the boards, but the noise arose over all and continually increased. It grew louder—louder—*louder!* And still the men chatted pleasantly, and smiled. Was it possible they heard not? Almighty God!—no, no! They heard!—they suspected!— they *knew!*—they were making a mockery of my horror!—this I thought, and this I think. But anything was better than this agony! Anything was more tolerable than this derision! I could bear those hypocritical smiles no longer! I felt that I must scream or die! and now—again!—hark! louder! louder! louder! *louder!*

"Villains!" I shrieked, "dissemble no more! I admit the deed! —tear up the planks! here, here!—it is the beating of his hideous heart!"

Questions for discussion

1. Although the narrator of the story admitted that he was nervous, he insisted that he was not insane. Reread the first two paragraphs. Do you believe him? Why or why not?

2. MOOD. The mood of a story is the feeling or frame of mind which the story creates in the reader. For most readers, the mood of "A Tell-Tale Heart" is one of rising horror. One of the ways in which Poe created this mood of horror was by using graphic details—details which made the horrible seem real. What was horrifying about Poe's descriptions of the evil eye, the midnight ritual, and the concealment of the body?
3. Poe intensified the mood of horror by using contrast. How did each of the following contrast?
   a. The narrator's daytime attitude toward the old man and his night-time attitude toward the old man.
   b. The narrator's feelings toward the old man on the night of the murder.
   c. The narrator's manner in the last scene of the story and the officers' manner.
4. Poe further emphasized the mood of horror in the last scene by making you believe that the narrator could hear the beating heart. How did Poe do this?
5. Think back to your answer to question 1. Did you become more convinced of the narrator's *sanity* or *insanity* as the story developed? Why?
6. What was the "tell-tale" heart? Was it the narrator's own heart beating? Was it his pulse throbbing in his temples? Was it his watch ticking? Was it a hallucination resulting from insanity and guilt? Give reasons to support your answer.

Vocabulary growth

WORDS ARE INTERESTING. Did you notice the interesting words in this story?

vex. This comes from a Latin word meaning "to shake or agitate." Today *vex* means "to make trouble for; disturb; annoy." Do you see how the old Latin meaning carries over into modern usage?

hearty. You will find it interesting to note how many words and phrases are based upon names of parts of the body: *head, hand, foot, face,* etc. You know the functions of the suffix *-y.* Do you know these expressions: *break one's heart, do one's heart good, eat one's heart out, have a heart, wear one's heart?* Are you sure you know what they mean? Now look up the meaning of *hearty* in your dictionary.

agony. This word goes back to ancient Greek times. In those days an *agonia* was a contest for victory. See how the word is used in the sixth line from the last in this story.

wane. This word goes back a thousand years to an Anglo-Saxon word meaning "to decrease, grow less." *Wane* is closely related to the word *want.* The opposite, or antonym, of *wane* is *wax.* If *wane* means "to grow less," what does *wax* mean? Curiously enough, *wax* is closely related to *waist,* which is the part of the body between the ribs and the hips. No doubt the word *waist* was invented by some middle-aged gentleman who observed sadly the effect of much good food upon his figure.

WORD PARTS. The suffixes *-ful* and *-ous* are used to make adjectives from nouns. They add meaning to the words in which they appear: *full of, having the qualities of, pertaining to.* You see these suffixes in *cautious, nervous, dreadful,* on pages 22–23. Work out the meaning of these words, using the meanings of the suffixes. Look for other words on the same pages with these suffixes.

For composition

1. This story is told in the first person. Rewrite the first two paragraphs in the third person to see how it changes. You might begin:

   "True! nervous—very, very dreadfully nervous he had been and is; but why *will* you say he is mad? The disease had sharpened his senses . . ."

2. Write the report turned in by the policeman which recounts his experiences from the moment he received the neighbor's call about a shriek in the dark.

3. Everyone has had moments of great anguish. This anguish may have been caused by any number of things—embarrassment, fear, anxiety, or sorrow, to name just a few. Write a paragraph in which you attempt to describe your feelings during such an experience.

4. Drug addiction is a source of true horror stories. If you have enough information, you might wish to discuss the agony involved in such situations.

Hit and Run

JOHN D. MacDONALD

A repair and repaint job on a front fender caught the eye of Investigator Walter Post. It was an important clue, but would it lead him to the hit-and-run driver he had been tracking down for a month?

Twenty-eight days after the woman died, Walter Post, special investigator for the Traffic Division, squatted on his heels in a big parking lot and ran his fingertips lightly along the front-right fender of the car which had killed her. It was a blue and gray four-door sedan, three years old, in the lower price range.

The repair job had probably been done in haste and panic. But it had been competently done. The blue paint was an almost perfect match. Some of it had got on the chrome stripping and had been wiped off, but not perfectly. The chrome headlight ring was a replacement, with none of the minute pits and rust flecks of the ring on the left headlight. He reached up into the fender well and brushed his fingers along the area where the undercoating had been flattened when the fender had been hammered out.

He stood up and looked toward the big insurance-company office building, large windows and aluminum panels glinting in the morning sun, and wondered where Mr. Wade Addams was, which window was his. A vice president, high up, looking down upon the world.

It had been a long hunt. Walter Post had examined many automobiles. The killing had occurred on a rainy Tuesday morning in September at 9:30, in the 1200 block of Harding Avenue. It was an old street of big elms and frame houses. It ran north and south. Residents in the new suburban areas south of the city used Harding Avenue in preference to Wright Boulevard when they drove to the center of the city. Harding Avenue had been resurfaced a year ago. There were few traffic lights. The people who lived on Harding Avenue had complained about fast traffic before Mary Berris was killed.

Mr. and Mrs. Steve Berris and their two small children had lived at 1237 Harding Avenue. He was the assistant manager of a supermarket. On that rainy morning she had put on her plastic rain cape to hurry across the street, apparently to see a neighbor on some errand. It was evident she had not intended to be gone long, as her two small children were left untended. The only witness was a thirteen-year-old girl, walking from her home to the bus stop.

Through careful and repeated interrogations of that girl after she had quieted down, authorities were able to determine that the street had been momentarily empty of traffic, that the death car had been proceeding toward the center of town at a high rate of speed, that Mary Berris had started to cross from right to left in front of the car, hurrying. Apparently, when she realized she had misjudged the speed and distance of the car, she had turned and tried to scamper back to the protection of the curb.

Walter Post guessed that the driver, assuming the young woman would continue across, had swerved to the right to go behind her. When she had turned back, the driver had hit the brakes. There were wet leaves on the smooth asphalt. The car had skidded. Mary Berris was struck and thrown an estimated twenty feet through the air, landing close to the curb. The car had swayed out of its skid and then accelerated.

The child had not seen the driver of the car. She said it was a pale car, a gray or blue, not a big car and not shiny new. Almost too late she realized she should look at the license number. But by then it was so far away that she could only tell that it was not an out-of-state license and that it ended, in her words, "in two fat numbers. Not sharp numbers like ones and sevens and fours. Fat ones, like sixes and eights and nines."

Mary Berris lived for nearly seventy hours with serious brain injuries, ugly contusions and abrasions and a fractured hip. She lived long enough for significant bruises to form, indicating from their shape and placement that the vehicle had struck her a glancing blow on the right hip and thigh, the curve of the bumper striking her right leg just below the knee. The fragments of glass from the lens of the shattered sealed-beam headlamp indicated three possible makes of automobile. No shellac or enamel was recovered from her clothing. It was believed that, owing to the glancing impact, the vehicle had not been seriously damaged. She did not regain consciousness before death.

For the first two weeks of the investigation Walter Post had the assistance of sufficient manpower to cover all places where repairs could have been made. The newspapers cooperated. Everyone in the metropolitan area was urged to look for the death car. But, as in so many other instances, the car seemed to disappear without a trace. Walter Post was finally left alone to continue the investigation, in addition to his other duties.

And, this time, he devoted more time to it than he planned. It seemed more personal. This was not a case of one walking drunk lurching into the night path of a driving drunk. This was a case of a young, pretty housewife—very pretty, according to the picture of her he had seen—mortally injured on a rainy Tuesday by somebody who had been in a hurry, somebody too callous to stop and clever enough to hide. He had talked to the broken husband and seen the small, puzzled kids, and heard the child witness say, "It made a terrible noise. A kind of—thick noise. And then she just went flying in the air, all loose in the air. And the car tried to go away so fast the wheels were spinning."

Walter Post would awaken in the night and think about Mary Berris and feel a familiar anger. This was his work, and he knew the cost of it and realized his own emotional involvement made him better at what he did. But this was a very small comfort in the bitter mood of the wakeful night. And he knew there would be no joy in solving the case because he would find at the end of his search not some monster, some symbol of evil, but merely another victim, a trembling human animal.

His wife Carolyn endured this time of his involvement as she had those which had gone before, knowing the cause of his remoteness, his brutal schedule of self-assigned work hours. Until this time of compulsion was ended, she and the children would live with—and rarely see—a weary man who kept pushing himself to the limit of his energy, who returned and ate and slept and went out again.

Operating on the assumption that the killer was a resident of the suburban areas south of the city, he had driven the area until he was able to block off one large section where, if you wanted to drive down into the center of the city, Harding Avenue was the most efficient route to take. With the cooperation of the clerks at the State Bureau of Motor Vehicle Registration, he compiled a discouragingly long list of all medium and low-priced sedans from one to four years old registered in the name of persons living in his chosen area, where the license numbers ended in 99, 98, 89, 88, 96, 69, 86, 68 and 66. He hoped he would not have to expand it to include threes and fives, which could also have given that impression of "fatness," in spite of the child witness's belief that the numbers were not threes or fives.

With his list of addresses he continued the slow process of elimination. He could not eliminate the darker or brighter colors until he was certain the entire car had not been repainted. He worked with a feeling of weary urgency, suspecting the killer would feel more at ease once the death car was traded in. He lost weight. He accomplished his other duties in an acceptable manner.

At nine on this bright October tenth, a Friday, just twenty-eight days and a few hours after Mary Berris had died, he had checked the residence of a Mr. Wade Addams. It was a long and impressive house on a wide curve of Saylor Lane. A slim, dark woman of about forty answered the door. She wore slacks and a sweater. Her features were too strong for prettiness, and her manner and expression were pleasant and confident.

"Yes?"

He smiled and said, "I just want to take up a few moments of your time. Are you Mrs. Addams?"

"Yes, but really, if you're selling something, I just—"

He took out his notebook. "This is a survey financed by the automotive industry. People think we're trying to sell cars, but we're not. This is a survey about how cars are used."

She laughed. "I can tell you one thing. There aren't enough cars in this family. My husband drives to work. We have a son, eighteen, in his last year of high school, and a daughter, fourteen, who needs a lot of taxi service. The big car is in for repairs, and today my husband took the little car to work. So you can see how empty the garage is. If Gary's marks are good at midyear, Wade is going to get him a car of his own."

"Could I have the make and year and model and color of your two cars, Mrs. Addams?"

She gave him the information on the big car first. And then she told him the make of the smaller car and said, "It's three years old. A four-door sedan. Blue and gray."

"Who usually drives it, Mrs. Addams?"

"It's supposed to be mine, but my husband and Gary and I all drive it. So I'm always the one who has it when it runs out of gas. I *never* can remember to take a look at the gauge."

"What does your husband do, Mrs. Addams?"

"He's a vice president at Surety Insurance."

"How long has your boy been driving?"

"Since it was legal. Don't they all? A junior license when he was sixteen, and his senior license last July when he turned eighteen. It makes me nervous, but what can you do? Gary is really quite a reliable boy. I shudder to think of what will happen when Nancy can drive. She's a scatterbrain. All you can do is depend on those young reflexes, I guess."

He closed his notebook. "Thanks a lot, Mrs. Addams. Beautiful place you have here."

"Thank you." She smiled at him. "I guess the automobile people are in a tizzy, trying to decide whether to make big cars or little cars."

"It's a problem," he said. "Thanks for your cooperation."

He had planned to check two more registrations in that immediate area. But he had a hunch about the Addams's car. Obviously Mrs. Addams hadn't been driving. He had seen too many of the guilty ones react. They had been living in terror. When questioned, they broke quickly and completely. Any questions always brought on the unmistakable guilt reactions of the amateur criminal.

So he had driven back into the city, shown his credentials to the guard at the gate of the executive parking area of the Surety Insurance Company and inspected the blue-gray car with the license that ended in 89.

He walked slowly back to his own car and stood beside it, thinking, a tall man in his thirties, dark, big-boned, a man with a thoughtful, slow-moving manner. The damage to the Addams car could be coincidence. But he was certain he had located the car. The old man or the boy had done it. Probably the boy. The public schools hadn't opened until the fifteenth.

He thought of the big job and the fine home and the pleasant, attractive woman. It was going to blow up that family as if you stuck a bomb under it. It would be hell, but not one tenth, one hundredth the hell Steve Berris was undergoing.

He went over his facts and assumptions. The Addamses lived in the right area to use Harding Avenue as the fast route to town. The car had been damaged not long ago in precisely the way he had guessed it would be. It fitted the limited description given.

He went into the big building. The information center in the lobby sent him up to the twelfth-floor receptionist. He told her his name, said he did not have an appointment but did not care to state his business. She raised a skeptical eyebrow, phoned Addams's secretary and asked him to wait a few minutes. He sat in a deep chair amid an efficient hush. Sometimes, when a door opened, he could hear a chattering drone of tabulating equipment.

Twenty minutes later a man walked quickly into the reception room. He was in his middle forties, a trim balding man with heavy glasses, a nervous manner and a weathered golfing tan. Walter stood as he approached.

"Mr. Post? I'm Wade Addams. I can spare a few minutes."

"You might want to make it more than a few minutes, Mr. Addams."

"I don't follow you."

"When and how did you bash in the front-right fender of your car down there in the lot?"

Addams stared at him. "If that fender is bashed in, Mr. Post, it happened since I parked it there this morning."

"It has been bashed in and repaired."

"That's nonsense!"

"Why don't we go down and take a look at it?" He kept his voice low.

Wade Addams was visibly irritated. "You'd better state your business in a—a less cryptic way, Mr. Post. I certainly have more to do than go down and stare at the fender on my own car."

"Do you happen to remember that hit-and-run on Harding Avenue? Mary Berris?"

"Of course I rem—" Wade Addams suddenly stopped talking. He stared beyond Post, frowning into the distance. "Surely you can't have any idea that—" He paused again, and Post saw his throat work as he swallowed. "This is some mistake."

"Let's go down and look at the fender."

Addams told the receptionist to tell his secretary he was leaving the building for a few moments. They went down to the lot. Post pointed out the unmistakable clues. There was a gleam of perspiration on Addams's forehead and upper lip. "I never noticed this. Not at all. My gosh, you don't look this carefully at a car."

"You have no knowledge of this fender's being bashed since you've owned the car?"

"Let's go back to my office, Mr. Post."

Addams had a big corner office, impressively furnished. Once they were alone, and Addams was seated behind his desk, he seemed better able to bring himself under control.

"Why have you—picked that car?"

Post explained the logic of his search and told of the subterfuge he had used with Mrs. Addams.

"Janet would know nothing about—"

"I know that, from talking to her."

"My wife is incapable of deceit. She considers it her great social handicap," he said, trying to smile.

"You didn't kill that woman either."

"No, I—"

"We're thinking of the same thing, Mr. Addams."

Addams got up quickly and walked restlessly over to the window. He turned suddenly, with a wide, confident smile. "Damn stupid of me, Mr. Post. I remember now. Completely slipped my mind. I drove that car over to Mercer last July. I—uh—skidded on a gravel road and had it fixed in a little country garage . . . hit it against a fence post when I went in the ditch."

Walter Post looked at him and shook his head slowly. "It won't work."

"I swear it's—"

"Mr. Addams, this is not a misdemeanor. In this state a hit-and-run killing is a mandatory murder charge. Second degree. The only way out of it is a valid insanity plea. In either case the criminal has to spend plenty of time locked up. You'd have to prove the date of the trip, show police officers exactly where you skidded, take them to the country garage, find people to back up the story. No, Mr. Addams. Not even a good try."

Addams went behind his desk and sat down heavily. "I don't know what to do. Get hold of a lawyer, I guess. All of a sudden I'm a hundred years old. I want to make myself believe that Gary bashed a fender and had it repaired on his own so he wouldn't lose his driving privilege."

"Why can't you believe that?"

"He has—changed, Mr. Post. In the last month. The teenage years are strange, murky years, if what I remember of my own is any clue. He's a huge youngster, Mr. Post. They all seem to grow so big lately. I've had trouble with him. The normal amount. If a kid doesn't have a streak of rebellion against authority in him—authority as represented by his male parent—then he isn't worth a damn. Gary has been a sunny type, usually. Reliable. Honest. He's traveled with a nice pack of kids. He's a pretty fair athlete and a B student. His contemporaries seem to like and respect him. Here's his picture. Taken last June."

Crew cut and a broad smiling face, a pleasant, rugged-looking boy, a good-looking kid.

"He's changed. Janet and I have discussed it, and we've tried to talk to him, but he won't talk. He's sour and moody and gloomy. Off his feed. He doesn't seem interested in dates or athletics or his studies. He spends a lot of time in his room with the door closed. He grunts at us and barks at his sister. We thought it was a phase and have hoped it would end soon. We've wondered if he's in some kind of trouble that he can't or won't tell us about."

"I appreciate your being so frank, Mr. Addams."

"I can't, in my heart, believe him capable of this. But I've read about all the polite, decent, popular kids from good homes who have got into unspeakable trouble. You know—you can live with them and not understand them at all."

"Were you here in the office on the ninth?"

"Yes, if it was a weekday."

"What time did you get in?"

Addams looked back in his appointment calendar. "A Tuesday. I'd called a section meeting for nine. I was in at eight-thirty, earlier than usual. I can't believe Gary—"

"A kid can panic, Mr. Addams. A good kid can panic just as quick as a bad kid. And once you run, it's too late to go back. Maybe he loaned the car to some other kid. Maybe your wife loaned it."

Addams looked across the desk at Walter Post, a gleam of hope apparent. "It's against orders for him to let any of his friends drive it. But it could have happened that way."

"That's what we have to find out, Mr. Addams."

"Can we—talk to my boy? Can we go together and talk to Gary?"

"Of course."

Wade Addams phoned the high school. He said he would be out in twenty minutes to speak to his son on a matter of importance, and he would appreciate their informing him and providing a place where they could talk privately.

When they arrived at the high school, they went to the administration office and were directed to a small conference room. Gary Addams was waiting for them and stood up when they came in and closed the door. He was big. He had a completely closed expression, watchful eyes.

"What's up, dad? I phoned the house to find out, but mom didn't know a thing. I guess I just got her worried."

Wade Addams said, "I was going to let Mr. Post here ask you some questions, Gary, but with his permission I think I would like to ask you myself."

Walter Post had to admire the man. The answers he would get would very probably shatter a good life and, unless the kid was one in ten thousand, his future would be ruined beyond repair. Yet Wade Addams was under control.

"Go ahead," Post said.

"You have acted strange for a month, Gary. You know that. Your mother and I have spoken to you. Now I'm desperately afraid I know what has been wrong."

"Do you?" the boy said with an almost insolent indifference.

"Will you sit down?"

"I'd just as soon stand, thanks."

Wade Addams sighed. "You'd better tell us about the front-right fender on the small car, Gary. You'd better tell us the whole thing."

Post saw the flicker of alarm in the boy's light-colored eyes as he glanced sideways at Post. He had hunted a killer, and now he felt sick at heart, as in all the times that had gone before.

"You better clue me, dad. That question is far out."

"Did you repair it yourself? Were you driving or was one of your friends driving when you hit that woman? Does that—clue you enough?" he asked bitterly.

The boy stiffened and stared at his father with a wild, naked astonishment. "No!" the boy said in an almost inaudible voice. "You couldn't possibly—you couldn't be trying to—"

"To what? I'm ordering you to tell me about that fender."

The boy changed visibly in a way Walter Post had seen once before and would always remember. It takes a curious variety of shock to induce that look of boneless lethargy. Once, at a major fire, he had seen a man who believed his whole family had perished, had seen that man confronted by his family. There was the same look of heavy, brooding wonder.

Gary Addams slid heavily into one of the wooden armchairs at the small conference table. He looked at the scarred table and said in a dull voice, "I'll tell you about that fender. The fourteenth of September was a Sunday. You can look it up. You and mom had gone to the club. Nancy was off someplace. School started the next day. I played tennis. I got back about four in the afternoon, dad. I decided to wash the car. I hadn't washed it in two weeks, and I figured you'd start to give me a hard time about it any day. That was when I found out somebody had bashed the right fender and had it fixed since the last time I'd washed it. You wash a car, and you can spot something like that right away."

"But, Gary, you didn't say anything."

"If anybody'd been home, I'd have gone right in and asked who clobbered the fender. You know, like a joke. But there wasn't anybody home. And it—it kept coming into my mind. About that woman." Wade Addams had moved to stand beside his son. The boy looked up at him with a dull agony. "Dad, I just couldn't stop thinking about it. We always go down Harding Avenue. Our car matches the description. And if—if you or mom had bashed a fender in some kind of harmless way, you wouldn't have kept it a secret. I couldn't imagine you or mom doing such a terrible thing, but I kept thinking about it, and it got worse and worse. I thought I was going to throw up. And ever since then, I haven't known what to—"

"Where were you on the day that woman was hit, son?" Walter Post asked.

The boy frowned at him. "Where was I? Oh, a guy picked me up real early, about dawn, and a bunch of us went up to his folks' place at the lake and swam and skied all day and got back late."

Wade Addams spoke to his son in a strange voice. "Let me get this straight. For the last month, Gary, you've been living with the idea that either your mother or I could have killed that woman and driven away?" Walter Post could see how strongly the man's hand was grasping the boy's shoulder.

"But nobody else ever drives the car!" the boy cried. "Nobody else."

Walter Post watched Wade Addams's face and saw the fierce indignation of the falsely accused change to a sudden understanding of what the boy had been enduring. In a trembling voice Wade Addams said, "We didn't do it, boy. Neither of us. Not one of the three of us. Believe me, son. You can come out of your nightmare. You can come home again."

When the boy began to cry, to sob in the hoarse clumsy way of the man-child years, Walter Post stepped quietly out into the corridor and closed the door and leaned against the wall and smoked a cigarette, tasting his own gladness, a depth of satisfaction he had never before experienced in this deadly occupation. It made him yearn for some kind of work where this could happen more often. And he now knew the probable answer to the killing.

When Addams and his son came out of the room, they had an identical look of pride and exhaustion. The boy shook hands with Post and went back to class.

"Now we go to your house and talk to your wife," Walter Post said. "We were too quick to think it was the boy. We should have talked to her first."

"I'm glad we did it just this way, Mr. Post. Very glad. About the car. I think now I can guess what—"

"Let's let your wife confirm it."

At 3:30 that afternoon Walter Post sat in the small office of Stewart Partchman, owner of Partchman Motors. With him were Partchman and a redheaded service manager named Finnigan and a mechanic named Dawes.

Finnigan was saying, "The reason I didn't let Thompson go, Mr. Partchman, is that he's always been a reliable little guy, and this is the first time he goofs. Dawes drove him out there to bring back the Addams job, around nine o'clock, and figured Thompson was following him right on back into town, and Thompson doesn't show up with the car until after lunch. He had some story about his wife being sick and stopping by his house to see how she was."

Partchman said angrily, "So it gave him time to take it someplace and hammer that fender out, then come back here and sneak the headlamp and chrome ring out of stock and get some paint onto it."

"It was in for a tune-up," Finnigan said, looking at the service sheet on the job, "new muffler, lube and oil change. It got in so late we couldn't deliver it back out there until the next day. I remember apologizing to Mrs. Addams over the phone. I didn't tell her why it was late. She was pretty decent about it."

The mechanic said, "Tommy has been jumpy lately. He's been making mistakes."

"How do you want to handle it?" Partchman asked Walter Post.

"Bring him in here right now, and everybody stay here and keep quiet and let me do the talking," Post said wearily.

Thompson was brought in, small, pallid, worried. His restless eyes kept glancing quickly at Post. Post let the silence become long and heavy after Thompson asked what was wanted of him. At last he said, "How did you feel during those three days, while you were wondering whether she was going to die?"

Thompson stared at him and moistened his lips. He started twice to speak. The tears began to run down his smudged cheeks. "I felt terrible," he whispered. "I felt just plain terrible." And he ground his fists into his eyes like a guilty child.

Walter Post took him in and turned him over to the experts from the Homicide Section and accomplished his share of the paperwork. He was home by six o'clock. He told Carolyn about it that evening, when he was lethargic with emotional reaction to the case. He talked to her about trying to get into some other line of investigatory work and tried to explain his reasons to her.

But they woke him up at three in the morning and told him to go out to River Road. He got there before the lab truck. He squatted in a floodlighted ditch and looked at the broken old body of a bearded vagrant and at the smear of green automotive enamel ground into the fabric of a shabby coat. He straightened up slowly, bemused by his own ready acceptance of the fact it was not yet time to leave this work. Somebody was driving in a personal terror through the misty night, in a car so significantly damaged it would wear—for Walter Post—the signs and stains of a sudden murder.

Questions for discussion

FLASHBACK. The structure of this plot is quite unlike that of the others you have read so far. The first three paragraphs occur on the afternoon of October 10. Then the forward movement of the plot is interrupted by a *flashback*; that is, by incidents which occurred before the opening of the story. This shift in time is made through the first sentence in the fourth paragraph, "It had been a long hunt."

Through this flashback, the author supplies the *exposition*, or information, you need to know. You learn about the details of the fatal accident, about the investigator's attitude toward his work, and about the information he has gathered. The flashback proceeds through the morning of October 10 and Investigator Post's call at the Addams' residence. Finally, you reach the point in the plot about the fender, which is where the story began. From there, the author proceeds chronologically, building to the climax and resolution of the plot.

1. Which person did Investigator Post suspect of having been the hit-and-run driver? What reasons did he have for his suspicion?
2. From the interview between Investigator Post and Mr. Wade Addams, what kind of person would you say Mr. Addams was? Give evidence to support your opinion.
3. What evidence made it reasonable for Mr. Addams to suspect Gary? What evidence caused him to have some doubts?
4. Point out details that built up a feeling of suspense in the scene between Mr. Addams and his son. What was your impression of Gary at the beginning of the scene? How did this impression change?
5. Do you think the denouement was satisfactory or too swift? Explain.
6. Go back to the point early in the story where the accident is described. List the factors that caused the accident. Do you feel that the author's use of the coincidence was natural and convincing or was it contrived and unconvincing? Explain.
7. What was Mr. Post's character? Was he hard and cold or sensitive and sympathetic toward the people with whom he was dealing? Support your answers with reference to the story.

Vocabulary growth

It is useful to have a large vocabulary, not just to impress your friends, but to understand more of what other people and books are saying. Vocabulary growth does not just happen, like measles or mumps. Vocabulary grows only through exercise—in your speech and writing and in your reading.

CONTEXT. How do you exercise your vocabulary in reading? There is one simple direction to follow: *When you come to a new word, try to figure out what it means.* Don't ignore it. Two things will help you: a knowledge of word parts and an understanding of context. The *context* of a word is the other words with which it is used. Let's see how context works to reveal meaning. On page 32 you find this sentence: "He worked with a feeling of weary urgency, suspecting the killer would feel more at ease once the death car was traded in." Just what is a feeling of *urgency?* You have often met the word *urge.* Someone will urge you to hurry so you won't be late. Pressure of necessity is suggested. *Urgent* is another form of the word. The sentence on page 32 suggests that Walter Post felt that he simply had to get information quickly if he was going to solve the case.

How about *lethargy?* On page 38 you find, "It takes a curious variety of shock to induce that look of boneless *lethargy.*" With the word boneless, it is clear that lethargy cannot mean vitally alive and alert. Perhaps you already are familiar with the word *lethal* as in "The fighter dealt a *lethal* blow to his opponent." And so you can come quite close to a good understanding of new words without stopping your reading at some tense point in the story.

For composition

1. Assume that you are a press reporter sent out to interview Walter Post. Write an account of this interview as it would appear in your newspaper.
2. Thompson's reputation with his employer was a good one. Apparently he was not a reckless, careless sort of person. Write an account of his confession that attempts to explain his side of the case.
3. Write an editorial dealing with the need for safe driving. Emphasize the ever-present hazard of the unexpected. Include also your ideas on the dangers of speeding. Be specific where possible to make your editorial forceful.

THE
PEOPLE
IN A
STORY

The People in a Story

From the stories you have read so far, it is clear that for a plot to exist, it must have *characters*, or people created by the author. Although these people are fictional, they must be believable and arouse your sympathy or interest if the story is to hold your attention.

Every author, in his own particular way, uses certain techniques to bring his characters to life. He may describe the appearance and personality of a character through direct statement. This method describes the character, but does not usually render him fully alive in the reader's mind.

Another way in which an author creates a character is by telling what other characters say about him, how they react to him, and what they think of him. But the most important and dramatic way of creating a memorable character is by *showing* him in action—being brave or selfish, kind or foolish—and revealing the man's state of mind—his questions and dilemmas, how he thinks and feels.

All three techniques may be used to create a character, but the final test is whether the character is true to life. He may be strange or eccentric, but he must be a recognizable human being who resembles us in some way. To be convincing, a character must have an interesting combination of strength and weakness, good and bad.

To be believable, a character must fit in with the part of the world in which he lives. A cowboy from Wyoming should not speak like a Harvard professor; a Harvard professor should not dress like a sea captain. Further, a timid character should not suddenly become a hero unless the author has prepared the reader for this change. Otherwise the character is inconsistent.

In the stories in this next section, you will meet characters who are worth knowing as individuals. You will participate in their lives for a little while. Although they are all different, they are human beings who may remind you of yourself and people you know.

James Thurber humorously portrays the secret and exciting world inside Walter Mitty.

Pepe Garcia, in "The Tiger's Heart," is regarded as a most confident man, but even he has his moments of fear. The real Pepe is presented through both his external and internal conflicts.

Cress Delahanty, in "The Road to the Isles," is a typically imaginative teenager with "problem" parents. She makes some important discoveries about people.

Finally, in "Luke Baldwin's Vow," you will meet a boy who finds that decisions are not easy to make when loyalty to a friend is involved.

The Secret Life of Walter Mitty

JAMES THURBER

There is adventure in the life of an airplane pilot, in the life of a surgeon, in the trial experiences of a criminal lawyer. Here is a story of adventure—with a difference.

"WE'RE going through!" The Commander's voice was like thin ice breaking. He wore his full-dress uniform, with the heavily braided white cap pulled down rakishly over one cold gray eye. "We can't make it, sir. It's spoiling for a hurricane, if you ask me." "I'm not asking you, Lieutenant Berg," said the Commander. "Throw on the power lights! Rev her up to 8,500! We're going through!" The pounding of the cylinders increased: ta-pocketa-pocketa-pocketa-*pocketa-pocketa*. The Commander stared at the ice forming on the pilot window. He walked over and twisted a row of complicated dials. "Switch on No. 8 auxiliary!" he shouted. "Switch on No. 8 auxiliary!" repeated Lieutenant Berg. "Full strength in No. 3 turret!" shouted the Commander. "Full strength in No. 3 turret!" The crew, bending to their various tasks in the huge, hurtling eight-engined Navy hydroplane, looked at each other and grinned. "The Old Man'll get us through," they said to one another. "The Old Man ain't afraid of Hell!" . . .

"Not so fast! You're driving too fast!" said Mrs. Mitty. "What are you driving so fast for?"

"Hmm?" said Walter Mitty. He looked at his wife, in the seat beside him, with shocked astonishment. She seemed grossly unfamiliar, like a strange woman who had yelled at him in a crowd. "You were up to fifty-five," she said. "You know I don't like to go more than forty. You were up to fifty-five." Walter Mitty drove on toward Waterbury in silence, the roaring of the SN202 through the worst storm in twenty years of Navy flying fading in the remote, intimate

47

airways of his mind. "You're tensed up again," said Mrs. Mitty. "It's one of your days. I wish you'd let Dr. Renshaw look you over."

Walter Mitty stopped the car in front of the building where his wife went to have her hair done. "Remember to get those overshoes while I'm having my hair done," she said. "I don't need overshoes," said Mitty. She put her mirror back into her bag. "We've been through that," she said, getting out of the car. "You're not a young man any longer." He raced the engine a little. "Why don't you wear your gloves? Have you lost your gloves?" Walter Mitty reached in a pocket and brought out the gloves. He put them on, but after she had turned and gone into the building and he had driven on to a red light, he took them off again. "Pick it up, brother!" snapped a cop as the light changed, and Mitty hastily pulled on his gloves and lurched ahead. He drove around the streets aimlessly for a time, and then he drove past the hospital on his way to the parking lot.

. . . "It's the millionaire banker, Wellington McMillan," said the pretty nurse. "Yes?" said Walter Mitty, removing his gloves slowly. "Who has the case?" "Dr. Renshaw and Dr. Benbow, but there are two specialists here, Dr. Remington from New York and Dr. Pritch-ard-Mitford from London. He flew over." A door opened down a long, cool corridor and Dr. Renshaw came out. He looked distraught and haggard. "Hello, Mitty," he said. "We're having the devil's own time with McMillan, the millionaire banker and close personal friend of Roosevelt. Obstreosis of the ductal tract. Tertiary. Wish you'd take a look at him." "Glad to," said Mitty.

In the operating room there were whispered introductions: "Dr. Remington, Dr. Mitty. Dr. Pritchard-Mitford, Dr. Mitty." "I've read your book on streptothricosis," said Pritchard-Mitford, shaking hands. "A brilliant performance, sir." "Thank you," said Walter Mitty. "Didn't know you were in the states, Mitty," grumbled Remington. "Coals to Newcastle, bringing Mitford and me up here for a tertiary." "You are very kind," said Mitty. A huge, complicated machine, connected to the operating table, with many tubes and wires, began at this moment to go pocketa-pocketa-pocketa. "The new anaesthetizer is giving away!" shouted an intern. "There is no one in the East who knows how to fix it!" "Quiet, man!" said Mitty, in a low, cool voice. He sprang to the machine, which was now going pocketa-pocketa-queep-pocketa-queep. He began fingering delicately a row of glistening dials. "Give me a fountain pen!" he snapped. Someone handed him a fountain pen. He pulled a faulty piston out of the machine and inserted the pen in its place. "That will hold for ten minutes," he said. "Get on with the operation." A nurse hurried over and whispered to Renshaw, and Mitty saw the man turn pale. "Coreopsis has set in," said Renshaw nervously. "If you would take over, Mitty?" Mitty looked at him and at the craven figure of Benbow, who drank, and at the grave, uncertain faces of the two great specialists. "If you wish," he said. They slipped a white gown on him; he adjusted a mask and drew on thin gloves; nurses handed him shining . . .

"Back it up, Mac! Look out for that Buick!" Walter Mitty jammed on the brakes. "Wrong lane, Mac," said the parking-lot attendant, looking at Mitty closely. "Gee. Yeh," muttered Mitty. He began cautiously to back out of the lane marked "Exit Only." "Leave her sit there," said the attendant. "I'll put her away." Mitty got out of the car. "Hey, better leave the key." "Oh," said Mitty, handing the man the ignition key. The attendant vaulted into the car, backed it up with insolent skill, and put it where it belonged.

They're so darn cocky, thought Walter Mitty, walking along Main Street; they think they know everything. Once he had tried to take his chains off, outside New Milford, and he had got them wound around the axles. A man had had to come out in a wrecking car and unwind them, a young, grinning garageman. Since then Mrs. Mitty always made him drive to a garage to have the chains taken off. The next time, he thought, I'll wear my right arm in a sling; they won't grin at me then. I'll have my right arm in a sling and they'll see I couldn't possibly take the chains off myself. He kicked at the slush on the sidewalk. "Overshoes," he said to himself and he began looking for a shoe store.

When he came out into the street again, with the overshoes in a box under his arm, Walter Mitty began to wonder what the other thing was his wife had told him to get. She had told him twice before they set out from their house for Waterbury. In a way he hated these weekly trips to town—he was always getting something wrong. Kleenex, he thought. Squibb's, razor blades? No. Toothpaste, toothbrush, bicarbonate, carborundum, initiative and referendum? He gave it up. But she would remember it. "Where's the what's-its-name?" she would ask. "Don't tell me you forgot the what's-its-name." A newsboy went by shouting something about the Waterbury trial.

. . . "Perhaps this will refresh your memory." The District Attorney suddenly thrust a heavy automatic at the quiet figure on the witness stand. "Have you ever seen this before?" Walter Mitty took the gun and examined it expertly. "This is my Webley-Vickers 50.80," he said calmly. An excited buzz ran around the courtroom. The Judge rapped for order. "You are a crack shot with any sort of firearms, I believe?" said the District Attorney, insinuatingly. "Objection!" shouted Mitty's attorney. "We have shown that the defendant could not have fired the shot. We have shown that he wore his right arm in a sling on the night of the fourteenth of July." Walter Mitty raised his hand briefly and the bickering attorneys were stilled. "With any known make of gun," he said evenly, "I could have killed Gregory Fitzhurst at three hundred feet *with my left hand*." Pandemonium broke loose in the courtroom. A woman's scream rose above the bedlam and suddenly a lovely, dark-haired girl was in Walter Mitty's arms The District Attorney struck at her savagely. Without rising from his chair, Mitty let the man have it on the point of the chin. "You miserable cur!" . . .

"Puppy biscuit," said Walter Mitty. He stopped walking and the buildings of Waterbury rose up out of the misty courtroom and surrounded him again. A woman who was passing laughed. "He said 'Puppy biscuit,'" she said to her companion. "That man said 'Puppy biscuit' to himself." Walter Mitty hurried on. He went into an A. & P., not the first one he came to but a smaller one farther up the street. "I want some biscuit for small, young dogs," he said to the clerk. "Any special brand, sir?" The greatest pistol shot in the world thought a moment. "It says 'Puppies Bark for It' on the box," said Walter Mitty.

His wife would be through at the hairdresser's in fifteen minutes, Mitty saw in looking at his watch, unless they had trouble drying it; sometimes they had trouble drying it. She didn't like to get to the hotel first; she would want him to be there waiting for her as usual. He found a big leather chair in the lobby, facing a window, and he put the overshoes and the puppy biscuit on the floor beside it. He picked up an old copy of *Liberty* and sank down into the chair. "Can Germany Conquer the World Through the Air?" Walter Mitty looked at the pictures of bombing planes and of ruined streets.

. . . "The cannonading has got the wind up in young Raleigh, sir," said the sergeant. Captain Mitty looked up at him through tousled hair. "Get him to bed," he said wearily, "with the others. I'll fly alone." "But you can't, sir," said the sergeant anxiously. "It takes two men to handle that bomber and the Archies are pounding hell out of the air. Von Richtman's circus is between here and Saulier." "Somebody's got to get that ammunition dump," said Mitty. "I'm going over. Spot of brandy?" He poured a drink for the sergeant and one for himself. War thundered and whined around the dugout and battered at the door. There was a rending of wood, and splinters flew through the room. "A bit of a near thing," said Captain Mitty carelessly. "The box barrage is closing in," said the sergeant. "We only live once, Sergeant," said Mitty, with his faint, fleeting smile. "Or do we?" He poured another brandy and tossed it off. "I never see a man could hold his brandy like you, sir," said the sergeant. "Begging your pardon, sir." Captain Mitty stood up and strapped on his huge Webley-Vickers automatic. "It's forty kilometres through hell, sir," said the sergeant. Mitty finished one last brandy. "After all," he said softly, "what isn't?" The pounding of the cannon increased; there was the rat-tat-tatting of machine guns, and from somewhere came the menacing pocketa-pocketa-pocketa of the new flame throwers. Walter Mitty walked to the door of the dugout humming "Auprès de Ma Blonde." He turned and waved to the sergeant. "Cheerio!" he said. . . .

Something struck his shoulder. "I've been looking all over this hotel for you," said Mrs. Mitty. "Why do you have to hide in this old chair? How did you expect me to find you?" "Things close in," said Walter Mitty vaguely. "What?" Mrs. Mitty said. "Did you get the what's-its-name? The puppy biscuit? What's in that box?" "Overshoes," said Mitty. "Couldn't you have put them on in the store?" "I was thinking," said Walter Mitty. "Does it ever occur to you that I am sometimes thinking?" She looked at him. "I'm going to take your temperature when I get you home," she said.

They went out through the revolving doors that made a faintly derisive whistling sound when you pushed them. It was two blocks to the parking lot. At the drugstore on the corner she said, "Wait here for me. I forgot something. I won't be a minute." She was more than a minute. Walter Mitty lighted a cigarette. It began to rain, rain with sleet in it. He stood up against the wall of the drugstore smoking. . . . He put his shoulders back and his heels together. "To hell with the handkerchief," said Walter Mitty scornfully. He took one last drag on his cigarette and snapped it away. Then, with that faint, fleeting smile playing about his lips, he faced the firing squad; erect and motionless, proud and disdainful, Walter Mitty, the Undefeated, inscrutable to the last.

Questions for discussion

1. The story begins realistically like any good action story about flying. At what point did you first realize that this was not a real action story?
2. Would the daydreams of most people have such a wide variety as Mitty's? Mitty's daydreams reveal an amazing range of technical understanding, a rich vocabulary, and a deeply dramatic quality. Cite instances of each of these from the story.
3. Is there any evidence in the story that would lead you to believe that Mitty has a practical, as well as a romantic streak?
4. When is daydreaming useful and wholesome? When is it undesirable? What do you think Mitty's purpose is in daydreaming? Do Mitty's daydreams hurt him in any way?
5. What is the author's attitude toward Mitty? Is he making fun of Mitty? Is he sympathetic? Give proof of your answer from the story.
6. One of the amusing contrasts of the story is the dramatic quality of Mitty's daydreams played against the practical concerns of Mrs. Mitty. Point out examples.
7. What is Mitty's relationship to his wife?
8. What kind of person is Walter Mitty? What do his daydreams show about him? Do you think he is a convincing character? Why or why not?
9. Why is this a humorous story? Is it also a sad story? Why?

Vocabulary growth

CONTEXT. On page 48 you read, "A door opened down a long, cool corridor and Dr. Renshaw came out. He looked *distraught* and *haggard*. 'Hello, Mitty,' he said. 'We're having the devil's own time with Mc-Millan. . . . Wish you'd take a look at him.' "

What does "distraught and haggard" mean? How much meaning can you get from the context? You know from the story that this is another case of "Mitty to the rescue." Obviously, he would not be rescuing someone happy, content, comfortable, and at ease. You can deduce, therefore, that "distraught" and "haggard" refer to something unpleasant.

Note that the doctor *looked* distraught and haggard. The words describe appearance. Can you now deduce how the doctor must have looked?

    a. On page 50 occurs the sentence, "Walter Mitty raised his hand briefly and the *bickering* attorneys were stilled." Reread the paragraph and from context clues work out the meaning of *bickering*.

    b. In the same paragraph occur the words *pandemonium* and *bedlam*. Work out their meaning from the context.

WORDS ARE INTERESTING. The word *bedlam* comes from Bethlehem Hospital in London long ago, where mentally ill people were treated. The name *Bethlehem* came to be shortened to *bedlam* from frequent use. The noise of the patients became associated with the word.

In *pandemonium*, the prefix *pan-* means "all." The suffix *-ium* often means "a place where," as in *aquarium* and *planetarium*. Thus, *Pandemonium* is the place where all demons dwell, a place of noise and confusion.

For composition

1. Everyone goes through unpleasant situations, such as explaining a car smashup, being turned down for a job, being criticized for doing poor work. Perhaps you have had such an experience recently. Write two accounts of the situation. In the first, report what actually happened. Then write an account of how you would have handled the situation so that you would have come out well.

2. If dreams are to come true, people must do something to make them come true. Write a short biographical sketch of some person who made a dream come true. The person might be yourself, or some well-known personality whom all the class will recognize.

The Tiger's Heart

JIM KJELGAARD

To do the impossible was not enough. To remain master of his village, Pepe Garcia had to do the impossible in his own way. You are about to enter village life in the exotic jungles of Latin America.

THE approaching jungle night was, in itself, a threat. As it deepened, an eerie silence enveloped the thatched village. People were silent. Tethered cattle stood quietly. Roosting chickens did not stir and wise goats made no noise. Thus it had been for countless centuries and thus it would continue to be. The brown-skinned inhabitants of the village knew the jungle. They had trodden its dim paths, forded its sulky rivers, borne its streaming heat and were intimately acquainted with its deer, tapir, crocodiles, screaming green parrots and countless other creatures.

That was the daytime jungle they could see, feel and hear, but at night everything became different. When darkness came, the jungle was alive with strange and horrible things which no man had ever seen and no man could describe. They were shadows that had no substance and one was unaware of them until they struck and killed. Then, with morning, they changed themselves back into the shape of familiar things. Because it was a time of the unknown, night had to be a time of fear.

Except, Pepe Garcia reflected, to the man who owned a rifle. As the night closed in, Pepe reached out to fondle his rifle and make sure that it was close beside him. As long as it was, he was king.

That was only just, for the rifle had cost him dearly. With eleven others from his village, Pepe had gone to help chop a right of way for the new road. They used machetes, the indispensable long knife of all jungle dwellers, and they had worked hard. Unlike the rest, Pepe had saved every peso he didn't have to spend for immediate

54

living expenses. With his savings, and after some haggling, he had bought his muzzle-loading rifle, a supply of powder, lead, and a mold in which he could fashion bullets for his rifle.

Eighty pesos the rifle had cost him. But it was worth the price. Though the jungle at night was fear itself, no man with a rifle had to fear. The others, who had only machetes with which to guard themselves from the terrors that came in the darkness, were willing to pay well for protection. Pepe went peacefully to sleep.

He did not know what awakened him, only that something was about. He listened intently, but there was no change in the jungle's monotonous night sounds. Still, something was not as it should be.

Then he heard it. At the far end of the village, near Juan Aria's hut, a goat bleated uneasily. Silence followed. The goat bleated again, louder and more fearful. There was a pattering rush of small hoofs, a frightened bleat cut short, again silence.

Pepe, who did not need to people the night with fantastic creatures because he owned a rifle, interpreted correctly what he had heard. A tiger, a jaguar, had come in the night, leaped the thorn fence with which the village was surrounded, and made off with one of Juan Aria's goats.

Pepe went peacefully back to sleep. With morning, certainly, Juan Aria would come to him.

(He did not awaken until the sun was up. Then he emerged from his hut, breakfasted on a papaya he had gathered the day before) and awaited his expected visitor. They must always come to him; it ill befitted a man with a rifle to seek out anyone at all.

Presently Pepe saw two men, Juan Aria and his brother, coming up one of the paths that wound through the village. Others stared curiously, but nobody else came because their flocks had not been raided. They had no wish to pay, or to help pay, a hunter.

Pepe waited until the two were near, then said, "*Buenos dias.*"

"*Buenos dias,*" they replied.

They sat down in the sun, looking at nothing in particular, not afraid any more, because the day was never a time of fear. By daylight, only now and again did a tiger come to raid a flock of goats, or kill a burro or a cow.

After a suitable lapse of time, Juan Aria said, "I brought my goats into the village last night, thinking they would be safe."

"And were they not?"

"They were not. Something came and killed one, a fine white and black nanny, my favorite. When the thing left, the goat went too. Never again shall I see her alive."

"What killed your goat?" Pepe inquired.

"A devil, but this morning I saw only the tracks of a tiger."

"Did you hear it come?"

"I heard it."

"Then why did you not defend your flock?"

Juan Aria gestured with eloquent hands. "To attack a devil, or a tiger, with nothing but a machete would be madness."

"That is true," Pepe agreed. "Let us hope that the next time it is hungry, this devil, or tiger, will not come back for another goat."

"But it will!"

Pepe relaxed, for Juan Aria's admission greatly improved Pepe's bargaining position. And it was true that, having had a taste of easy game, the tiger would come again. Only death would end his forays, and since he knew where to find Juan Aria's goats, he would continue to attack them.

Pepe said, "That is bad, for a man may lose many goats to a tiger."

"Unless a hunter kills him," Juan Aria said.

"Unless a hunter kills him," Pepe agreed.

"That is why I have come to you, Pepe," Juan Aria said. A troubled frown overspread his face. "I hope you will follow and kill this tiger, for you are the only man who can do so."

"It would give me pleasure to kill him, but I cannot work for nothing."

"Nor do I expect you to. Even a tiger will not eat an entire goat, and you are sure to find what is left of my favorite nanny. Whatever the tiger has not eaten, you may have for your pay."

Pepe bristled. "You are saying that I should put myself and my rifle to work for carrion left by a tiger?"

"No, no!" Juan Aria protested. "In addition I will give you one live goat!"

"Three goats."

"I am a poor man!" the other wailed. "You would bankrupt me!"

"No man with twenty-nine goats is poor, though he may be if a tiger raids his flock a sufficient number of times," Pepe said.

"I will give you one goat and two kids."

"Two goats and one kid."

"You drive a hard bargain," Juan Aria said, "but I cannot deny you now. Kill the tiger."

Affecting an air of nonchalance, as befitted the owner of a firearm, Pepe took his rifle from the fine blanket upon which it lay when he was not carrying it. He looked to his powder horn and bullet pouch, strapped his machete on, and sauntered toward Juan Aria's hut. A half-dozen worshipful children followed.

"Begone!" Pepe ordered.

They fell behind, but continued to follow until Pepe came to that place where Juan Aria's flock had passed the night. He glanced at the dust, and saw the tiger's great paw marks imprinted there. It was a huge cat, lame in the right front paw, or it might have been injured in battle with another tiger.

Expertly, Pepe located the place where it had gone back over the thorn fence. Though the tiger had carried the sixty-pound goat in its jaws, only a couple of thorns were disturbed at the place where it had leaped.

Though he did not look around, Pepe was aware of the villagers watching him and he knew that their glances would be very respectful. Most of the men went into the jungle from time to time to work with their machetes, but none would work where tigers were known to be. Not one would dare take a tiger's trail. Only Pepe dared and, because he did, he must be revered.

Still affecting nonchalance, Pepe sauntered through the gate. Behind him, he heard the village's collective sigh of mingled relief and admiration. A raiding tiger was a very real and terrible threat, and goats and cattle were not easily come by. The man with a rifle, the man able to protect them, must necessarily be a hero.

Once in the jungle, and out of the villagers' sight, Pepe underwent a transformation.

He shed his air of indifference and became as alert as the little doe that showed him only her white tail. A rifle might be a symbol of power, but unless a man was also a hunter, a rifle did him no good. Impressing the villagers was one thing: hunting a tiger was quite another.

Pepe knew the great cats were dappled death incarnate. They could move with incredible swiftness and were strong enough to kill an ox. They feared nothing.

Jungle-born, Pepe slipped along as softly as a jungle shadow. His machete slipped a little, and he shifted it to a place where his legs would not be bumped. From time to time he glanced at the ground before him.

To trained eyes, there was a distinct trail. It consisted of an occasional drop of blood from the dead goat, a bent or broken plant, a few hairs where the tiger had squeezed between trees, paw prints in soft places. Within the first quarter mile Pepe knew many things about this tiger.

He was not an ordinary beast, or he would have gone only far enough from the village so his nostrils could not be assailed by its unwelcome scents and eaten what he wanted there, then covered the remainder of the goat with sticks and leaves. He was not old, for his was not the lagging gait of an old cat, and the ease with which he had leaped the thorn fence with a goat in his jaws was evidence of his strength.

Pepe stopped to look to the loading and priming of his rifle. There seemed to be nothing amiss, and there had better not be. When he saw the tiger, he must shoot straight and true. Warned by some super jungle sense, Pepe slowed his pace. A moment later he found his game.

He came upon it suddenly in a grove of scattered palms. Because he had not expected it there, Pepe did not see it until it was nearer than safety allowed.

The tiger crouched at the base of a palm whose fronds waved at least fifty feet above the roots. Both the beast's front paws were on what remained of the dead goat. It did not snarl or grimace, or even twitch its tail. But there was a lethal quality about the great cat and an extreme tension. The tiger was bursting with raw anger that seemed to swell and grow.

Pepe stopped in his tracks and cold fear crept up his spine. But he did not give way to fear. With deliberate, studied slowness he brought the rifle to his shoulder and took aim. He had only one bullet and there would be no time to reload, but even a tiger could not withstand the smash of that enormous leaden ball right between the eyes. Pepe steadied the rifle.

His finger tightened slowly on the trigger, for he must not let nervousness spoil his aim. When the hammer fell Pepe's brain and body became momentarily numb.

There was no satisfying roar and no puff of black powder smoke wafting away from the muzzle. Instead there was only a sudden hiss, as though cold water had spilled on a hot stone, and the metallic click of the falling hammer. Pepe himself had loaded the rifle, but he could not have done so correctly. Only the powder in the priming pan flashed.

It was the spark needed to explode the anger in the tiger's lithe and deadly body. He emitted a coughing snarl and launched his charge. Lord of the jungle, he would crush this puny man who dared interfere with him.

Pepe jerked back to reality, but he took time to think of his rifle, leaning it lovingly against a tree and in the same motion jerking his machete from its sheath.

It was now a hopeless fight, to be decided in the tiger's favor, because not within the memory of the village's oldest inhabitant had any man ever killed a tiger with a machete. But it was as well to fight hopelessly, as to turn and run, for if he did that he would surely be killed. No tiger that attacked anything was ever known to turn aside.

Machete in hand, Pepe studied the onrushing cat. He had read the tracks correctly, for from pad to joint the tiger's right front foot was swollen to almost twice the size of the other. It must have stepped on a poisonous thorn or been bitten by a snake.

Even with such a handicap, a tiger was more than a match for a man armed only with a machete—but Pepe watched the right front paw carefully. If he had any advantage, it lay there. Then the tiger, a terrible, pitiless engine of destruction, flung himself at Pepe. Pepe had known from the first that the tiger's initial strike would be exactly this one, and he was ready for it. He swerved, bending his body outward as the great cat brushed past him. With all the strength in his powerful right arm, he swung the machete. He stopped his downward stroke just short of the tiger's silken back, for he knew suddenly that there was just one way to end this fight.

The tiger whirled, and hot spittle from his mouth splashed on the back of Pepe's left hand. Holding the machete before him, like a sword, he took a swift backward step. The tiger sprang, launching himself from the ground as though his rear legs were made of powerful steel springs, and coming straight up. His flailing left paw flashed at Pepe. It hooked in his shirt, ripping it away from the arm as though it were paper, and burning talons sank into the flesh. Red blood welled out.

Pepe did not try again to slash with the machete, but thrust, as he would have thrust with a knife or sword. The machete's point met the tiger's throat, and Pepe put all his strength and weight behind it. The blade explored its way into living flesh, and the tiger gasped. Blood bubbled over the machete.

With a convulsive effort the tiger pulled himself away. But blood was rushing from his throat now and he shook his head, then stumbled and fell. He pulled himself erect, looked with glazing eyes at Pepe and dragged himself toward him. There was a throttled snarl. The tiger slumped to the ground. The tip of his tail twitched and was still.

Pepe stared, scarcely seeing the blood that flowed from his lacerated arm. He had done the impossible, he had killed a tiger with a machete. Pepe brushed a hand across his eyes and took a trembling forward step.

He picked up his rifle and looked again to the priming. There seemed to be nothing wrong. Repriming, Pepe clasped the rifle with his elbow and seized the machete's hilt. Bracing one foot against the tiger's head, he drew the machete out.

Then he held his rifle so close to the machete wound that the muzzle caressed silken fur. He pulled the trigger. The wound gaped wider and smoke-blackened fur fringed it. All traces of the machete wound were obliterated. Pepe knew a second's anguished regret, then steeled himself, for this was the way it must be.

Everybody had a machete. In his village, the man who owned a rifle must remain supreme.

Questions for discussion

1. Is Pepe an admirable character? Give reasons and examples to support your answer.
2. Pepe had to choose between being hailed as a courageous hero, and being "master" of his village. In what way was he master of the village? What were the reasons for his choice?
3. If Pepe had told the villagers what had really happened, what ad-

mission would he have had to make about the gun? What would this admission have done to his position in the village?

4. The gun did two things for Pepe. It gave him a satisfying way of earning a living. What else?

5. What evidence is there that Pepe was shrewd and crafty? That he was superstitious? What kind of person was Pepe? Look carefully at the picture of him (a) before the tiger arrived (b) while he waited for Juan (c) while bargaining with Juan (d) while in the forest.

6. Pepe had it in his power to rid the natives of their superstitious beliefs about "tigers and devils." He chose not to. Why? What does this tell you about Pepe's character?

7. ". . . not within the memory of the village's oldest inhabitants had any man ever killed a tiger with a machete." The whole story turns upon the fact stated in this sentence. Why is it so important to the story?

8. Were you surprised by the ending of the story? Show how the author prepared you for this ending. What clues does he give you about Pepe, his regard for the gun, and the reasons for his using it?

9. Does Pepe's victory over the tiger seem reasonable as you read it? What does the author tell you about Pepe that makes the outcome of the fight more believable?

Vocabulary growth

WORDS ARE INTERESTING. The word *eerie* has an interesting history. Originally it meant "timid, or cowardly." Thus, it was a term applied to persons and animals. Later, the word came to mean "inspiring fear, weird, uncanny." The aspect of cowardice is no longer present in the word. Note its use in the second sentence of the story, ". . . an eerie silence enveloped the thatched village." Reread the next four sentences to see how they build meaning into the word *eerie*. By the way, you will be interested to see what the dictionary tells you about *uncanny*.

CONTEXT. Use the context clues to discover the meaning of the unfamiliar words which appear in the following sentences:

a. On page 54, read the sentence, "They used machetes . . ." What clue tells you what a *machete* is?

b. What do you learn about *papaya* from this sentence? "Then he . . . breakfasted on a papaya he had gathered the day before. . . ."

c. On page 54, read the sentence, "Only death would end his forays. . . ." Read the rest of the paragraph and explain the meaning of *forays*.

For composition

Reread the first two paragraphs. Can you feel with the natives the fear of the mysterious and unknown? Note the sentence, "Because it was a time of the unknown, night had to be a time of fear." Do people fear the unknown more than the known? Do superstitions arise out of the unknown? Do people today have any fear about ominous dangers? Do people today have any superstitions about science itself? Write a composition on the topic "Superstitions of Our Time" or "What Modern Man Fears."

Road to the Isles

JESSAMYN WEST

Everyone is continually making discoveries about himself and about other people. Sometimes these discoveries can come as a shock. On the night of the dance festival, Cress made some important discoveries.

I T was the last Thursday in January, about nine in the evening, cold and raining. The three Delahantys sat close about the living-room fireplace—Mr. Delahanty at the built-in desk working on his schedule, Mrs. Delahanty on the sofa reading, and between them, crosswise in the wing chair, their fourteen-year-old daughter, Crescent. Cress was apparently studying the program of the folk-dance festival in which she was to appear the next evening. For the most part, however, she did not even see the program. She saw, instead, herself, infinitely graceful, moving through the figures of the dance that had been so difficult for her to master.

The high-school folk-dancing class was made up of two kinds of performers—those with natural ability, who had themselves elected the class, and those who, in the language of the physical-education department, were "remedials." The remedials had been sent into the class willy-nilly in an effort to counteract in them defects ranging from antisocial attitudes to what Miss Ingols, the gym teacher, called "a general lack of grace." Cress had achieved the class under this final classification but now, at midterm, had so far outgrown it as to be the only remedial with a part in the festival.

The first five numbers on the program, "Tsiganotchka," "Ladies' Whim," "Meitschi Putz Di," "Hiawatha," and "Little Man in a Fix," Cress ignored. It was not only that she was not in these but that they were in no way as beautiful as "Road to the Isles," in which Mary Lou Hawkins, Chrystal O'Conor, Zelma Mayberry, Bernadine Deevers, and Crescent Delahanty took part. The mere sight of her

63

name beside that of Bernadine Deevers, Tenant High School's most gifted dancer—most gifted *person*, really—instantly called up to Cress a vision of herself featly footing it in laced kirtle and starched skirts, a vision of herself dancing not only the outward steps of "Road to the Isles" but its inner meaning: what Miss Ingols had called "the achievement of the impossible."

Cress thought that she was particularly adapted to dancing that meaning because she had so recently come that way herself. If she had been given three wishes when school opened in September, two of them would have been that Bernadine be her friend and that she herself succeed in the folk-dancing class. Both had then seemed equally impossible. Now not only did she have a part in the festival but Bernadine was her dear friend and coming to spend the weekend with her. At the minute the evening reached what she considered its peak of mellowness, she intended to speak to her father and mother about the festival and Bernadine's visit. She was exceedingly uncertain about their performances on both these occasions.

The rain suddenly began to fall harder. Cress's father, hearing it on the roof, watched with gratification as the water streamed across the dark windowpanes. "Just what the oranges have been a-thirsting for," he said.

Mrs. Delahanty closed her book. "How's the schedule coming?" she asked her husband.

"O.K., I guess," said Mr. Delahanty.

Cress looked up from the festival program with embarrassment. The schedule was one of the things she wanted to speak to her father about. She hoped he wouldn't mention it while Bernadine was visiting them. Every winter, as work on the ranch slackened, he drew up a schedule for the better ordering of his life. And every spring, as work picked up, he abandoned it as easily as if it had never been. Last winter, he had made a plan called "A Schedule of Exercises to Ensure Absolute Fitness," which included not only the schedule of exercises and the hours at which he proposed to practice them but a list of the weaknesses they were to counteract. He had even gone so far, last winter, as to put on a pair of peculiar short pants and run six times around the orchard without stopping, arms flailing, chest pumping—a very embarrassing sight, and one that Cress could not possibly have explained to Bernadine.

This winter, the subject of her father's schedule-making was not in itself so unsuitable. He had bought a new encyclopedia set and was mapping out a reading program that would enable him, by a wise use of his spare time, to cover the entire field of human knowledge in a year. The name of the schedule, written at the top of a sheet of Cress's yellow graph paper, was, in fact, "Human Knowledge in a Year." There was nothing about this plan that would call for embarrassing public action, like running around the orchard in shorts, but it was so incredibly naïve and dreamy that Cress hoped her father would not speak of it. Bernadine was far too sophisticated for schedules.

"Where are you now on your schedule, John?" Mrs. Delahanty asked.

Mr. Delahanty, who liked to talk about his plans almost as much as he liked to make them, put down his pen and picked up the sheet of paper on which he had been writing. "I've got all the subjects I want to read up about listed, and the times I'll have free *for* reading listed. Nothing left to do now but decide what's the best time for what. For instance, if you were me, Gertrude, would you spend the fifteen minutes before breakfast on art? Or on archeology, say?"

"You don't ever have fifteen minutes before breakfast," Mrs. Delahanty said.

Mr. Delahanty picked up his pen. "I thought you wanted to discuss this."

"Oh, I do!" said Mrs. Delahanty. "Well if *I* had fifteen minutes before breakfast, *I'd* read about archeology."

"Why?" asked Mr. Delahanty.

"It's more orderly that way," Mrs. Delahanty said.

"Orderly?" asked Mr. Delahanty.

"A-r-c," Mrs. Delahanty spelled, "comes before a-r-t."

Mr. Delahanty made an impatient sound. "I'm not going at this alphabetically, Gertrude. Cut and dried. What I'm thinking about is what would make the most interesting morning reading. The most interesting and inspiring."

"Art is supposed to be more inspiring," Mrs. Delahanty told him. "If that's what you're after."

This seemed to decide Mr. Delahanty. "No, I think science should be the morning subject," he said, and wrote something at the top of a sheet—"Science," Cress supposed. "That's better," he said. "That leaves art for the evening, when I'll have time to read aloud to you."

"Don't change your schedule around for my sake, John," said Mrs. Delahanty, who hated being read to about anything.

"I'm not. All personal consideration aside, that's a more logical arrangement. Now the question is, which art?"

This seemed to Cress the moment for which she had been waiting. "Dancing is one of the earliest and most important of the arts," she said quickly.

"Oho!" said her father. "I thought you were in a coma."

"I've been rehearsing," said Cress.

"Rehearsing!" exclaimed Mr. Delahanty.

"In my mind," Cress said.

"So that's what was going on—'Ladies' Whim,' 'Tsiganotchka'—"

"Father," Cress interrupted, "I've told you and told you the t's silent. Why don't you take the program and practice the names? I'll help you." Cress got up and took the program across to her father.

"Practice them," said Mr. Delahanty with surprise, reading through the dances listed. "What do I care how they're pronounced? 'Korbushka,' 'Kohanotchka,' " he said, mispronouncing wildly. "I'm not going to Russia."

"But you're going to the folk-dance festival," Cress reminded him.

"I don't *have* to go. If you don't want—"

"I do, Father. You know I want you to go. Only I don't want you to mispronounce the names."

"Look, Cress," Mr. Delahanty said. "I promise you I'll keep my mouth shut the whole time I'm there. No one will know you have a father who can't pronounce. Mute I'll come and mute I'll go."

"I don't want you to be mute," Cress protested. "And even if I did, you couldn't very well be mute the whole time Bernadine's here. And Bernadine's the star of the program."

"To Bernadine," said Mr. Delahanty, referring to the program once again, "I shall speak of 'Badger,' and 'The Lumberman's Two Step.' I can pronounce them fine and they ought to hold Bernadine. She's not going to be here long, is she?"

"Friday to Monday," said Mrs. Delahanty.

"In that case," said Mr. Delahanty, "maybe I should find another one. How about 'The Irish Jollity,' Cress? Do I say that all right?"

"Now, John!" Mrs. Delahanty reproved her husband.

"It's all right for him to joke about it to me, Mother. But he mustn't before Bernadine. Bernadine's serious about dancing. She's going to be a great artist."

"A great dancer?" Mrs. Delahanty asked.

"She hasn't decided what kind of an artist yet," Cress said. "Only to be great in something."

"Well, well," said Mr. Delahanty. "I'm beginning to look forward to meeting Bernadine."

"You already have," Cress told him. "Bernadine was one of the girls who rode with us to the basketball game."

Mr. Delahanty squinted his eyes, as if trying to peer backward to the Friday two weeks before when he had provided Cress and four of her friends with transportation to an out-of-town game. He shook his head. "Can't recall any Bernadine," he said.

"She was the one in the front seat with us," Cress reminded him.

"That girl!" exclaimed Mr. Delahanty, remembering. "But her name wasn't Bernadine, was it?"

"No," Cress told him. "That's what I wanted to explain to you, because tomorrow's Friday, too."

Mr. Delahanty left desk and schedule and walked over in front of the fireplace. From this position, he could get a direct view of his daughter.

"What's this you're saying, Cress?" he asked. "Her name isn't Bernadine because tomorrow's Friday. Is that what you said?"

"Yes, it is," Cress told him, seriously. "Only it's not just tomorrow. Her name isn't Bernadine on any Friday."

Mr. Delahanty appealed to his wife. "Do you hear what I hear, Gertrude?"

"Mother," Cress protested, "this isn't anything funny. In fact, it's a complete tragedy."

"Well, Cress dear," her mother said reasonably, "I haven't said a word. And your father's just trying to get things straight."

"He's trying to be funny about a tragedy," Cress insisted obstinately.

"Now, Cress," Mr. Delahanty urged, "you're jumping to conclusions. Though I admit I think it's queer to have a name on Fridays you don't have the rest of the week. And I don't see anything tragic about it."

"That's what I'm trying to tell you, only you keep acting as if it's a joke."

"What is Bernadine's name on Fridays, Cress?" asked her mother.

"Nedra," said Cress solemnly.

Mr. Delahanty snapped his fingers. "Yes, sir," he said, "that's it! That's what they called her, all right."

"Of course," said Cress. "Everyone does on Fridays, out of respect for her sorrow."

"Just what *is* Bernadine's sorrow, Cress?" her mother asked.

"Bernadine never did say—out and out, that is. Once in a while she tries to. But she just can't. It overwhelms her. But we all know what, generally speaking, must have happened."

"What?" asked Mr. Delahanty. "Generally speaking?"

Cress looked at her father suspiciously, but his face was all sympathetic concern.

"On some Friday in the past," she said, "Nedra had to say no to someone. Someone she loved."

"How old is Berna—Nedra?" Mrs. Delahanty asked.

"Sixteen," Cress said. "Almost."

"Well, it couldn't have been too long ago then, could it?" her mother suggested.

"Was this person," Mr. Delahanty ventured, "this person Nedra said no to, a male?"

"Of course," said Cress. "I told you it was a complete tragedy, didn't I? His name was Ned. That much we know."

"Then the Nedra is in honor of—Ned?" asked her mother.

"In honor and loving memory," Cress told her. "On the very next Friday, Ned died."

Mr. Delahanty said nothing. Mrs. Delahanty said, "Poor boy!"

"I think he was probably more than a boy," Cress said. "He owned two drugstores."

After the elder Delahantys had thought about this for a while Mr. Delahanty asked, "This 'no' Bernadine—Nedra—said, was it to a proposal of marriage?"

"We don't ever ask about that," Cress told her father disapprovingly. "It doesn't seem like good taste to us."

"No, I don't suppose it is," Mr. Delahanty admitted.

"Anyway," Cress said, "that's Bernadine's tragedy and we all respect it and her wish to be called Nedra on Fridays. And tomorrow is a Friday, and it would be pretty awful to have her upset before the festival."

Mr. Delahanty stepped briskly back to his desk. "Don't you worry for a second, Cress," he said. "As far as I'm concerned, the girl's name is Nedra."

"Thank you, Father," Cress said. "I knew you'd understand. Now I'd better go to bed." At the door to the hallway, she turned and spoke once again. "If I were you, Father, I wouldn't say anything about your schedule to Bernadine."

"I hadn't planned on talking to her about it. But what's wrong with it?" Mr. Delahanty sounded a little testy.

"Oh, nothing," Cress assured him. "I think it's dear and sweet of you to make schedules. Only," she explained, "it's so idealistic."

After Cress left the room, Mr. Delahanty said, "What the hell's wrong with being idealistic?"

Cress thought that her friend, in her costume for "Fado Blanquita," the Spanish dance in which she performed the solo part, looked like the queen of grace and beauty. And she said so.

"This does rather suit my type," Bernadine admitted. She was leaning out from the opened casement window of Cress's room into the shimmering, rain-washed air. She tautened her costume's already tight bodice, fluffed up its already bouffant skirt, and extended her hands in one of the appealing gestures of the dance toward the trees of the orange orchard upon which the window opened.

"Is your father a shy man?" she asked.

Mr. Delahanty, who had been working near the driveway to the house when the two girls got off the school bus an hour before, had, instead of lingering to greet them, quickly disappeared behind a row of trees. Now, in rubber boots, carrying a light spade that he was using to test the depth to which the night before's rain had penetrated the soil, he came briefly into sight, waved his spade, and once again disappeared.

"No," said Cress, who thought her father rather bold, if anything. "He's just busy. After the rain, you know."

"Rain, sunshine. Sunshine, rain," Bernadine said understandingly. She moved her hands about in the placid afternoon air as if scooping up samples. "Farming is an awfully elemental life, I expect. My father"—Bernadine's father, J. M. Deevers, was vice-president of the Tenant First National Bank—"probably doesn't know one element from another. I expect your father's rather an elemental type, too, isn't he? Fundamentally, I mean?"

"I don't know, Nedra," Cress said humbly.

"He's black-haired," Bernadine said. "It's been my experience that black-haired men are very elemental." She brought her expressive hands slowly down to her curving red satin bodice. "You must have a good deal of confidence in your family to let them go tonight," she went on briskly.

"Let them!" Cress repeated, amazed at the word.

"Perhaps they're different from my family. Mine always keep me on pins and needles about what they're going to say and do next."

"Mine, too," Cress admitted, though loyalty to her father and mother would not permit her to say how greatly they worried her. She never went anyplace with them that she was not filled with a tremulous concern lest they do or say something that would discredit them all. She stayed with them. She attempted to guide them. She hearkened to every word said to them, so that she could prompt them with the right answers. But *let* them! "They always just take it for granted that where I go, they go," she said. "There's not much question of letting."

"Mine used to be that way," Bernadine confided. "But after what happened at the festival last year, I put my foot down. 'This year,' I told them, 'you're not going.' "

"What happened last year?" asked Cress, who had not then been a dancer.

"After the program was over last year, Miss Ingols asked for parent participation in the dancing. And my father participated. He danced the 'Hopak,' and pretty soon he was lifting Miss Ingols off the floor at every other jump."

"Oh, Nedra," Cress said. "How terrible! What did Ingols do?"

"Nothing," said Bernadine. "That was the disgusting part. As a matter of fact, she seemed to enjoy it. But you can imagine how I suffered."

Cress nodded. She could. She was thinking how she would suffer if her father, in addition to mispronouncing all the dances, went out on the gymnasium floor and, before all her friends, misdanced them.

"Are your parents the participating type?" Bernadine asked.

Cress nodded with sad conviction. "Father is. And Mother is if encouraged."

"You'd better warn them right away," Bernadine said. "Your father just came in the back door. You could warn him now."

Cress walked slowly down the hallway toward the kitchen. Before the evening was over, her father, too, would probably be jouncing Miss Ingols around, and even calling Bernadine Bernadine—then all would be ruined completely, all she had looked forward to for so long. In the kitchen, she noted signs of the special supper her mother was cooking because of Bernadine: the cole-slaw salad had shreds of green peppers and red apples mixed through it tonight to make it festive; the party sherbet glasses, with their long, icicle stems, awaited the lemon pudding. But her mother was out of the kitchen—on the back porch telling her father to hurry, because they would have to have dinner early if they were to get to the festival in time. "Festival!" Cress heard her father say. "I wish I'd never heard of that festival. How did Cress ever come to get mixed up in this dancing business, anyway?" he asked. "She's no dancer. Why, the poor kid can hardly get through a room without knocking something over. Let alone dance!"

"That's *why* she's mixed up with it," her mother explained. "To overcome her awkwardness. And she *is* better."

"But is she good enough?" asked her father. "I'd hate to think of her making a spectacle of herself—to say nothing of having to sit and watch it."

"Now, John," Cress heard her mother say soothingly. "You're always too concerned about Cress. Will she do this right? Will she do that right? Stop worrying. Cress'll probably be fine."

"Maybe fall on her ear, too," her father said morosely. "They oughtn't to put so much responsibility on kids. Performing in public. Doesn't it worry you any?"

"Certainly it worries me. But all parents worry. And remember, we'll have the star of the performance with us. You can concentrate on Nedra if watching Cress is too much for you."

"That Nedra! The only dance I can imagine that girl doing is one in which she would carry somebody's head on a platter."

Cress had started back down the hall before her father finished this sentence, but she had not gone so far as to miss its final word.

She stopped in the bathroom to have a drink of water and to see how she looked in the mirror over the washbasin. She looked different. For the first time in her life, she saw herself through other eyes than her own. Through her parents' eyes. Did parents worry about the figures their *children* cut? Were they embarrassed for *them*, and did they wonder if they were behaving suitably, stylishly, well? Cress felt a vacant, hollow space beneath her heart, which another glass of water did nothing to fill. Why, *I'm* all right, Cress thought. *I* know how to behave. I'll get by. *They're* the ones . . . but she looked at her face again and it was wavering, doubtful—not the triumphant face she had imagined, smiling in sureness as she danced the come-and-go figures of "Road to the Isles."

She went back to her room full of thought. Bernadine was changing her costume, and her muffled voice came from under all her skirts. "Did you tell them?" this muffled voice asked.

"No," said Cress, "I didn't."

"Why not? Won't you be worried?"

"They're the ones who are worrying. About me."

"About you?"

"Father thinks I may fall on my ear."

Bernadine, clear of her skirts, nodded in smiling agreement. "It's a possibility that sometimes occurs to *me*, Cress dear."

Cress gazed at her friend speculatively. "They're worried about you, too," she said.

"Me?" asked Bernadine, her smile fading.

"Father said the only dance he could imagine you doing was one with a head on a platter."

"Salome!" Bernadine exclaimed with pleasure. "Your father's imaginative, isn't he? Sympathetically imaginative?"

"I guess so," Cress said, and in her confusion told everything. "He keeps schedules."

"Schedules?"

"For the better ordering of his life."

Bernadine laughed again. "How precious!" she said.

Then, as if remembering after too long a lapse the day and her bereavement, she said, "Neddy was like that, too."

"Neddy," repeated Cress, pain for the present making Bernadine's past seem not only past but silly. "Oh, shut up about Neddy, *Bernadine!*"

Bernadine gave a little gasp. "Have you forgotten it's Friday?" "I don't care what day it is," Cress said. She walked over to her bed, picked up the pillow, and lay down. Then she put the pillow over her face.

Questions for discussion

1. What discovery did Cress make about her parents and especially about her father? What did she learn about herself? About Bernadine?
2. In a sudden moment of insight near the end of the story, Cress changed a great deal. In what ways did she change?
3. Before Cress changed, she was patronizing to her parents. That is, out of her "superior" knowledge and experience she "graciously" consented to put up with them. What incidents in the story show this attitude?
4. How would you describe Mrs. Delahanty's attitude toward her husband?
5. What evidence is there that Mr. Delahanty realizes how and why Cress worries about him?
6. What is Bernadine's attitude toward Mr. Delahanty? Cite examples from the story.
7. In many stories, a character changes and is quite different at the end from what he was at the beginning. The writer must prepare the reader for a change such as this in order to make his story believable. The change in Cress's attitude toward her parents is a gradual one. At what point does it begin to change?
8. Does Cress seem natural and real? Why or why not?
9. CHARACTER. A writer can portray a character *directly* by describing his appearance and telling what kind of a person he is. The writer may also portray a character *indirectly* through what the character says and does, and through what other people say about him. By what means is Mr. Delahanty's character portrayed? By what means do we learn about Cress?

Vocabulary growth

WORD FORMATION. In English, many words are made by adding prefixes and suffixes to base words. Thus, the words *act, inaction, active, inactive, activate* all grow out of the common base word, *act*. Find the base word from which each of the following is formed. Make at least one other word from the same base.

remedial	midterm	knowledge
infinitely	festival	reasonably
antisocial	unsuitable	idealistic
classification	enable	discredit

CONTEXT. On page 64, you read that Cress had a vision of herself "featly footing it in laced kirtle. . . ." Reread the sentence and try to figure out a meaning for *featly*. Check your estimate with the dictionary. On page 66, Mr. Delahanty says, "Mute I'll come and mute I'll go." Reread the passage and figure out a meaning for *mute*. Check your estimate with the dictionary.

For composition

1. Discuss in a light vein: "My Worries About My Parents"; "My Parents' Worries About Me."
2. Write a paragraph on "A Dream That I Made Come True."
3. If you were permitted to read Cress's diary, what would you find recorded there for Thursday night? For Friday night, the night after the dance festival?

Luke Baldwin's Vow

MORLEY CALLAGHAN

An orphan boy goes to live with his uncle and grows to love the uncle's old, half-blind dog. What can he do when the uncle decides that the dog is useless and must be put away?

THAT summer when twelve-year-old Luke Baldwin came to live with his Uncle Henry in the house on the stream by the sawmill, he did not forget that he had promised his dying father he would try to learn things from his uncle; so he used to watch him very carefully.

Uncle Henry, who was the manager of the sawmill, was a big, burly man weighing more than two hundred and thirty pounds, and he had a rough-skinned, brick-colored face. He looked like a powerful man, but his health was not good. He had aches and pains in his back and shoulders which puzzled the doctor. The first thing Luke learned about Uncle Henry was that everybody had great respect for him. The four men he employed in the sawmill were always polite and attentive when he spoke to them. His wife, Luke's Aunt Helen, a kindly, plump, straightforward woman, never argued with him. "You should try and be like your Uncle Henry," she would say to Luke. "He's so wonderfully practical. He takes care of everything in a sensible, easy way."

Luke used to trail around the sawmill after Uncle Henry not only because he liked the fresh clean smell of the newly cut wood and the big piles of sawdust, but because he was impressed by his uncle's precise, firm tone when he spoke to the men.

Sometimes Uncle Henry would stop and explain to Luke something about a piece of lumber. "Always try and learn the essential facts, son," he would say. "If you've got the facts, you know what's useful and what isn't useful, and no one can fool you."

He showed Luke that nothing of value was ever wasted around

75

the mill. Luke used to listen, and wonder if there was another man in the world who knew so well what was needed and what ought to be thrown away. Uncle Henry had known at once that Luke needed a bicycle to ride to his school, which was two miles away in town, and he bought him a good one. He knew that Luke needed good, serviceable clothes. He also knew exactly how much Aunt Helen needed to run the house, the price of everything, and how much a woman should be paid for doing the family washing. In the evenings Luke used to sit in the living room watching his uncle making notations in a black notebook which he always carried in his vest pocket, and he knew that he was assessing the value of the smallest transaction that had taken place during the day.

Luke promised himself that when he grew up he, too, would be admired for his good, sound judgment. But, of course, he couldn't always be watching and learning from his Uncle Henry, for too often when he watched him he thought of his own father; then he was lonely. So he began to build up another secret life for himself around the sawmill, and his companion was the eleven-year-old collie, Dan, a dog blind in one eye and with a slight limp in his left hind leg. Dan was a fat, slow-moving old dog. He was very affectionate and his eye was the color of amber. His fur was amber too. When Luke left for school in the morning, the old dog followed him for half a mile down the road, and when he returned in the afternoon, there was Dan waiting at the gate.

Sometimes they would play around the millpond or by the dam, or go down the stream to the lake. Luke was never lonely when the dog was with him. There was an old rowboat that they used as a pirate ship in the stream, and they would be pirates together, with Luke shouting instructions to Captain Dan and with the dog seeming to understand and wagging his tail enthusiastically. Its amber eye was alert, intelligent, and approving. Then they would plunge into the brush on the other side of the stream, pretending they were hunting tigers. Of course, the old dog was no longer much good for hunting; he was too slow and too lazy. Uncle Henry no longer used him for hunting rabbits or anything else.

When they came out of the brush, they would lie together on the cool, grassy bank being affectionate with each other, with Luke talking earnestly, while the collie, as Luke believed, smiled with the good eye. Lying in the grass, Luke would say things to Dan he could not say to his uncle or his aunt. Not that what he said was important; it was just stuff about himself that he might have told to his own father or mother if they had been alive. Then they would go back to the house for dinner, and after dinner Dan would follow him down the road to Mr. Kemp's house, where they would ask old Mr. Kemp if they could go with him to round up his four cows. The old man was always glad to see them. He seemed to like watching Luke and the collie running around the cows, pretending they were riding on a vast range in the foothills of the Rockies.

Uncle Henry no longer paid much attention to the collie, though once when he tripped over him on the veranda he shook his head and said thoughtfully, "Poor old fellow, he's through. Can't use him for anything. He just eats and sleeps and gets in the way."

One Sunday during Luke's summer holidays, when they had returned from church and had had their lunch, they had all moved out to the veranda where the collie was sleeping. Luke sat down on the steps, his back against the veranda post, Uncle Henry took the rocking chair, and Aunt Helen stretched herself out in the hammock, sighing contentedly. Then Luke, eyeing the collie, tapped the step with the palm of his hand, giving three little taps like a signal, and the old collie, lifting his head, got up stiffly with a slow wagging of the tail as an acknowledgment that the signal had been heard, and began to cross the veranda to Luke. But the dog was sleepy; his bad eye was turned to the rocking chair; in passing, his left front paw went under the rocker. With a frantic yelp, the dog went bounding down the steps and hobbled around the corner of the house, where he stopped, hearing Luke coming after him. All he needed was the touch of Luke's hand. Then he began to lick the hand methodically, as if apologizing.

"Luke," Uncle Henry called sharply, "bring that dog here."

When Luke led the collie back to the veranda, Uncle Henry nodded and said, "Thanks, Luke." Then he took out a cigar, lit it, put his big hands on his knees, and began to rock in the chair while he frowned and eyed the dog steadily. Obviously he was making some kind of an important decision about the collie.

"What's the matter, Uncle Henry?" Luke asked nervously.

"That dog can't see any more," Uncle Henry said.

"Oh, yes, he can," Luke said quickly. "His bad eye got turned to the chair, that's all, Uncle Henry."

"And his teeth are gone, too," Uncle Henry went on, paying no attention to what Luke had said. Turning to the hammock, he called, "Helen, sit up a minute, will you?"

When she got up and stood beside him, he went on, "I was thinking about this old dog the other day, Helen. It's not only that he's just about blind, but did you notice that when we drove up after church he didn't even bark?"

"It's a fact he didn't, Henry."

"No, not much good even as a watchdog now."

"Poor old fellow. It's a pity, isn't it?"

"And no good for hunting either. And he eats a lot, I suppose."

"About as much as he ever did, Henry."

"The plain fact is the old dog isn't worth his keep any more. It's time we got rid of him."

"It's always so hard to know how to get rid of a dog, Henry."

"I was thinking about it the other day. Some people think it's best to shoot a dog. I haven't had any shells for that shotgun for over a year. Poisoning is a hard death for a dog. Maybe drowning is the easiest and quickest way. Well, I'll speak to one of the mill hands and have him look after it."

Crouching on the ground, his arms around the old collie's neck, Luke cried out, "Uncle Henry, Dan's a wonderful dog! You don't know how wonderful he is!"

"He's just a very old dog, son," Uncle Henry said calmly. "The time comes when you have to get rid of any old dog. We've got to be practical about it. I'll get you a pup, son. A smart little dog that'll be worth its keep. A pup that will grow up with you.

"I don't want a pup!" Luke cried, turning his face away. Circling around him, the dog began to bark, then flick his long pink tongue at the back of Luke's neck.

Aunt Helen, catching her husband's eye, put her finger on her lips, warning him not to go on talking in front of the boy. "An old dog like that often wanders off into the brush and sort of picks a place to die when the time comes. Isn't that so, Henry?"

"Oh, sure," he agreed quickly. "In fact, when Dan didn't show up yesterday, I was sure that was what had happened." Then he yawned and seemed to forget about the dog.

But Luke was frightened, for he knew what his uncle was like. He knew that if his uncle had decided that the dog was useless and that it was sane and sensible to get rid of it, he would be ashamed of himself if he were diverted by any sentimental consideration. Luke knew in his heart that he couldn't move his uncle. All he could do, he thought, was keep the dog away from his uncle, keep him out of the house, feed him when Uncle Henry wasn't around.

Next day at noontime Luke saw his uncle walking from the mill toward the house with old Sam Carter, a mill hand. Sam Carter was a dull, stooped, slow-witted man of sixty with an iron-gray beard, who was wearing blue overalls and a blue shirt. He hardly ever spoke to anybody. Watching from the veranda, Luke noticed that his uncle suddenly gave Sam Carter a cigar, which Sam put in his pocket. Luke had never seen his uncle give Sam a cigar or pay much attention to him.

Then, after lunch, Uncle Henry said lazily that he would like Luke to take his bicycle and go into town and get him some cigars.

"I'll take Dan," Luke said.

"Better not, son," Uncle Henry said. "It'll take you all afternoon. I want those cigars. Get going, Luke."

His uncle's tone was so casual that Luke tried to believe they were not merely getting rid of him. Of course he had to do what he was told. He had never dared to refuse to obey an order from his uncle. But when he had taken his bicycle and had ridden down the path that followed the stream to the town road and had got about a quarter of a mile along the road, he found that all he could think of was his uncle handing old Sam Carter the cigar.

Slowing down, sick with worry now, he got off the bike and stood uncertainly on the sunlit road. Sam Carter was a gruff, aloof old man who would have no feeling for a dog. Then suddenly Luke could go no farther without getting some assurance that the collie would not be harmed while he was away. Across the fields he could see the house.

Leaving the bike in the ditch, he started to cross the field, intending to get close enough to the house so Dan could hear him if he whistled softly. He got about fifty yards away from the house and whistled and waited, but there was no sign of the dog, which might be asleep at the front of the house, he knew, or over at the sawmill. With the saws whining, the dog couldn't hear the soft whistle. For a few minutes Luke couldn't make up his mind what to do, then he decided to go back to the road, get on his bike, and go back the way he had come until he got to the place where the river path joined the road. There he could leave his bike, go up the path, then into the tall grass and get close to the front of the house and the sawmill without being seen.

He had followed the river path for about a hundred yards, and when he came to the place where the river began to bend sharply toward the house his heart fluttered and his legs felt paralyzed, for he saw the old rowboat in the one place where the river was deep, and in the rowboat was Sam Carter with the collie.

The bearded man in the blue overalls was smoking the cigar; the dog, with a rope around its neck, sat contentedly beside him, its tongue going out in a friendly lick at the hand holding the rope. It was all like a crazy dream picture to Luke; all wrong because it looked so lazy and friendly, even the curling smoke from Sam Carter's cigar. But as Luke cried out, "Dan! Dan! Come on, boy!" and the dog jumped at the water, he saw that Sam Carter's left hand was hanging deep in the water, holding a foot of rope with a heavy stone at the end. As Luke cried out wildly, "Don't! Please don't!" Carter dropped the stone, for the cry came too late; it was blurred by the screech of the big saws at the mill. But Carter was startled, and he stared stupidly at the riverbank, then he ducked his head and began to row quickly to the bank.

But Luke was watching the collie take what looked like a long, shallow dive, except that the hind legs suddenly kicked up above the surface, then shot down, and while he watched, Luke sobbed and trembled, for it was as if the happy secret part of his life around the sawmill was being torn away from him. But even while he watched, he seemed to be following a plan without knowing it, for he was already fumbling in his pocket for his jackknife, jerking the blade open, pulling off his pants, kicking his shoes off, while he muttered fiercely and prayed that Sam Carter would get out of sight.

It hardly took the mill hand a minute to reach the bank and go slinking furtively around the bend as if he felt that the boy was following him. But Luke hadn't taken his eyes off the exact spot in the water where Dan had disappeared. As soon as the mill hand was out of sight, Luke slid down the bank and took a leap at the water, the sun glistening on his slender body, his eyes wild with eagerness as he ran out to the deep place, then arched his back and dived, swimming under water, his open eyes getting used to the greenish-gray haze of the water, the sandy bottom, and the imbedded rocks.

His lungs began to ache, then he saw the shadow of the collie floating at the end of the taut rope, rock-held in the sand. He slashed at the rope with his knife. He couldn't get much strength in his arm because of the resistance of the water. He grabbed the rope with his left hand, hacking with his knife. The collie suddenly drifted up slowly, like a water-soaked log. Then his own head shot above the surface, and, while he was sucking in the air, he was drawing in the rope, pulling the collie toward him and treading water. In a few strokes he was away from the deep place and his feet touched the bottom.

Hoisting the collie out of the water, he scrambled toward the bank, lurching and stumbling in fright because the collie felt like a dead weight.

He went on up the bank and across the path to the tall grass, where he fell flat, hugging the dog and trying to warm him with his own body. But the collie didn't stir, the good amber eye remained closed. Then suddenly Luke wanted to act like a resourceful, competent man. Getting up on his knees, he stretched the dog out on its belly, drew him between his knees, felt with trembling hands for the soft places on the flanks just above the hipbones, and rocked back and forth, pressing with all his weight, then relaxing the pressure as he straightened up. He hoped that he was working the dog's lungs like a bellows. He had read that men who had been thought drowned had been saved in this way.

"Come on, Dan. Come on, old boy," he pleaded softly. As a little water came from the collie's mouth, Luke's heart jumped, and he muttered over and over, "You can't be dead, Dan! You can't, you can't! I won't let you die, Dan!" He rocked back and forth tirelessly, applying the pressure to the flanks. More water dribbled from the mouth. In the collie's body he felt a faint tremor. "Oh, gee, Dan, you're alive," he whispered. "Come on, boy. Keep it up."

With a cough the collie suddenly jerked his head back, the amber eye opened, and there they were looking at each other. Then the collie, thrusting his legs out stiffly, tried to hoist himself up, staggered, tried again, then stood there in a stupor. Then he shook himself like any other wet dog, turned his head, eyed Luke, and the red tongue came out in a weak flick at Luke's cheek.

"Lie down, Dan," Luke said. As the dog lay down beside him, Luke closed his eyes, buried his head in the wet fur, and wondered why all the muscles of his arms and legs began to jerk in a nervous reaction, now that it was all over. "Stay there, Dan," he said softly, and he went back to the path, got his clothes, and came back beside Dan and put them on. "I think we'd better get away from this spot, Dan," he said. "Keep down, boy. Come on." And he crawled on through the tall grass till they were about seventy-five yards from the place where he had undressed. There they lay down together.

In a little while he heard his aunt's voice calling, "Luke. Oh, Luke! Come here, Luke!"

"Quiet, Dan," Luke whispered. A few minutes passed, and then Uncle Henry called, "Luke, Luke!" and he began to come down the path. They could see him standing there, massive and imposing, his hands on his hips as he looked down the path; then he turned and went back to the house.

As he watched the sunlight shine on the back of his uncle's neck, the exultation Luke had felt at knowing the collie was safe beside him turned to bewildered despair, for he knew that even if he should be forgiven for saving the dog when he saw it drowning, the fact was that his uncle had been thwarted. His mind was made up to get rid of Dan, and in a few days' time, in another way, he would get rid of him, as he got rid of anything around the mill that he believed to be useless or a waste of money.

As he lay back and looked up at the hardly moving clouds, he began to grow frightened. He couldn't go back to the house, nor could he take the collie into the woods and hide him and feed him there unless he tied him up. If he didn't tie him up, Dan would wander back to the house.

"I guess there's just no place to go, Dan," he whispered sadly. "Even if we start off along the road, somebody is sure to see us."

But Dan was watching a butterfly that was circling crazily above them. Raising himself a little, Luke looked through the grass at the corner of the house, then he turned and looked the other way to the wide blue lake. With a sigh he lay down again, and for hours they lay there together, until there was no sound from the saws in the mill and the sun moved low in the western sky.

"Well, we can't stay here any longer, Dan," he said at last. "We'll just have to get as far away as we can. Keep down, old boy," and he began to crawl through the grass, going farther away from the house. When he could no longer be seen, he got up and began to trot across the field toward the gravel road leading to town.

On the road, the collie would turn from time to time as if wondering why Luke shuffled along, dragging his feet wearily, head down. "I'm stumped, that's all, Dan," Luke explained. "I can't seem to think of a place to take you."

When they were passing the Kemp place, they saw the old man sitting on the veranda, and Luke stopped. All he could think of was that Mr. Kemp had liked them both and it had been a pleasure to help him get the cows in the evening. Dan had always been with them. Staring at the figure of the old man on the veranda, he said in a worried tone, "I wish I could be sure of him, Dan. I wish he was a dumb, stupid man who wouldn't know or care whether you were worth anything. . . . Well, come on." He opened the gate bravely, but he felt shy and unimportant.

"Hello, son. What's on your mind?" Mr. Kemp called from the veranda. He was a thin, wiry man in a tan-colored shirt. He had a gray, untidy mustache, his skin was wrinkled and leathery, but his eyes were always friendly and amused.

"Could I speak to you, Mr. Kemp?" Luke asked when they were close to the veranda.

"Sure. Go ahead."

"It's about Dan. He's a great dog, but I guess you know that as well as I do. I was wondering if you could keep him here for me."

"Why should I keep Dan here, son?"

"Well, it's like this," Luke said, fumbling the words awkwardly. "My uncle won't let me keep him any more . . . says he's too old." His mouth began to tremble, then he blurted out the story.

"I see, I see," Mr. Kemp said slowly, and he got up and came over to the steps and sat down and began to stroke the collie's head. "Of course, Dan's an old dog, son," he said quietly. "And sooner or later you've got to get rid of an old dog. Your uncle knows that. Maybe it's true that Dan isn't worth his keep."

"He doesn't eat much, Mr. Kemp. Just one meal a day."

"I wouldn't want you to think your uncle was cruel and unfeeling, Luke," Mr. Kemp went on. "He's a fine man . . . maybe just a little bit too practical and straightforward."

"I guess that's right," Luke agreed, but he was really waiting and trusting the expression in the old man's eyes.

"Maybe you should make him a practical proposition."

"I—I don't know what you mean."

"Well, I sort of like the way you get the cows for me in the evenings," Mr. Kemp said, smiling to himself. "In fact, I don't think you need me to go along with you at all. Now, supposing I gave you seventy-five cents a week. Would you get the cows for me every night?"

"Sure I would, Mr. Kemp. I like doing it, anyway."

"All right, son. It's a deal. Now I'll tell you what to do. You go back to your uncle, and before he has a chance to open up on you, you say right out that you've come to him with a business proposition. Say it like a man, just like that. Offer to pay him the seventy-five cents a week for the dog's keep."

"But my uncle doesn't need seventy-five cents, Mr. Kemp," Luke said uneasily.

"Of course not," Mr. Kemp agreed. "It's the principle of the thing. Be confident. Remember that he's got nothing against the dog. Go to it, son. Let me know how you do," he added, with an amused smile. "If I know your uncle at all, I think it'll work."

"I'll try it, Mr. Kemp," Luke said. "Thanks very much." But he didn't have any confidence, for even though he knew that Mr. Kemp was a wise old man who would not deceive him, he couldn't believe that seventy-five cents a week would stop his uncle, who was an important man. "Come on, Dan," he called, and he went slowly and apprehensively back to the house.

When they were going up the path, his aunt cried from the open window, "Henry, Henry, in heaven's name, it's Luke with the dog!"

Ten paces from the veranda, Luke stopped and waited nervously for his uncle to come out. Uncle Henry came out in a rush, but when he saw the collie and Luke standing there, he stopped stiffly, turned pale, and his mouth hung open loosely.

"Luke," he whispered, "that dog had a stone around his neck."

"I fished him out of the stream," Luke said uneasily.

"Oh, oh, I see," Uncle Henry said, and gradually the color came back to his face. "You fished him out, eh?" he asked, still looking at the dog uneasily. "Well, you shouldn't have done that. I told Sam Carter to get rid of the dog, you know."

"Just a minute, Uncle Henry," Luke said, trying not to falter. He gained confidence as Aunt Helen came out and stood beside her husband, for her eyes seemed to be gentle, and he went on bravely, "I want to make you a practical proposition, Uncle Henry."

"A what?" Uncle Henry asked, still feeling insecure, and wishing the boy and the dog weren't confronting him.

"A practical proposition," Luke blurted out quickly. "I know Dan isn't worth his keep to you. I guess he isn't worth anything to anybody. but me. So I'll pay you seventy-five cents a week for his keep."

"What's this?" Uncle Henry asked, looking bewildered. "Where would you get seventy-five cents a week, Luke?"

"I'm going to get the cows every night for Mr. Kemp."

"Oh, for heaven's sake, Henry," Aunt Helen pleaded, looking distressed, "let him keep the dog!" and she fled into the house.

"None of that kind of talk!" Uncle Henry called after her. "We've got to be sensible about this!" But he was shaken himself, and overwhelmed with a distress that destroyed all his confidence. As he sat down slowly in the rocking chair and stroked the side of his big face, he wanted to say weakly, "All right, keep the dog," but he was ashamed of being so weak and sentimental. He stubbornly refused to yield to this emotion; he was trying desperately to turn his emotion into a bit of good, useful common sense, so he could justify his distress. So he rocked and pondered. At last he smiled. "You're a smart little shaver, Luke," he said slowly. "Imagine you working it out like this. I'm tempted to accept your proposition."

"Gee, thanks, Uncle Henry."

"I'm accepting it because I think you'll learn something out of this," he went on ponderously.

"Yes, Uncle Henry."

"You'll learn that useless luxuries cost the smartest men hard-earned money."

"I don't mind."

"Well, it's a thing you'll have to learn sometime. I think you'll learn, too, because you certainly seem to have a practical streak in you. It's a streak I like to see in a boy. O.K., son," he said, and he smiled with relief and went into the house.

Turning to Dan, Luke whispered softly, "Well, what do you know about that?"

As he sat down on the step with the collie beside him and listened to Uncle Henry talking to his wife, he began to glow with exultation. Then gradually his exultation began to change to a vast wonder that Mr. Kemp should have had such a perfect understanding of Uncle Henry. He began to dream of someday being as wise as old Mr. Kemp and knowing exactly how to handle people. It was possible, too, that he had already learned some of the things about his uncle that his father had wanted him to learn.

Putting his head down on the dog's neck, he vowed to himself fervently that he would always have some money on hand, no matter what became of him, so that he would be able to protect all that was truly valuable from the practical people in the world.

Questions for discussion

1. In what way was Luke's first impression of his uncle a favorable one?
2. What did Luke learn about Uncle Henry at the end of the story?
3. At the end of the story, Luke wants to be as wise as Mr. Kemp. In what way? At the end, Luke makes a vow to himself. What is this vow?
4. Uncle Henry was upset when he saw Luke returning with the dog. Which of the following are the most likely reasons for his being upset? Find instances in the story to support your answer:
   a. He was angry at Luke and the dog.
   b. He was angry that his plan for getting rid of the dog had failed.
   c. He was ashamed because Luke had discovered what had happened.
   d. He was ashamed of having ordered the hired man to drown the dog.
   e. He was distressed because he realized how much the dog meant to Luke.
5. Sam, the mill hand, accepted Uncle Henry's cigar, tied a rope around the dog's neck, and took him out on the lake. How did Sam feel about this job?
6. Uncle Henry's character is very carefully and clearly drawn in this story. The reader learns a great deal about him from the opinions of others: the sawmill workers and Aunt Helen, for example. Find the passages in which their opinions are given. What did Luke's father think of Uncle Henry? How did you know what Mr. Kemp thought of him?
7. Did Uncle Henry decide everything on a practical basis, or did he take the feelings of other people into account? Is he ever really touched by the human side of things? Cite evidence from the story.

8. Can you state the central idea of the story? Read over the last page of the story for clues to the main idea.

9. What are values? A value is something that you think is important, such as honesty, success, self-approval, freedom of choice. Some things are more important to you than others. So it may be said that everyone has a *scale* of values, running from the least to the most important. Your values help you to decide what to do in a new situation. What did Uncle Henry value the most? What did Luke value more highly?

10. In many situations a person must choose between one value and another. In such a case, there is a *conflict of values*. Luke had one value of loyalty and obedience to his uncle. What other value was this in conflict with? Uncle Henry placed a high value on practicality. What value was this in conflict with?

Vocabulary growth

WORD FORMATION. If you know how words are put together, you can often figure out the meaning of a new word that looks long and complicated. Certain noun suffixes are especially useful to know because they add little or no meaning to the word. Their function is to make a noun out of an adjective or verb. Among them are *-ness, -ance, -ation* (*-tion, -ion*), and *-ment*.

a. The following words appear in "Luke Baldwin's Vow." Find the base word to which the noun suffix has been added.

notation	instruction	consideration
transaction	attention	assurance
judgment	exultation	eagerness

b. By adding one of the noun endings given above, make nouns out of the following verbs and adjectives. Check your spelling with the dictionary.

untidy	propose	busy
friendly	(to) state	weak
amuse	rid	appear
awkward	express	protect

For composition

1. Have you thought about your own scale of values? What are the most important things in your life? Here are some possibilities: *physical comfort, making a contribution to society, your family, your religious*

faith, popularity, earning a great deal of money. You will think of others. Write a paper in which you state what is your highest value. You can show how much this value means to you by pointing out what things you would be willing to give up in order to live by this value.

2. Many humorous family stories revolve about a pet. Do you remember when someone left the bird cage open and the parakeet escaped? Do you remember when the new puppy got up on the table and helped himself to the birthday cake? Write an account of a similar incident.

3. You may believe that people make too much of pets. If so, you will have instances and examples in mind. Write a paper on the subject, "Pets in Their Proper Place."

THE TIME
AND PLACE
OF A
STORY

The Time and Place of a Story

To present characters convincingly in a significant conflict, an author must place what happens in some *setting*. The setting of a story may include the historical period in which it takes place, the geographical area in which it occurs, the specific place of the action, and even the time of day and the weather.

In some stories, the setting is extremely important. For example, you feel that what happens in "The Tiger's Heart" could not have happened in any other place but this village and jungle in South America. Sometimes the setting is less important, as in "The Secret Life of Walter Mitty." Here the action and the chief character are universal, and place and time are not so crucial to the development of the story.

Often the setting of a story is presented through direct description. A skillful author, however, can also present the setting indirectly through dialogue or incidental references during the action of the story. Either way, the setting can contribute much to the general atmosphere or mood of a story. Clearly, a story that takes place on a lonely farm will have a very different mood from a story that takes place in a city high school.

The setting may also help to explain the personality and behavior of a character. A person working in a large, busy city like New York or Chicago at the present time undoubtedly will be different from a person working on a cattle ranch in the late nineteenth century.

In the three stories that follow, setting is so closely interwoven with plot and character that it becomes an essential part of each story. The authors illustrate how setting can contribute to the overall impact of a story.

In "Antaeus" by Borden Deal, what happens to the main character depends on his living in a treeless and grassless city and on his being part of a gang of boys who have a hideout on a barren tar roof.

Walter D. Edmonds sets "Water Never Hurt a Man" on the Erie Canal in the nineteenth century. The setting determines not only the

91

occupation of the boy's father and the type of characters in the story, but also plays a major role in what happens to a boy who suddenly finds himself confronting the adult world one stormy night.

The strange and mysterious setting of "By the Waters of Babylon" by Stephen Vincent Benét is crucial in establishing the mood and atmosphere of the story. Before you have finished this story, you will also discover that the setting contributes a great deal to the story's powerful impact and significance.

Antaeus

BORDEN DEAL

Antaeus (an tē′ əs) was a giant in Greek mythology, whose mother was Gaea, the earth goddess. No one could defeat him in wrestling because each time his body touched the earth, his strength was renewed. He was finally defeated by Hercules, who strangled him while holding him in the air.

The following story is about a modern Antaeus, who discovered that in a big city, a friendly gang of boys is easier to find than woods or an acre of cotton.

THIS was during the wartime, when lots of people were coming North for jobs in factories and war industries, when people moved around a lot more than they do now and sometimes kids were thrown into new groups and new lives that were completely different from anything they had ever known before. I remember this one kid, T.J. his name was, from somewhere down South, whose family moved into our building during that time. They'd come North with everything they owned piled into the back seat of an old-model sedan that you wouldn't expect could make the trip, with T.J. and his three younger sisters riding shakily on top of the load of junk.

Our building was just like all the others there, with families crowded into a few rooms, and I guess there were twenty-five or thirty kids about my age in that one building. Of course, there were a few of us who formed a gang and ran together all the time after school, and I was the one who brought T.J. in and started the whole thing.

The building right next door to us was a factory where they made walking dolls. It was a low building with a flat, tarred roof that had a parapet all around it about head-high and we'd found out a long time before that no one, not even the watchman, paid any attention

93

to the roof because it was higher than any of the other buildings around. So my gang used the roof as a headquarters. We could get up there by crossing over to the fire escape from our own roof on a plank and then going on up. It was a secret place for us, where nobody else could go without our permission.

I remember the day I first took T.J. up there to meet the gang. He was a stocky, robust kid with a shock of white hair, nothing sissy about him except his voice—he talked in this slow, gentle voice like you never heard before. He talked different from any of us and you noticed it right away. But I liked him anyway, so I told him to come on up.

We climbed up over the parapet and dropped down on the roof. The rest of the gang were already there.

"Hi," I said. I jerked my thumb at T.J. "He just moved into the building yesterday."

He just stood there, not scared or anything, just looking, like the first time you see somebody you're not sure you're going to like.

"Hi," Blackie said. "Where are you from?"

"Marion County," T.J. said.

We laughed. "Marion County?" I said. "Where's that?"

He looked at me for a moment like I was a stranger, too. "It's in Alabama," he said, like I ought to know where it was.

"What's your name?" Charley said.

"T.J.," he said, looking back at him. He had pale blue eyes that looked washed-out but he looked directly at Charley, waiting for his reaction. He'll be all right, I thought. No sissy in him . . . except that voice. Who ever talked like that?

"T.J.," Blackie said. "That's just initials. What's your real name? Nobody in the world has just initials."

"I do," he said. "And they're T.J. That's all the name I got."

His voice was resolute with the knowledge of his rightness and for a moment no one had anything to say. T.J. looked around at the rooftop and down at the black tar under his feet. "Down yonder where I come from," he said, "we played out in the woods. Don't you-all have no woods around here?"

"Naw," Blackie said. "There's the park a few blocks over, but it's full of kids and cops and old women. You can't do a thing."

T.J. kept looking at the tar under his feet. "You mean you ain't got no fields to raise nothing in? . . . no watermelons or nothing?"

"Naw," I said scornfully. "What do you want to grow something for? The folks can buy everything they need at the store."

He looked at me again with that strange, unknowing look. "In Marion County," he said, "I had my own acre of cotton and my own acre of corn. It was mine to plant and make ever' year."

He sounded like it was something to be proud of, and in some obscure way it made the rest of us angry. "Jesus!" Blackie said. "Who'd want to have their own acre of cotton and corn? That's just work. What can you do with an acre of cotton and corn?"

T.J. looked at him. "Well, you get part of the bale offen your acre," he said seriously. "And I fed my acre of corn to my calf."

We didn't really know what he was talking about, so we were more puzzled than angry; otherwise, I guess, we'd have chased him off the roof and wouldn't let him be part of our gang. But he was strange and different and we were all attracted by his stolid sense of rightness and belonging, maybe by the strange softness of his voice contrasting our own tones of speech into harshness.

He moved his foot against the black tar. "We could make our own field right here," he said softly, thoughtfully. "Come spring we could raise us what we want to . . . watermelons and garden truck and no telling what all."

"You'd have to be a good farmer to make these tar roofs grow any watermelons," I said. We all laughed.

But T.J. looked serious. "We could haul us some dirt up here," he said. "And spread it out even and water it and before you know it we'd have us a crop in here." He looked at us intently. "Wouldn't that be fun?"

"They wouldn't let us," Blackie said quickly.

"I thought you said this was you-all's roof," T.J. said to me. "That you-all could do anything you wanted to up here."

"They've never bothered us," I said. I felt the idea beginning to catch fire in me. It was a big idea and it took a while for it to sink in but the more I thought about it the better I liked it. "Say," I said to the gang. "He might have something there. Just make us a regular roof garden, with flowers and grass and trees and everything. And all ours, too," I said. "We wouldn't let anybody up here except the ones we wanted to."

"It'd take a while to grow trees," T.J. said quickly, but we weren't paying any attention to him. They were all talking about it suddenly, all excited with the idea after I'd put it in a way they could catch hold of it. Only rich people had roof gardens, we knew, and the idea of our own private domain excited them.

"We could bring it up in sacks and boxes," Blackie said. "We'd have to do it while the folks weren't paying any attention to us, for we'd have to come up to the roof of our building and then cross over with it."

"Where could we get the dirt?" somebody said worriedly.

"Out of those vacant lots over close to school," Blackie said. "Nobody'd notice if we scraped it up."

I slapped T.J. on the shoulder. "Man, you had a wonderful idea," I said, and everybody grinned at him, remembering that he had started it. "Our own private roof garden."

He grinned back. "It'll be ourn," he said. "All ourn." Then he looked thoughtful again. "Maybe I can lay my hands on some cotton seed, too. You think we could raise us some cotton?"

We'd started big projects before at one time or another, like any gang of kids, but they'd always petered out for lack of organization and direction. But this one didn't . . . somehow or other T.J. kept it going all through the winter months. He kept talking about the watermelons and the cotton we'd raise, come spring, and when even that wouldn't work he'd switch around to my idea of flowers and grass and trees, though he was always honest enough to add that it'd take a while to get any trees started. He always had it on his mind and he'd mention it in school, getting them lined up to carry dirt that afternoon, saying in a casual way that he reckoned a few more weeks ought to see the job through.

Our little area of private earth grew slowly. T.J. was smart enough to start in one corner of the building, heaping up the carried earth two or three feet thick, so that we had an immediate result to look at, to contemplate with awe. Some of the evenings T.J. alone was carrying earth up to the building, the rest of the gang distracted by other enterprises or interests, but T.J. kept plugging along on his own and eventually we'd all come back to him again and then our own little acre would grow more rapidly.

He was careful about the kind of dirt he'd let us carry up there and more than once he dumped a sandy load over the parapet into the areaway below because it wasn't good enough. He found out the kinds of earth in all the vacant lots for blocks around. He'd pick it up and feel it and smell it, frozen though it was sometimes, and then he'd say it was good growing soil or it wasn't worth anything and we'd have to go on somewhere else.

Thinking about it now, I don't see how he kept us at it. It was hard work, lugging paper sacks and boxes of dirt all the way up the stairs of our own building, keeping out of the way of the grown-ups so they wouldn't catch on to what we were doing. They probably wouldn't have cared, for they didn't pay much attention to us, but we wanted to keep it secret anyway. Then we had to go through the trap door to our roof, teeter over a plank to the fire escape, then climb two or three stories to the parapet and drop down onto the roof. All that for a small pile of earth that sometimes didn't seem worth the effort. But T.J. kept the vision bright within us, his words shrewd and calculated toward the fulfillment of his dream; and he worked harder than any of us. He seemed driven toward a goal that we couldn't see, a particular point in time that would be definitely marked by signs and wonders that only he could see.

The laborious earth just lay there during the cold months, inert and lifeless, the clods lumpy and cold under our feet when we walked over it. But one day it rained and afterward there was a softness in the air and the earth was live and giving again with moisture and warmth. That evening T.J. smelled the air, his nostrils dilating with the odor of the earth under his feet.

"It's spring," he said, and there was a gladness rising in his voice that filled us all with the same feeling. "It's mighty late for it, but it's spring. I'd just about decided it wasn't never gonna get here at all."

We were all sniffing at the air, too, trying to smell it the way that T.J. did, and I can still remember the sweet odor of the earth under our feet. It was the first time in my life that spring and spring earth had meant anything to me. I looked at T.J. then, knowing in a faint way the hunger within him through the toilsome winter months, knowing the dream that lay behind his plan. He was a new Antaeus, preparing his own bed of strength.

"Planting time," he said. "We'll have to find us some seed."

"What do we do?" Blackie said. "How do we do it?"

"First we'll have to break up the clods," T.J. said. "That won't be hard to do. Then we plant the seed and after a while they come up. Then you got you a crop." He frowned. "But you ain't got it raised yet. You got to tend it and hoe it and take care of it and all the time it's growing and growing, while you're awake and while you're asleep. Then you lay it by when it's growed and let it ripen and then you got you a crop."

"There's those wholesale seed houses over on Sixth," I said. "We could probably swipe some grass seed over there."

T.J. looked at the earth. "You-all seem mighty set on raising some grass," he said. "I ain't never put no effort into that. I spent all my life trying not to raise grass."

"But it's pretty," Blackie said. "We could play on it and take sunbaths on it. Like having our own lawn. Lots of people got lawns."

"Well," T.J. said. He looked at the rest of us, hesitant for the first time. He kept on looking at us for a moment. "I did have it in mind to raise some corn and vegetables. But we'll plant grass."

He was smart. He knew where to give in. And I don't suppose it made any difference to him, really. He just wanted to grow something, even if it was grass.

"Of course," he said, "I do think we ought to plant a row of watermelons. They'd be mighty nice to eat while we was a-laying on that grass."

We all laughed. "All right," I said. "We'll plant us a row of watermelons."

Things went very quickly then. Perhaps half the roof was covered with the earth, the half that wasn't broken by ventilators, and we swiped pocketfuls of grass seed from the open bins in the wholesale seed house, mingling among the buyers on Saturdays and during the school lunch hour. T.J. showed us how to prepare the earth, breaking up the clods and smoothing it and sowing the grass seed. It looked rich and black now with moisture, receiving of the seed, and it seemed that the grass sprang up overnight, pale green in the early spring.

We couldn't keep from looking at it, unable to believe that we had created this delicate growth. We looked at T.J. with understanding now, knowing the fulfillment of the plan he had carried alone within his mind. We had worked without full understanding of the task but he had known all the time.

We found that we couldn't walk or play on the delicate blades, as we had expected to, but we didn't mind. It was enough just to look at it, to realize that it was the work of our own hands, and each evening the whole gang was there, trying to measure the growth that had been achieved that day.

One time a foot was placed on the plot of ground . . . one time only, Blackie stepping onto it with sudden bravado. Then he looked at the crushed blades and there was shame in his face. He did not do it again. This was his grass, too, and not to be desecrated. No one said anything, for it was not necessary.

T.J. had reserved a small section for watermelons and he was still trying to find some seed for it. The wholesale house didn't have any watermelon seed and we didn't know where we could lay our hands on them. T.J. shaped the earth into mounds, ready to receive them, three mounds lying in a straight line along the edge of the grass plot.

We had just about decided that we'd have to buy the seed if we were to get them. It was a violation of our principles, but we were anxious to get the watermelons started. Somewhere or other, T.J. got his hands on a seed catalogue and brought it one evening to our roof garden.

"We can order them now," he said, showing us the catalogue. "Look!"

We all crowded around, looking at the fat, green watermelons pictured in full color on the pages. Some of them were split open, showing the red, tempting meat, making our mouths water.

"Now we got to scrape up some seed money," T.J. said, looking at us. "I got a quarter. How much you-all got?"

We made up a couple of dollars between us and T.J. nodded his head. "That'll be more than enough. Now we got to decide what kind to get. I think them Kleckley Sweets. What do you-all think?"

He was going into esoteric matters beyond our reach. We hadn't even known there were different kinds of melons. So we just nodded our heads and agreed that Yes, we thought the Kleckley Sweets too.

"I'll order them tonight," T.J. said. "We ought to have them in a few days."

"What are you boys doing up here?" an adult voice said behind us.

It startled us, for no one had ever come up here before, in all the time we had been using the roof of the factory. We jerked around and saw three men standing near the trap door at the other end of the roof. They weren't policemen, or night watchmen, but three men in plump business suits, looking at us. They walked toward us.

"What are you boys doing up here?" the one in the middle said again.

We stood still, guilt heavy among us, levied by the tone of voice, and looked at the three strangers.

The men stared at the grass flourishing behind us. "What's this?" the man said. "How did this get up here?"

"Sure is growing good, ain't it?" T.J. said conversationally. "We planted it."

The men kept looking at the grass as if they didn't believe it. It was a thick carpet over the earth now, a patch of deep greenness startling in the sterile industrial surroundings.

"Yes sir," T.J. said proudly. "We toted that earth up here and planted that grass." He fluttered the seed catalogue. "And we're just fixing to plant us some watermelon."

The man looked at him then, his eyes strange and faraway. "What do you mean, putting this on the roof of my building?" he said. "Do you want to go to jail?"

T.J. looked shaken. The rest of us were silent, frightened by the authority of his voice. We had grown up aware of adult authority, of policemen and night watchmen and teachers, and this man sounded like all the others. But it was a new thing to T.J.

"Well, you wan't using the roof," T.J. said. He paused a moment and added shrewdly, "So we just thought to pretty it up a little bit."

"And sag it so I'd have to rebuild it," the man said sharply. He started turning away, saying to another man beside him, "See that all that junk is shoveled off by tomorrow."

"Yes sir," the man said.

T.J. started forward. "You can't do that," he said. "We toted it up here and it's our earth. We planted it and raised it and toted it up here."

The man stared at him coldly. "But it's my building," he said. "It's to be shoveled off tomorrow."

"It's our earth," T.J. said desperately. "You ain't got no right!"

The men walked on without listening and descended clumsily through the trap door. T.J. stood looking after them, his body tense with anger, until they had disappeared. They wouldn't even argue with him, wouldn't let him defend his earth-rights.

He turned to us. "We won't let 'em do it," he said fiercely. "We'll stay up here all day tomorrow and the day after that and we won't let 'em do it."

We just looked at him. We knew that there was no stopping it. He saw it in our faces and his face wavered for a moment before he gripped it into determination.

"They ain't got no right," he said. "It's our earth. It's our land. Can't nobody touch a man's own land."

We kept on looking at him, listening to the words but knowing that it was no use. The adult world had descended on us even in our richest dream and we knew there was no calculating the adult world, no fighting it, no winning against it.

We started moving slowly toward the parapet and the fire escape, avoiding a last look at the green beauty of the earth that T.J. had planted for us . . . had planted deeply in our minds as well as in our experience. We filed slowly over the edge and down the steps to the plank, T.J. coming last, and all of us could feel the weight of his grief behind us.

"Wait a minute," he said suddenly, his voice harsh with the effort of calling. We stopped and turned, held by the tone of his voice, and looked up at him standing above us on the fire escape.

"We can't stop them?" he said, looking down at us, his face strange in the dusky light. "There ain't no way to stop 'em?"

"No," Blackie said with finality. "They own the building."

We stood still for a moment, looking up at T.J., caught into inaction by the decision working in his face. He stared back at us and his face was pale and mean in the poor light, with a bald nakedness in his skin like cripples have sometimes.

"They ain't gonna touch my earth," he said fiercely. "They ain't gonna lay a hand on it! Come on."

He turned around and started up the fire escape again, almost running against the effort of climbing. We followed more slowly, not knowing what he intended. By the time we reached him, he had seized a board and thrust it into the soil, scooping it up and flinging it over the parapet into the areaway below. He straightened and looked at us.

"They can't touch it," he said. "I won't let 'em lay a dirty hand on it!"

We saw it then. He stooped to his labor again and we followed, the gusts of his anger moving in frenzied labor among us as we scattered along the edge of earth, scooping it and throwing it over the parapet, destroying with anger the growth we had nurtured with such tender care. The soil carried so laboriously upward to the light and the sun cascaded swiftly into the dark areaway, the green blades of grass crumpled and twisted in the falling.

It took less time than you would think . . . the task of destruction is infinitely easier than that of creation. We stopped at the end, leaving only a scattering of loose soil, and when it was finally over a stillness stood among the group and over the factory building. We looked down at the bare sterility of black tar, felt the harsh texture of it under the soles of our shoes, and the anger had gone out of us, leaving only a sore aching in our minds like overstretched muscles.

T.J. stood for a moment, his breathing slowing from anger and effort, caught into the same contemplation of destruction as all of us. He stooped slowly, finally, and picked up a lonely blade of grass left trampled under our feet and put it between his teeth, tasting it, sucking the greenness out of it into his mouth. Then he started walking toward the fire escape, moving before any of us were ready to move, and disappeared over the edge.

We followed him but he was already halfway down to the ground, going on past the board where we crossed over, climbing down into the areaway. We saw the last section swing down with his weight and then he stood on the concrete below us, looking at the small pile of anonymous earth scattered by our throwing. Then he walked across the place where we could see him and disappeared toward the street without glancing back, without looking up to see us watching him.

They did not find him for two weeks. Then the Nashville police caught him just outside the Nashville freight yards. He was walking along the railroad track; still heading south, still heading home.

As for us, who had no remembered home to call us . . . none of us ever again climbed the escape-way to the roof.

Questions for discussion

1. T.J. did not begin his acquaintance with the gang by telling them about other gangs to which he had belonged. Instead, he asked ques-

tions. What did he want to know? In what ways did T.J. show he was different from the other boys?

2. A leader has (a) ideas and vision, (b) ability to inspire others with confidence in his ideas and vision, (c) ability to make plans toward a definite goal and to organize others to achieve that goal. Which of these qualities did T.J. have? Point to specific evidence in the story to support your opinion.

3. What did T.J.'s project reveal about him? What did he feel when the project was threatened? Do you think he was right to do what he did? Explain.

4. Why do you think the story is called "Antaeus"? What do Antaeus and T.J. have in common? What do you think the author is trying to say through this story?

5. Explain why the setting for this story—a Northern industrial city— is central to what happens.

Vocabulary growth

CONTEXT. From the context, try to determine the meaning of the italicized words in the following sentences:

a. "... the task of destruction is *infinitely* easier than that of creation." (page 102)

b. "... the bare *sterility* of black tar. ..." (page 102)

c. "T.J. stood for a moment ... caught in the same *contemplation* of destruction as all of us." (page 102)

For composition

1. People will usually support a leader who has qualities they admire and respect and who excels in these qualities. Write a character sketch of a person you know whom you admire as a leader.

2. Imagine that Blackie, Charley, and the narrator of the story are discussing their past acquaintance with T.J. Write an account of their conversation.

3. Sometimes a place, an event, or even an object can have a deep meaning for a person. Write a composition in which you describe something that means a lot to you, or has meant a lot to you in the past.

Water Never Hurt a Man

WALTER D. EDMONDS

Today, if the son of a lawyer, or the son of an electrician wishes to follow in his father's footsteps, he goes to school for training. In the early years of our country, a boy could learn a profession or trade by working alongside his father.

Life on the Erie Canal in the 1830's was rugged, adventurous and exciting. Towboats were pulled forward by horses that trod a towpath which ran along the edge of the canal. They moved thousands of tons of manufactured goods westward to the settlers, and towed thousands of tons of farm goods back to the East.

Young John Brace, in his eagerness to be a part of all this wonder of the canal, could not know in advance the great price to be paid in hard work. What he did know was that he had often seen his father standing proudly in the bow of the *Bacconola*, directing the towboat safely through the heavy traffic. John's heart must have leaped when one day his father finally said, "John's old enough to be a driver boy, he's coming along with me."

HE trudged with his hands tight fists in his pockets, his head bowed to the wind and rain. Ahead of him in the darkness, so that he could hear the squdge of their hoofs, the towing team bowed their necks against the collars. He could not see them in the darkness. When he lifted his face the rain cut at his eyes; and when lightning split the darkness he shut his eyes tight and pulled his head closer into his coat collar, waiting blindly for the thunder. Once in a lull he looked back. He could barely make out the bow lantern and the arrows of gray rain slanting against it. Between him and the light he caught glimpses of the tow rope, dipped slightly between the team's heaves, and the roughened water in the canal. Somewhere back of the light his father stood by the rudder-sweep, his beard curled and wet, his eyes slits, sighting for the bank. John wanted to go back, wanted to tie-by for the night, wanted to be in the bunk with his head buried in the friendly, musty smell of the blanket, where the storm could not reach him. He had gone back once, but his father had reached for his belt, saying, "Go on back. Watter never hurt a man. It keeps his hide from cracking."

John had gone back to the team. They did not need his guidance. But it was his place to keep the rope from fouling if a packet boat coming their way signaled to pass. He was afraid of his father at night, afraid of the big belt and strong hands with hair on the fingers over the knuckles. He caught up with the plodding horses and let the rain have its way. At each stroke of lightning his small back stiffened. It was his first year on the canal and he was afraid of storms at night.

He had been proud that spring when his father said, "John's old enough to be a driver boy, he's coming along with me and the *Bacconola.*" He had showed his dollar to his brothers and sisters, first pay in advance, and his father had bought him a pair of cowhide boots from the cobbler when he came to the village. Later, when the frost was out of the mud, John would go barefoot.

He was proud of his father. In Westernville, with other small boys, he had heard the dock loafers talking about his father, George Brace, bully of the Black River Canal. In some strange way they had news of every fight his father fought a day after it happened. "George licked the Amsterdam Bully Wednesday mornin'. Lock fifty-nine. It tuk nineteen minits only." "George is a great hand. Them big ditch bezabors is learning about George." A stranger had said, "Wait till Buffalo Joe meets up with him." There was silence then. Buffalo Joe Buller, he was bully of the western end of the Erie. A pea-souper, a Canadian, he fought the Erie bullies down one by one, and when he licked them he marked them with his boot in the Canadian style. It had a cross of nails to mark the beaten man's face. "You wait," said the stranger.

Little John, listening then, felt shivers down his back. But now, with the wind and rain, and the lightning tumbling the clouds apart, he forgot. They were on the long haul westward, to Buffalo, with plows aboard, full drafted in Rome. They had had to leave three hundred weight on the dock.

He felt his muddy boots slip in the towpath. He heard the squelching of the horses. Squelch-squelch, a steady rhythm as they kept step.

Once the lightning caught his eyes; and he had a clear view of trees beyond the canal-side meadow, their budded twigs bent down, like old women with their backs to the storm, and the flat, sharp wall of a canal house, sixty yards behind him. He had not even seen it as he passed. The rain was finding a channel down his neck. It crept farther, bit by bit, with a cold touch. He could feel his fists white in his pockets from clenching them. His legs ached with the slippery going. They had had supper at six, tied up by the bank, and John had eaten his plate of beans. He had felt sleepy afterward, barely noticing his father's big body bent over the dishpan. It was warm in the cabin, with the little stove roaring red hot, and his small hat hanging beside his father's cap on the door.

He had been almost asleep when his father's hand shook him roughly, then tumbled him from his chair. "Get out, John. Them plows we've got has to get west for spring plowing. We'll pick up Bob in Syracuse, then we'll have a better chance to rest. Get out now," and he had reached for his belt.

What did John care for the old plows anyway? But it hadn't then begun to storm, and he had gone, with a tired sense of importance. One had to keep freight moving on the old Erie. The old *Bacconola* always made fast hauls. He had been proud and shouted in a high voice to the tired horses and kicked one with his new boots.

But now he did not care about the plows. He wished the crazy old *Bacconola* would spring a leak in her flat bottom, so they would have to stop till the hurry-up boat came along and patched her up. He thought of her now, bitterly, with her scabs of orange paint. "Crummy old blister," he called her to himself and made names to himself, which he said aloud to the horses in a shrill voice. He was only twelve, with all the bitterness of twelve, and the world was a hateful thing.

A water rat went off the towpath with a splash, and a frog squeaked.

He glanced up to see a team on the opposite towpath heading east. "Hey, there!" yelled the driver in a hoarse voice; but John was too tired to answer. He liked to yell back in the daytime and crack his whip. But he had dropped his whip a while back. He would get a licking for that in the morning. But he didn't care. To hell with the whip and the driver and Pa.

"Hey, there!" shouted the other driver, a voice in the rain. "All right, all right, you dirty pup. Eat rain, if you want to and go drownd."

The rain took the voice, and the boat came by, silently, noiseless as oil, with its bow light a yellow torch against the rain. The steersman gave a toot upon the horn, but the sound bubbled through the water in it, and the steersman swore.

They were still on the long level, alone once more. It must be midnight. If only the lock would show. In Syracuse, Bob would come. He took turns driving and steering and cooking—a little man with a bent shoulder who had dizzy spells once in a while.

At the lock John could sit down and rest and listen to the tender snarling at his sluices while the boat went down, and heaving at his gate beam, while John's father heaved against the other. He was crazy, the lock-keeper was; all lock-keepers were crazy. John's father always said so. John had seen a lot of them in their week of hauling, but he did not see why they were crazy. They looked no different even if they were. He hoped the lock-keeper would be asleep, so it would take a while to wake him.

Squelch, squelch-squelch, squelch. The horses kept plodding. Suddenly John caught a break in the rhythm. One foot sounded light. He pushed his way up beside them against the wind and laid a wet hand against a side. He could not see, but the side felt hot and wet, and he got a smell of sweat. Yes, he could feel the off horse limping. Hope filled him. He waited till the boat came up where he was, a small figure, shrunk with cold. The boat's bow, round and sullen, slipped along, the bow light hanging over and showing an old mullein stalk in silhouette against the water.

"Pa!"

His voice was thin against the wind.

He saw his father's figure, rain dripping from the visor of his cap, straight and big, almighty almost, breast to the wind.

"Pa!"

The head turned.

"Hey, there! What you doin'? Get on back! Or I'll soap you proper."

"Pa! Prince has got a limp in his front foot. Pa!"

The voice turned hoarse with passion, "Get on back, you little pup. Fifty-nine's just round the next bend. Take your whip and tar him. Or I'll tar you proper."

John sobbed aloud. For a bare moment he thought of staying still and letting the boat pass on. He would run away and join the railroad.

He would get run over by an engine there, just when things went well, and they would be sorry. He started to draw himself a picture of his body coming home in a black box, and his mother crying, and his father looking ashamed and sorry, and then the lightning made a blue flare and he saw the straight figure of his father ahead, on the *Bacconola*, which seemed struck still, a pill-box in the flat country, and he was afraid and went running desperately, hoping he could get back to the team before he was missed.

He caught the horses on the bend and, lifting his face to the storm, saw the lock lanterns dimly ahead. And even then his ears caught, coming up behind him, the harsh blast of a tin horn.

He looked back and saw a light, two rope lengths behind the *Bacconola*. Even while he watched over his shoulder, he saw that it was creeping up.

"John!" His father's voice beat down the sound of rain. "Lay into them brutes and beat into the lock!"

He could imagine his father glaring back. If only he had not dropped his whip. He would have liked to ask his father for the big bull whip that cracked like forty guns, but he knew what would happen if he did. He shrieked at the horses and fumbled for a stone to throw. But they had heard and recognized the note in his father's voice, and they were bending earnestly against the collars. A sudden excitement filled John as his father's horn rang out for the lock. The wind took the sound and carried it back, and the other boat's horn sounded a double toot for passing. John yelled shrilly. The horses seemed to stand still, and there was an odd effect in the rain of the canal sliding under them inch by inch laboriously, as if with his own feet he turned the world backward.

Minutes crept at them out of the rain, and the lights of the lock did not seem to stir. Then John heard the squelching of the team behind his back. Little by little they were coming up, past the *Bacconola*, until he could hear them panting through the rain, and saw them close behind, behind dim puffs of steamy breath. He watched them frantically. Then the lightning came once more, a triple bolt, and the thunder shook him, and when he opened his eyes once more he saw the lock lanterns a hundred yards ahead.

At that instant the driver of the boat behind yelled, "Haw!" and the following team swung across his towrope, and they were snarled.

The horses stopped of themselves, shuddering. They were old

hands, and knew enough not to move, for fear of being thrown from the towpath. The boats came drifting on, placidly as water-logged sticks. The light of the following boat showed a dark bow coming up. John heard his father roaring oaths, and saw by the bow light of the other boat a tall, clean-shaven man as big as his father crouched to jump ashore. Then both boats came in by the towpath, and both men jumped. They made no sound except for the thump of their shoes, but John saw them dim against the lantern light, their fists coming at each other in slow, heavy swings.

The strange team was panting close beside him, and he did not hear the blows landing. There was a pushing upward in his chest, which hurt, and his fists made small balls in the pockets of his trousers. The other boater and his father were standing breast to breast, their faces still, cut, stonelike things in the yellow light, and the rain walling them in. He saw his father lift his hand, and the other man slip, and he would have yelled, for all his cold, if the lightning had not come again, so blue that his eyes smarted. He doubled up, hiding his face, and wept. . . .

A hand caught him by the shoulder.

"A little puny girly boy," said a voice. "I wouldn't lick you proper! Not a little girly baby like you. But I'll spank you just to learn you to let us come by!"

John opened his eyes to see a boy, about his own height but broader built, squinting at him through the rain.

"Take off your pants, dearie," said the boy in a mock voice, digging in his fingers till John winced. "Joe Buller can handle your Captain smart enough. Me, I'll just paddle you to learn you."

John, looking up, was afraid. He did not know what to do, but without warning his hands acted for him, and he struck at the square face with all his might. A pain shot up his arm, making his elbow tingle, and the boy fell back. John could feel the surprise in that body stock still in the rain, and had an instant of astonished pride.

Then panic laid hold of him and he tried to run. But the other boy jumped on his back. They went down flat in the mud, the older boy on John's shoulders, pummeling him till his head sang, and forcing his face into the track, and crying, "Eat it, you lousy little skunk. Eat it, eat it, eat it, eat it."

John could taste the mud in his mouth, with a salty taste, and he began to squirm, twisting his head to escape the brown suffocation.

He heaved himself behind, throwing the boy unexpectedly forward, twisted round, and kicked with all his might. The boy yelled and jumped back on him. And again they went down, this time the boy bent seriously to business. And this time John realized how it was to be hurt. At the third blow something burst loose in his inside and he screamed. He was crying madly. The other boy was heavier, but John squirmed over on his back, and as the brown hand came down on his face he caught it in both his own and bit with all the strength of his jaws. The hand had a slippery, muddy taste, but in a second it was warm in his mouth, and there was a sick, salt warmth on his tongue. The boy struck him once in the eyes and once on the nose, but John held on and bit. Then the boy howled and tore loose and ran back. There was another stroke of lightning, and John saw him doubled up, holding his hand to his mouth; and he got stiffly up, turned his back to the thunder and saw his father bent over the other boater, taking off his shoe.

John walked up to them. His father's face was bleeding a trickle of blood from the right eye into his beard, but he was grinning.

"I'll take his boot for a souvenir," he said. "How'd you come out, Johnny?"

"Oh, pretty good. I guess that other feller won't bother us no more," said John, examining the fallen man. He lay half stunned, by the water's edge, a smooth, big man, with frightened, pale eyes. And one crumpled arm was in the water. John's father looked at the man and then at the boot he had in his hand.

"I'd ought to mark him by the rights of it; but he ain't worth the work, the way he laid down. Who'd ever know his name was Buller?"

Buller. . . . John gazed up admiringly at his big father and studied how the blood ran from the outer corner of the eye and lost its way in the black beard, which the rain had soaked. His father had licked the western bully proper.

"Hey, there!"

The hail came in a thin, cracking voice. Turning, they saw the lock-keeper, white-bearded, peering at them from under the battered umbrella he held with both hands against the wind. The tails of his nightshirt whipped round the tops of his boots.

"Hey, there, you. There'll be some down boats by pretty quick, so you want to hurry along now, while the level's right."

John was aware of his father standing looking down at him.

"Shall we tie-by where we be?" asked his father.

John felt pains coming into the back of his neck where he had been pummeled, and his knuckles ached.

"We can stay here a spell," said his father. "The storm's comin' on again. There'll be bad lightnin' I make no doubt."

As he spoke there came a flash, and John whirled to see if the other driver boy was still visible. He was proud to see him sitting by the towpath, nursing his hurt hand. John did not notice the thunder. He was elaborating a sentence in his mind.

He made a hole in the mud with the toe of his boot, spat into it, and covered it, the way he had seen his father do at home on a Sunday.

"Why," he said, in his high voice, eying the old *Bacconola*, "I guess them poor bezabor farmers will be wantin' them plows for the spring plowing, I guess."

"Me, I'm kind of tuckered," said his father, raising his shoulders to loose the wet shirt off his back. "And the rain's commencing too."

John said importantly, "Watter never hurt a man, it keeps his hide from cracking."

His father jumped aboard. He took his horn and tooted it for the lock. John ran ahead and put back the other boat's team and cried to their own horses to go on. They took up the slack wearily, and presently little ripples showed on the *Bacconola's* bow, and the lantern showed the shore slipping back. On the stern, George Brace blew a blast for the lock. The old lock-keeper was standing by the sluices, drops of water from his beard falling between his feet.

The boat went down, and the horses took it out. Ahead, the team and the boy left the lantern light and entered once more the darkness. The rope followed. And once more the *Bacconola* was alone with its own lantern.

Presently, though, in a stroke of light, George saw his son beside the boat.

"What's the matter? Hey, there!" he asked.

"Say, Pa! Will you chuck me your bull whip here ashore? Them horses is getting kind of dozey. They need soaping proper."

"Where's your whip?"

"I guess I left it a while back. I guess it was in that kind of scrummage we had. I guess it needs a heavier whip anyhow. I guess a man couldn't spare the time going back for it."

"Sure," said George.

He reached down and took it from its peg, recoiled it, and tossed it ashore. The boat went ahead, slowly, with a sound of water, and of rain falling, and of wind.

Questions for discussion

1. Is this story about John or about his father? Cite evidence from the story to support your answer.

2. The story begins in the middle of things. For several paragraphs the reader is not certain who the characters are, or where they are. Then, in a flashback, the information is given. Find this flashback. What does it tell the reader?

3. Early in the story, John's father says, "Watter never hurt a man." Why did he say this? Later in the story, John himself repeats the words. Why?

4. The story shows a great change that takes place in John. What is he thinking about at the beginning of the story? What is he thinking about at the end? What is the change, then, in John?

5. How does the writer make the sudden change in John seem reasonable? When is the reader definitely sure that John is going to "give what it takes" to get the boat into Syracuse?

6. Can you admire a person and still be afraid of him? John feared his father. Find examples of this. Did John also admire his father? Cite evidence from the story.

7. Was George Brace another bully like the man he had defeated? Did he have certain admirable qualities? What sort of a father was he? Just as they had a chance to get into the lock, "John was aware of his father standing looking down at him." What was the father thinking? Give proof for your answer.

8. There are several conflicts in the story: the fight between the Braces and the other boat; the conflict between John and his father; the conflict between John and the demands of his job; the conflict within John himself. Which of these is the major conflict, and the basis of the plot? Point out the ups and downs that make the outcome of the major conflict uncertain. At what point in the story is this conflict settled?

9. What is the theme of this story? What is the story basically about? (It is not about a fight on the Erie Canal.)

10. SETTING. Describe briefly the setting of this story. Point out specific details that show how the setting contributes to the overall atmosphere and mood. In what ways does the setting have an important effect on the characters?

Vocabulary growth

CONTEXT. When you are reading a story as exciting as "Water Never Hurt a Man," you do not want to stop to look up words in a dictionary. If you meet a new word, you can make a check mark in the margin and look the word up later. But if the word is important in the story, you may be missing something. It is better to make a guess than to ignore the word completely. This is the point at which context clues help you. They will not tell you everything about the word, but they may give you enough meaning so that you can get on with your reading.

In "Water Never Hurt a Man," the word *bow* is important, and there are context clues that give you all the meaning you need. You know the word as a verb meaning "to bend the body." You also know the word in the phrase "bow and arrows," and you know its meaning in the phrase "ribbons and bows." But none of these meanings fits *bow* as it is used in this story.

We first meet the word in the sentence, "He could barely make out the *bow* lantern. . . ." Then again on page 107 another boat came by "with its *bow* light a yellow torch against the rain."

From these two uses, we might think that *bow* refers to a kind of light. But now on page 107 we get another clue: "The boat's *bow*, round and sullen, slipped along. . . ." From this sentence, we know that a *bow* is part of a boat. But which part of a boat is it?

Two other clues tell us. On page 109 we read, "The light of the following boat showed a dark *bow* coming up." Obviously, it would be the front part of a boat that you would see coming up behind you.

There are other clues in the story, but those mentioned are enough. While reading "Water Never Hurt a Man," all you need to know is that a *bow* is part of a boat. By the way, how is the word pronounced?

On page 111 we read, "He was *elaborating* a sentence in his mind." From the context, figure out the meaning of *elaborating*.

For composition

1. Writers of historical fiction do a great deal of research before they write their stories and novels. What can you learn from good historical fiction that you do not learn from a straight history text? Write a paragraph to explain. Cite specific examples from "Water Never Hurt a Man."

2. You are a reporter on a Syracuse newspaper. You have heard rumors of the fight between Brace and Buller. You must investigate the facts and write an account of the story. Your lead is: "The long, brutal reign of Buffalo Joe Buller came to an end last night on the rain-soaked banks of the canal below this city."

By the Waters of Babylon

STEPHEN VINCENT BENÉT

Here is the story of a young man's adventure into the unknown.
Physical danger and even the threat of death could not stop him. As
you read, you will be surprised to discover where and when the adventure
begins.

THE north and the west and the south are good hunting ground,
but it is forbidden to go east. It is forbidden to go to any of the Dead
Places except to search for metal and then he who touches the metal
must be a priest or the son of a priest. Afterwards, both the man and
the metal must be purified. These are the rules and the laws; they are
well made. It is forbidden to cross the great river and look upon the
place that was the Place of the Gods—this is most strictly forbidden.
We do not even say its name though we know its name. It is there
that spirits live, and demons—it is there that there are the ashes of
the Great Burning. These things are forbidden—they have been forbidden since the beginning of time.

My father is a priest; I am the son of a priest. I have been in the
Dead Places near us, with my father—at first, I was afraid. When
my father went into the house to search for the metal, I stood by
the door and my heart felt small and weak. It was a dead man's
house, a spirit house. It did not have the smell of man, though there
were old bones in a corner. But it is not fitting that a priest's son
should show fear. I looked at the bones in the shadow and kept my
voice still.

Then my father came out with the metal—a good, strong piece.
He looked at me with both eyes but I had not run away. He gave
me the metal to hold—I took it and did not die. So he knew that I
was truly his son and would be a priest in my time. That was when
I was very young—nevertheless, my brothers would not have done it,

though they are good hunters. After that, they gave me the good piece of meat and the warm corner by the fire. My father watched over me—he was glad that I should be a priest. But when I boasted or wept without a reason, he punished me more strictly than my brothers. That was right.

After a time, I myself was allowed to go into the dead houses and search for metal. So I learned the ways of those houses—and if I saw bones, I was no longer afraid. The bones are light and old—sometimes they will fall into dust if you touch them. But that is a great sin.

I was taught the chants and the spells—I was taught how to stop the running of blood from a wound and many secrets. A priest must know many secrets—that was what my father said. If the hunters think we do all things by chants and spells, they may believe so—it does not hurt them. I was taught how to read in the old books and how to make the old writings—that was hard and took a long time. My knowledge made me happy—it was like a fire in my heart. Most of all, I liked to hear of the Old Days and the stories of the gods. I asked myself many questions that I could not answer, but it was good to ask them. At night, I would lie awake and listen to the wind— it seemed to me that it was the voice of the gods as they flew through the air.

We are not ignorant like the Forest People—our women spin wool on the wheel, our priests wear a white robe. We do not eat grubs from the tree, we have not forgotten the old writings, although they are hard to understand. Nevertheless, my knowledge and my lack of knowledge burned in me—I wished to know more. When I was a man at last, I came to my father and said, "It is time for me to go on my journey. Give me your leave."

He looked at me for a long time, stroking his beard, then he said at last, "Yes. It is time." That night, in the house of the priest-hood, I asked for and received purification. My body hurt but my spirit was a cool stone. It was my father himself who questioned me about my dreams.

He bade me look into the smoke of the fire and see—I saw and told what I saw. It was what I have always seen—a river, and, beyond it, a great Dead Place and in it the gods walking. I have always thought about that. His eyes were stern when I told him—he was no longer my father but a priest. He said, "This is a strong dream."

"It is mine," I said, while the smoke waved and my head felt light. They were singing the Star song in the outer chamber and it was like the buzzing of bees in my head.

He asked me how the gods were dressed and I told him how they were dressed. We know how they were dressed from the book, but I saw them as if they were before me. When I had finished, he threw the sticks three times and studied them as they fell.

"This is a very strong dream," he said. "It may eat you up."

"I am not afraid," I said and looked at him with both eyes. My voice sounded thin in my ears but that was because of the smoke.

He touched me on the breast and the forehead. He gave me the bow and the three arrows.

"Take them," he said. "It is forbidden to travel east. It is forbidden to cross the river. It is forbidden to go to the Place of the Gods. All these things are forbidden."

"All these things are forbidden," I said, but it was my voice that spoke and not my spirit. He looked at me again.

"My son," he said. "Once I had young dreams. If your dreams do not eat you up, you may be a great priest. If they eat you, you are still my son. Now go on your journey."

I went fasting, as is the law. My body hurt but not my heart. When the dawn came, I was out of sight of the village. I prayed and purified myself, waiting for a sign. The sign was an eagle. It flew east.

Sometimes signs are sent by bad spirits. I waited again on the flat rock, fasting, taking no food. I was very still—I could feel the sky above me and the earth beneath. I waited till the sun was beginning to sink. Then three deer passed in the valley, going east—they did not wind me or see me. There was a white fawn with them—a very great sign.

I followed them, at a distance, waiting for what would happen. My heart was troubled about going east, yet I knew that I must go. My head hummed with my fasting—I did not even see the panther spring upon the white fawn. But, before I knew it, the bow was in my hand. I shouted and the panther lifted his head from the fawn. It is not easy to kill a panther with one arrow but the arrow went through his eye and into his brain. He died as he tried to spring— he rolled over, tearing at the ground. Then I knew I was meant to go east—I knew that was my journey. When the night came, I made my fire and roasted meat.

It is eight suns' journey to the east and a man passes by many Dead Places. The Forest People are afraid of them but I am not. Once I made my fire on the edge of a Dead Place at night and, next morning, in the dead house, I found a good knife, little rusted. That was small to what came afterward but it made my heart feel big. Always when I looked for game, it was in front of my arrow, and twice I passed hunting parties of the Forest People without their knowing. So I knew my magic was strong and my journey clean, in spite of the law.

Toward the setting of the eighth sun, I came to the banks of the great river. It was half-a-day's journey after I had left the god-road—we do not use the god-roads now for they are falling apart into great blocks of stone, and the forest is safer going. A long way off, I had seen the water through trees but the trees were thick. At last, I came out upon an open place at the top of a cliff. There was the great river below, like a giant in the sun. It is very long, very wide. It could eat all the streams we know and still be thirsty. Its name is Ou-dis-sun, the Sacred, the Long. No man of my tribe had seen it, not even my father, the priest. It was magic and I prayed.

Then I raised my eyes and looked south. It was there, the Place of the Gods.

How can I tell what it was like—you do not know. It was there, in the red light, and they were too big to be houses. It was there with the red light upon it, mighty and ruined. I knew that in another moment the gods would see me. I covered my eyes with my hands and crept back into the forest.

Surely, that was enough to do, and live. Surely it was enough to spend the night upon the cliff. The Forest People themselves do not come near. Yet, all through the night, I knew that I should have to cross the river and walk in the places of the gods, although the gods ate me up. My magic did not help me at all and yet there was a fire in my bowels, a fire in my mind. When the sun rose, I thought, "My journey has been clean. Now I will go home from my journey." But, even as I thought so, I knew I could not. If I went to the Place of the Gods, I would surely die, but, if I did not go, I could never be at peace with my spirit again. It is better to lose one's life than one's spirit, if one is a priest and the son of a priest.

Nevertheless, as I made the raft, the tears ran out of my eyes.

The Forest People could have killed me without fight, if they had come upon me then, but they did not come. When the raft was made, I said the sayings for the dead and painted myself for death. My heart was cold as a frog and my knees like water, but the burning in my mind would not let me have peace. As I pushed the raft from the shore, I began my death song—I had the right. It was a fine song.

"I am John, son of John," I sang. "My people are the Hill People.
　They are the men.
I go into the Dead Places but I am not slain.
I take the metal from the Dead Places but I am not blasted.
I travel upon the god-roads and am not afraid. E-yah! I have killed
　the panther, I have killed the fawn!
E-yah! I have come to the great river. No man has come there before.
It is forbidden to go east, but I have gone, forbidden to go on the
　great river, but I am there.
Open your hearts, you spirits, and hear my song.
　Now I go to the Place of the Gods, I shall not return.
My body is painted for death and my limbs weak, but my heart is big
　as I go to the Place of the Gods!"

All the same, when I came to the Place of the Gods, I was afraid, afraid. The current of the great river is very strong—it gripped my raft with its hands. That was magic, for the river itself is wide and calm. I could feel evil spirits about me, in the bright morning; I could feel their breath on my neck as I was swept down the stream. Never have I been so much alone—I tried to think of my knowledge, but it was a squirrel's heap of winter nuts. There was no strength in my knowledge any more and I felt small and naked as a new-hatched bird— alone upon the great river, the servant of the gods.

Yet, after a while, my eyes were opened and I saw. I saw both banks of the river—I saw that once there had been god-roads across it, though now they were broken and fallen like broken vines. Very great they were, and wonderful and broken—broken in the time of the Great Burning when the fire fell out of the sky. And always the current took me nearer to the Place of the Gods, and the huge ruins rose before my eyes.

I do not know the customs of rivers—we are the People of the Hills. I tried to guide my raft with the pole but it spun around. I thought the river meant to take me past the Place of the Gods and out into the Bitter Water of the legends. I grew angry then—my heart felt strong. I said aloud, "I am a priest and the son of a priest!" The gods heard me—they showed me how to paddle with the pole on one side of the raft. The current changed itself—I drew near to the Place of the Gods.

When I was very near, my raft struck and turned over. I can swim in our lakes—I swam to the shore. There was a great spike of rusted metal sticking out into the river—I hauled myself up upon it and sat there, panting. I had saved my bow and two arrows and the knife I found in the Dead Place but that was all. My raft went whirling downstream toward the Bitter Water. I looked after it, and thought if it had trod me under, at least I would be safely dead. Nevertheless, when I had dried my bowstring and re-strung it, I walked forward to the Place of the Gods.

It felt like ground underfoot; it did not burn me. It is not true what some of the tales say, that the ground there burns forever, for I have been there. Here and there were the marks and stains of the Great Burning, on the ruins, that is true. But they were old marks and old stains. It is not true either, what some of our priests say, that it is an island covered with fogs and enchantments. It is not. It is a great Dead Place—greater than any Dead Place we know. Everywhere in it there are god-roads, though most are cracked and broken. Everywhere there are the ruins of the high towers of the gods.

How shall I tell what I saw? I went carefully, my strung bow in my hand, my skin ready for danger. There should have been the wailings of spirits and the shrieks of demons, but there were not. It was very silent and sunny where I had landed—the wind and the rain and the birds that drop seeds had done their work—the grass grew in the cracks of the broken stone. It is a fair island—no wonder the gods built there. If I had come there, a god, I also would have built.

How shall I tell what I saw? The towers are not all broken— here and there one still stands, like a great tree in a forest, and the birds nest high. But the towers themselves look blind, for the gods are gone. I saw a fish-hawk, catching fish in the river. I saw a little dance of white butterflies over a great heap of broken stones and columns. I went there and looked about me—there was a carved stone with cut-letters, broken in half. I can read letters but I could not understand these. They said UBTREAS. There was also the shattered image of a man or a god. It had been made of white stone and he wore his hair tied back like a woman's. His name was ASHING, as I read on the cracked half of a stone. I thought it wise to pray to ASHING, though I do not know that god.

How shall I tell what I saw? There was no smell of man left, on stone or metal. Nor were there many trees in that wilderness of stone. There are many pigeons, nesting and dropping in the towers—the gods must have loved them, or, perhaps, they used them for sacrifices. There are wild cats that roam the god-roads, green-eyed, unafraid of man. At night they wail like demons but they are not demons. The wild dogs are more dangerous, for they hunt in a pack, but them I did not meet till later. Everywhere there are the carved stones, carved with magical numbers or words.

I went north—I did not try to hide myself. When a god or a demon saw me, then I would die, but meanwhile I was no longer afraid. My hunger for knowledge burned in me—there was so much that I could not understand. After awhile, I knew that my belly was hungry. I could have hunted for my meat, but I did not hunt. It is known that the gods did not hunt as we do—they got their food from enchanted boxes and jars. Sometimes these are still found in the Dead Places—once, when I was a child and foolish, I opened such a jar and tasted it and found the food sweet. But my father found out and punished me for it strictly, for, often, that food is death. Now, though, I had long gone past what was forbidden, and I entered the likeliest towers, looking for the food of the gods.

I found it at last in the ruins of a great temple in the mid-city. A mighty temple it must have been, for the roof was painted like the sky at night with its stars—that much I could see, though the colors were faint and dim. It went down into great caves and tunnels—perhaps they kept their slaves there. But when I started to climb down, I heard the squeaking of rats, so I did not go—rats are unclean, and there must have been many tribes of them, from the squeaking. But near there, I found food, in the heart of a ruin, behind a door that still opened. I ate only the fruits from the jars—they had a very sweet taste. There was drink, too, in bottles of glass—the drink of the gods was strong and made my head swim. After I had eaten and drunk, I slept on the top of a stone, my bow at my side.

When I woke, the sun was low. Looking down from where I lay,

I saw a dog sitting on his haunches. His tongue was hanging out of his mouth; he looked as if he were laughing. He was a big dog, with a gray-brown coat, as big as a wolf. I sprang up and shouted at him but he did not move—he just sat there as if he were laughing. I did not like that. When I reached for a stone to throw, he moved swiftly out of the way of the stone. He was not afraid of me; he looked at me as if I were meat. No doubt I could have killed him with an arrow, but I did not know if there were others. Moreover, night was falling.

I looked about me—not far away there was a great, broken god-road, leading north. The towers were high enough, but not so high, and while many of the dead-houses were wrecked, there were some that stood. I went toward this god-road, keeping to the heights of the ruins, while the dog followed. When I had reached the god-road, I saw that there were others behind him. If I had slept later, they would have come upon me asleep and torn out my throat. As it was, they were sure enough of me; they did not hurry. When I went into the dead-house, they kept watch at the entrance—doubtless they thought they would have a fine hunt. But a dog cannot open a door and I knew, from the books, that the gods did not like to live on the ground but on high.

I had just found a door I could open when the dogs decided to rush. Ha! They were surprised when I shut the door in their faces—it was a good door, of strong metal. I could hear their foolish baying beyond it but I did not stop to answer them. I was in darkness—I found stairs and climbed. There were many stairs, turning around till my head was dizzy. At the top was another door—I found the knob and opened it. I was in a long small chamber—on one side of it was a bronze door that could not be opened, for it had no handle. Perhaps there was a magic word to open it but I did not have the word. I turned to the door in the opposite side of the wall. The lock of it was broken and I opened it and went in.

Within, there was a place of great riches. The god who lived there must have been a powerful god. The first room was a small ante-room—I waited there for some time, telling the spirits of the place that I came in peace and not as a robber. When it seemed to me that they had had time to hear me, I went on. Ah, what riches! Few, even, of the windows had been broken—it was all as it had been. The great windows that looked over the city had not been broken at all though they were dusty and streaked with many years. There were coverings on the floors, the colors not greatly faded, and the chairs were soft and deep. There were pictures upon the walls, very strange, very wonderful—I remember one of a bunch of flowers in a jar—if you came close to it, you could see nothing but bits of color, but if you stood away from it, the flowers might have been picked yesterday. It made my heart feel strange to look at this picture—and to look at the figure of a bird, in some hard clay, on a table and see it so like our birds. Everywhere there were books and writings, many in tongues that I could not read. The god who lived there must have been a wise god and full of knowledge. I felt I had right there, as I sought knowledge also.

Nevertheless, it was strange. There was a washing-place but no water—perhaps the gods washed in air. There was a cooking-place but no wood, and though there was a machine to cook food, there was no place to put fire in it. Nor were there candles or lamps—there were things that looked like lamps but they had neither oil nor wick. All these things were magic, but I touched them and lived—the magic had gone out of them. Let me tell one thing to show. In the washing-place, a thing said "Hot" but it was not hot to the touch—another thing said "Cold" but it was not cold. This must have been a strong magic but the magic was gone. I do not understand—they had ways—I wish that I knew.

It was close and dry and dusty in their house of the gods. I have said the magic was gone but that is not true—it had gone from the magic things but it had not gone from the place. I felt the spirits about me, weighing upon me. Nor had I ever slept in a Dead Place before—and yet, tonight, I must sleep there. When I thought of it, my tongue felt dry in my throat, in spite of my wish for knowledge. Almost I would have gone down again and faced the dogs, but I did not.

I had not gone through all the rooms when the darkness fell. When it fell, I went back to the big room looking over the city and made fire. There was a place to make fire and a box with wood in it, though I do not think they cooked there. I wrapped myself in a floor-covering and slept in front of the fire—I was very tired.

Now I tell what is very strong magic. I woke in the midst of the night. When I woke, the fire had gone out and I was cold. It seemed to me that all around me there were whisperings and voices. I closed my eyes to shut them out. Some will say that I slept again, but I do not think that I slept. I could feel the spirits drawing my spirit out of my body as a fish is drawn on a line.

Why should I lie about it? I am a priest and the son of a priest. If there are spirits, as they say, in the small Dead Places near us, what spirits must there not be in that great Place of the Gods? And would not they wish to speak? After such long years? I know that I felt myself drawn as a fish is drawn on a line. I had stepped out of my body—I could see my body asleep in front of the cold fire, but it was not I. I was drawn to look out upon the city of the gods.

It should have been dark, for it was night, but it was not dark. Everywhere there were lights—lines of light—circles and blurs of light —ten thousand torches would not have been the same. The sky itself was alight—you could barely see the stars for the glow in the sky. I thought to myself "This is strong magic" and trembled. There was a roaring in my ears like the rushing of rivers. Then my eyes grew used to the light and my ears to the sound. I knew that I was seeing the city as it had been when the gods were alive.

That was a sight indeed—yes, that was a sight: I could not have seen it in the body—my body would have died. Everywhere went the gods, on foot and in chariots—there were gods beyond number and counting and their chariots blocked the streets. They had turned night to day for their pleasure—they did not sleep with the sun. The noise of their coming and going was the noise of many waters. It was magic what they could do—it was magic what they did.

I looked out of another window—the great vines of their bridges were mended and the god-roads went east and west. Restless, restless, were the gods and always in motion! They burrowed tunnels under rivers—they flew in the air. With unbelievable tools they did giant works—no part of the earth was safe from them, for, if they wished for a thing, they summoned it from the other side of the world. And always, as they labored and rested, as they feasted and made love, there was a drum in their ears—the pulse of the giant city, beating and beating like a man's heart.

Were they happy? What is happiness to the gods? They were great, they were mighty, they were wonderful and terrible. As I looked upon them and their magic, I felt like a child—but a little more, it seemed to me, and they would pull down the moon from the sky. I saw them with wisdom beyond wisdom and knowledge beyond knowledge. And yet not all they did was well done—even I could see that—and yet their wisdom could not but grow until all was peace.

Then I saw their fate come upon them and that was terrible past speech. It came upon them as they walked the streets of their city. I have been in the fights with the Forest People—I have seen men die. But this was not like that. When gods war with gods, they use weapons we do not know. It was fire falling out of the sky and a mist that poisoned. It was the time of the Great Burning and the Destruction. They ran about like ants in the streets of their city— poor gods, poor gods! Then the towers began to fall. A few escaped— yes, a few. The legends tell it. But, even after the city had become a Dead Place, for many years the poison was still in the ground. I saw it happen, I saw the last of them die. It was darkness over the broken city and I wept.

All this, I saw. I saw it as I have told it, though not in the body. When I woke in the morning, I was hungry, but I did not think first of my hunger for my heart was perplexed and confused. I knew the reason for the Dead Places but I did not see why it had happened. It seemed to me it should not have happened, with all the magic they had. I went through the house looking for an answer. There was so much in the house I could not understand—and yet I am a priest and the son of a priest. It was like being on one side of the great river, at night, with no light to show the way.

Then I saw the dead god. He was sitting in his chair, by the window, in a room I had not entered before and, for the first moment, I thought that he was alive. Then I saw the skin on the back of his hand—it was like dry leather. The room was shut, hot and dry—no doubt that had kept him as he was. At first I was afraid to approach him—then the fear left me. He was sitting looking out over the city— he was dressed in the clothes of the gods. His age was neither young nor old—I could not tell his age. But there was wisdom in his face and great sadness. You could see that he would have not run away. He had sat at his window, watching his city die—then he himself had died. But it is better to lose one's life than one's spirit—and you could see from the face that his spirit had not been lost. I knew, that, if I touched him, he would fall into dust—and yet, there was something unconquered in the face.

That is all of my story, for then I knew he was a man—I knew then that they had been men, neither gods nor demons. It is a great knowledge, hard to tell and believe. They were men—they went a dark road, but they were men. I had no fear after that—I had no fear going home, though twice I fought off the dogs and once I was hunted for two days by the Forest People. When I saw my father again, I prayed and was purified. He touched my lips and my breast, he said, "You went away a boy. You come back a man and a priest." I said, "Father, they were men! I have been in the Place of the Gods and seen it! Now slay me, if it is the law—but still I know they were men."

He looked at me out of both eyes. He said, "The law is not always the same shape—you have done what you have done. I could not have done it my time, but you come after me. Tell!"

I told and he listened. After that, I wished to tell all the people but he showed me otherwise. He said, "Truth is a hard deer to hunt. If you eat too much truth at once, you may die of the truth. It was not idly that our fathers forbade the Dead Places." He was right—it is better the truth should come little by little. I have learned that, being a priest. Perhaps, in the old days, they ate knowledge too fast.

Nevertheless, we make a beginning. It is not for the metal alone we go to the Dead Places now—there are the books and the writings. They are hard to learn. And the magic tools are broken—but we can look at them and wonder. At least, we make a beginning. And, when I am chief priest we shall go beyond the great river. We shall go to the Place of the Gods—the place newyork—not one man but a company. We shall look for the images of the gods and find the god ASHING and the others—the gods Lincoln and Baltimore and Moses. But they were men who built the city, not gods or demons. They were men. I remember the dead man's face. They were men who were here before us. We must build again.

Questions for discussion

1. The priest's son broke the law of his tribe, but in the end he was not punished. Were his actions the same kind of crimes as robbery or murder?
2. What punishment did the youth face for breaking the law? Why was he not punished? Should he have been? Why?
3. What did the priest mean when he said, "The law is not always the same shape."?

4. What is the difference between questioning authority and defying authority? Was the priest's son defiant, or was he merely questioning? How does the priest's son feel at the close of the story?
5. The priest's son was willing to suffer the penalty for breaking the law in order to get what he wanted. What was it that he wanted? What were his reasons for going toward the "forbidden east"?
6. What was the great shattering discovery the priest's son made? Did he admire the ways of the gods? What was his explanation of their destruction?
7. The priest's son met both external and internal obstacles. What external obstacles did he have to overcome? Within himself, one side of the conflict was his desire for knowledge. What was the other side of the conflict? At what point in the story did he finally resolve this conflict?
8. When the young man himself became a priest, he followed his father's advice not to tell his people all about his discovery right away. Why? What is the main idea behind this story?
9. Setting plays an important part in this story. Give at least three reasons why this is so.

Vocabulary growth

VARIANT MEANINGS. Most words in common use have more than one meaning. Some of them like *law* have many meanings. The laws of a country are passed by people in power—dictators, kings, elected councils, legislatures, and so on. They are interpreted by courts and enforced by police, marshals, and in some countries by soldiers.

But there are other kinds of law. What is moral law, for example? Who enforces it? What is an economic law? What makes it work? What is a law of physics or chemistry? All of these kinds of law have something in common. What is it? Your dictionary will help you.

For composition

1. This story raises the troublesome question of how to behave towards authority. You might think through some of the questions below and write a statement of your views on "Young People and Authorities."
   a. What authorities are there besides the law?
   b. What would happen if no one ever questioned authorities?
   c. What is the difference between questioning and defying authority?
   d. What would happen if everyone decided for himself which laws he would obey and which he would break?

2. What would happen in your community if a bomb fell on it? Write a narrative with the title "When the Bomb Fell."

3. You are one of the Hill People. Write the story of the return of the priest's son, and tell what he said. Read the last two pages of the story carefully before beginning.

4. The Hill People were guided and protected from danger by their customs and the wisdom of the priest. The young man ventured into places where none of his forefathers had ever been. He was prepared by unusual learning, tough discipline, favored treatment, and ritual ceremonies. Compare his preparation with that of the astronauts who have gone to places no previous generation had seen. In what ways are they given favored treatment, tough discipline, and special training? Are there any ritual ceremonies?

5. Usually everyone has a dream. Is your dream a strong dream that might eat you up, as the father in this story cautioned his son? To what sources will you look for guidance? What customs of past generations may help you? Will science, mathematics, technology, and medicine serve you, as they do the astronauts? Will religion be important? Will your parents, teachers, and classmates understand your dream?

THE
IDEA
BEHIND A
STORY

The Idea Behind a Story

So far, the stories you have read have shown how a writer of fiction blends plot, character, and setting for the purpose of conveying an idea about people or a particular situation. The idea the author wants to communicate to his readers is called the *theme* of the story. The theme is not the plot or the action; the theme is the general truth or commentary on life and people that underlies the story.

The theme is not stated openly, but is left for you to figure out. The theme need not be a moral, or lesson, in the ordinary sense of the word. It should, however, give you something to think about. It may even challenge your own values and opinions. A writer does not ask you to agree with him. But he does say: "Here is what I have observed. Take a look at it."

This does not mean, of course, that every short story must be serious. A fiction writer may choose to present his theme in a light, humorous narrative. For example, "The Secret Life of Walter Mitty" makes you smile or laugh as you learn something important about how people—including yourself—can try to escape the everyday world.

A well-written story, then, presents an important or provocative theme through plot, character, and setting; and these four elements are so artistically fused that you participate in an experience that is both vivid and enriching. Thus, fiction becomes not an "escape" from real life, but a means of gaining a deep and rewarding insight into people and life.

The four stories in this next section all contain themes worthy of thought and discussion. In "The Feeling of Power," Isaac Asimov humorously envisions the possible fate of man if he continues to concentrate upon machines and computers.

In "The Parsley Garden," William Saroyan deals with a human question that has always troubled people: how to deal with humiliation. Saroyan emphasizes that dignity and self-respect are necessary to every person.

131

The destructive effects of an unjust accusation are dramatized in "The Piece of String" by the French short story writer, Guy de Maupassant. Finally, "A Visit to Grandmother" by William Melvin Kelley illustrates the long and painful misunderstanding that can exist between a parent and a child.

The Feeling of Power

ISAAC ASIMOV

Long, long ago in the 1960's, Earth scientists were building machines to imitate the human brain. In time, they succeeded to a degree. But now, at the time of this story, all of this early work has been forgotten. Men have become dependent upon computers, and there is a certain dissatisfaction with them.

JEHAN Shuman was used to dealing with the men in authority on long-embattled Earth. He was only a civilian but he originated programming patterns that resulted in self-directing war computers of the highest sort. Generals consequently listened to him. Heads of congressional committees, too.

There was one of each in the special lounge of New Pentagon. General Weider was space-burnt and had a small mouth puckered almost into a cipher. Congressman Brant was smooth-cheeked and clear-eyed. He smoked Denebian tobacco with the air of one whose patriotism was so notorious, he could be allowed such liberties.

Shuman, tall, distinguished, and Programmer-first-class, faced them fearlessly.

He said, "This, gentlemen, is Myron Aub."

"The one with the unusual gift that you discovered quite by accident," said Congressman Brant placidly. "Ah." He inspected the little man with the egg-bald head with amiable curiosity.

The little man, in return, twisted the fingers of his hands anxiously. He had never been near such great men before. He was only an aging low-grade Technician who had long ago failed all tests designed to smoke out the gifted ones among mankind and had settled into the rut of unskilled labor. There was just this hobby of his that the great Programmer had found out about and was now making such a frightening fuss over.

133

General Weider said, "I find this atmosphere of mystery childish."

"You won't in a moment," said Shuman. "This is not something we can leak to the firstcomer. ——Aub!" There was something imperative about his manner of biting off that one-syllable name, but then he was a great Programmer speaking to a mere Technician. "Aub! How much is nine times seven?"

Aub hesitated a moment. His pale eyes glimmered with a feeble anxiety. "Sixty-three," he said.

Congressman Brant lifted his eyebrows. "Is that right?"

"Check it for yourself, Congressman."

The congressman took out his pocket computer, nudged the milled edges twice, looked at its face as it lay there in the palm of his hand, and put it back. He said, "Is this the gift you brought us here to demonstrate. An illusionist?"

"More than that, sir. Aub has memorized a few operations and with them he computes on paper."

"A paper computer?" said the general. He looked pained.

"No, sir," said Shuman patiently. "Not a paper computer. Simply a sheet of paper. General, would you be so kind as to suggest a number?"

"Seventeen," said the general.

"And you, Congressman?"

"Twenty-three."

"Good! Aub, multiply those numbers and please show the gentlemen your manner of doing it."

"Yes, Programmer," said Aub, ducking his head. He fished a small pad out of one shirt pocket and an artist's hairline stylus out of the other. His forehead corrugated as he made painstaking marks on the paper.

General Weider interrupted him sharply. "Let's see that."

Aub passed him the paper, and Weider said, "Well, it looks like the figure seventeen."

Congressman Brant nodded and said, "So it does, but I suppose anyone can copy figures off a computer. I think I could make a passable seventeen myself, even without practice."

"If you will let Aub continue, gentlemen," said Shuman without heat.

Aub continued, his hand trembling a little. Finally he said in a low voice, "The answer is three hundred and ninety-one."

Congressman Brant took out his computer a second time and flicked it, "By Godfrey, so it is. How did he guess?"

"No guess, Congressman," said Shuman. "He computed that result. He did it on this sheet of paper."

"Humbug," said the general impatiently. "A computer is one thing and marks on paper are another."

"Explain, Aub," said Shuman.

"Yes, Programmer. ——Well, gentlemen, I write down seventeen and just underneath it, I write twenty-three. Next, I say to myself: seven times three——"

The congressman interrupted smoothly, "Now, Aub, the problem is seventeen times twenty-three."

"Yes, I know," said the little Technician earnestly, "but I *start* by saying seven times three because that's the way it works. Now seven times three is twenty-one."

"And how do you know that?" asked the congressman.

"I just remember it. It's always twenty-one on the computer. I've checked it any number of times."

"That doesn't mean it always will be, though, does it?" said the congressman.

"Maybe not," stammered Aub. "I'm not a mathematician. But I always get the right answers, you see."

"Go on."

"Seven times three is twenty-one, so I write down twenty-one. Then one times three is three, so I write down a three under the two of twenty-one."

"Why under the two?" asked Congressman Brant at once.

"Because——" Aub looked helplessly at his superior for support. "It's difficult to explain."

Shuman said, "If you will accept his work for the moment, we can leave the details for the mathematicians."

Brant subsided.

Aub said, "Three plus two makes five, you see, so the twenty-one becomes a fifty-one. Now you let that go for a while and start fresh. You multiply seven and two, that's fourteen, and one and two, that's two. Put them down like this and it adds up to thirty-four. Now if you put the thirty-four under the fifty-one this way and add them, you get three hundred and ninety-one and that's the answer."

There was an instant's silence and then General Weider said,

"I don't believe it. He goes through this rigmarole and makes up numbers and multiplies and adds them this way and that, but I don't believe it. It's too complicated to be anything but hornswoggling."

"Oh no, sir," said Aub in a sweat. "It only *seems* complicated because you're not used to it. Actually, the rules are quite simple and will work for any numbers."

"Any numbers, eh?" said the general. "Come then." He took out his own computer (a severely styled GI model) and struck it at random. Make a five seven three eight on the paper. That's five thousand seven hundred and thirty-eight."

"Yes, sir," said Aub, taking a new sheet of paper.

"Now," (more punching of his computer), "seven two three nine. Seven thousand two hundred and thirty-nine."

"Yes, sir."

"And now multiply those two."

"It will take some time," quavered Aub.

"Take the time," said the general.

"Go ahead, Aub," said Shuman crisply.

Aub set to work, bending low. He took another sheet of paper and another. The general took out his watch finally and stared at it. "Are you through with your magic-making, Technician?"

"I'm almost done, sir. ——Here it is, sir. Forty-one million, five hundred and thirty-seven thousand, three hundred and eighty-two." He showed the scrawled figures of the result.

General Weider smiled bitterly. He pushed the multiplication contact on his computer and let the numbers whirl to a halt. And then he stared and said in a surprised squeak, "Great Galaxy, the fella's right."

The President of the Terrestrial Federation had grown haggard in office and, in private, he allowed a look of settled melancholy to appear on his sensitive features. The Denebian war, after its early start of vast movement and great popularity, had trickled down into a sordid matter of maneuver and countermaneuver, with discontent rising steadily on Earth. Possibly, it was rising on Deneb, too.

And now Congressman Brant, head of the important Committee on Military Appropriations was cheerfully and smoothly spending his half-hour appointment spouting nonsense.

"Computing without a computer," said the president impatiently, "is a contradiction in terms."

"Computing," said the congressman, "is only a system for handling data. A machine might do it, or the human brain might. Let me give you an example." And, using the new skills he had learned, he worked out sums and products until the president, despite himself, grew interested.

"Does this always work?"

"Every time, Mr. President. It is foolproof."

"Is it hard to learn?"

"It took me a week to get the real hang of it. I think you would do better."

"Well," said the president, considering, "it's an interesting parlor game, but what is the use of it?"

"What is the use of a newborn baby, Mr. President? At the moment there is no use, but don't you see that this points the way toward liberation from the machine. Consider, Mr. President," the congressman rose and his deep voice automatically took on some of the cadences he used in public debate, "that the Denebian war is a war of computer against computer. Their computers forge an impenetrable shield of counter-missiles against our missiles, and ours forge one against theirs. If we advance the efficiency of our computers, so do they theirs, and for five years a precarious and profitless balance has existed.

"Now we have in our hands a method for going beyond the computer, leapfrogging it, passing through it. We will combine the mechanics of computation with human thought; we will have the equivalent of intelligent computers; billions of them. I can't predict what the consequences will be in detail but they will be incalculable. And if Deneb beats us to the punch, they may be unimaginably catastrophic."

The president said, troubled, "What would you have me do?"

"Put the power of the administration behind the establishment of a secret project on human computation. Call it Project Number, if you like. I can vouch for my committee, but I will need the administration behind me."

"But how far can human computation go?"

"There is no limit. According to Programmer Shuman, who first introduced me to this discovery——"

"I've heard of Shuman, of course."

"Yes. Well, Dr. Shuman tells me that in theory there is nothing the computer can do that the human mind can not do. The computer merely takes a finite amount of data and performs a finite number of operations upon them. The human mind can duplicate the process."

The president considered that. He said, "If Shuman says this, I am inclined to believe him—in theory. But, in practice, how can anyone know how a computer works?"

Brant laughed genially. "Well, Mr. President, I asked the same question. It seems that at one time computers were designed directly by human beings. Those were simple computers, of course, this being before the time of the rational use of computers to design more advanced computers."

"Yes, yes. Go on."

"Technician Aub apparently had, as his hobby, the reconstruction of some of these ancient devices and in so doing he studied the details of their workings and found he could imitate them. The multiplication I just performed for you is an imitation of the workings of a computer."

"Amazing!"

The congressman coughed gently, "If I may make another point, Mr. President—— The further we can develop this thing, the more we can divert our Federal effort from computer production and computer maintenance. As the human brain takes over, more of our energy can be directed into peacetime pursuits and the impingement of war on the ordinary man will be less. This will be most advantageous for the party in power, of course."

"Ah," said the president, "I see your point. Well, sit down, Congressman, sit down. I want some time to think about this. ——But meanwhile, show me that multiplication trick again. Let's see if I can't catch the point of it."

Programmer Shuman did not try to hurry matters. Loesser was conservative, very conservative, and liked to deal with computers as his father and grandfather had. Still, he controlled the West European computer combine, and if he could be persuaded to join Project Number in full enthusiasm, a great deal would be accomplished.

But Loesser was holding back. He said, "I'm not sure I like the idea of relaxing our hold on computers. The human mind is a capricious thing. The computer will give the same answer to the same problem each time. What guarantee have we that the human mind will do the same?"

"The human mind, Computer Loesser, only manipulates facts. It doesn't matter whether the human mind or a machine does it. They are just tools."

"Yes, yes. I've gone over your ingenious demonstration that the mind can duplicate the computer but it seems to me a little in the air. I'll grant the theory but what reason have we for thinking that theory can be converted to practice?"

"I think we have reason, sir. After all, computers have not always existed. The cave men with their triremes, stone axes, and railroads had no computers."

"And possibly they did not compute."

"You know better than that. Even the building of a railroad or a ziggurat called for some computing, and that must have been without computers as we know them."

"Do you suggest they computed in the fashion you demonstrate?"

"Probably not. After all, this method—we call it 'graphitics,' by the way, from the old European word 'grapho' meaning 'to write'— is developed from the computers themselves so it cannot have antedated them. Still, the cave men must have had *some* method, eh?"

"Lost arts! If you're going to talk about lost arts——"

"No, no. I'm not a lost art enthusiast, though I don't say there may not be some. After all, man was eating grain before hydroponics, and if the primitives ate grain, they must have grown it in soil. What else could they have done?"

"I don't know, but I'll believe in soil-growing when I see someone grow grain in soil. And I'll believe in making fire by rubbing two pieces of flint together when I see that, too."

Shuman grew placative. "Well, let's stick to graphitics. It's just part of the process of etherealization. Transportation by means of bulky contrivances is giving way to direct mass-transference. Communications devices become less massive and more efficient constantly. For that matter, compare your pocket computer with the massive jobs of a thousand years ago. Why not, then, the last step of doing away with computers altogether? Come, sir, Project Number is a going concern; progress is already headlong. But we want your help. If patriotism doesn't move you, consider the intellectual adventure involved."

Loesser said skeptically, "What progress? What can you do beyond multiplication? Can you integrate a transcendental function?"

"In time, sir. In time. In the last month I have learned to handle division. I can determine, and correctly, integral quotients and decimal quotients."

"Decimal quotients? To how many places?"

Programmer Shuman tried to keep his tone casual. "Any number!"

Loesser's lower jaw dropped. "Without a computer?"

"Set me a problem."

"Divide twenty-seven by thirteen. Take it to six places."

Five minutes later, Shuman said, "Two point oh seven six nine two three."

Loesser checked it. "Well, now, that's amazing. Multiplication didn't impress me too much because it involved integers after all, and I thought trick manipulation might do it. But decimals—"

"And that is not all. There is a new development that is, so far, top secret and which, strictly speaking, I ought not to mention. Still—— We may have made a break-through on the square root front."

"Square roots?"

"It involves some tricky points and we haven't licked the bugs yet, but Technician Aub, the man who invented the science and who has an amazing intuition in connection with it, maintains he has the problem almost solved. And he is only a Technician. A man like yourself, a trained and talented mathematician ought to have no difficulty."

"Square roots," muttered Loesser, attracted.

"Cube roots, too. Are you with us?"

Loesser's hand thrust out suddenly, "Count me in."

General Weider stumped his way back and forth at the head of the room and addressed his listeners after the fashion of a savage teacher facing a group of recalcitrant students. It made no difference to the general that they were the civilian scientists heading Project Number. The general was the over-all head, and he so considered himself at every waking moment.

He said, "Now square roots are all fine. I can't do them myself and I don't understand the methods, but they're fine. Still, the Project will not be sidetracked into what some of you call the fundamentals. You can play with graphitics any way you want to after the war is over, but right now we have specific and very practical problems to solve."

In a far corner, Technician Aub listened with painful attention. He was no longer a Technician, of course, having been relieved of his duties and assigned to the Project, with a fine-sounding title and good pay. But, of course, the social distinction remained and the highly placed scientific leaders could never bring themselves to admit him to their ranks on a footing of equality. Nor, to do Aub justice, did he, himself, wish it. He was as uncomfortable with them as they with him.

The general was saying, "Our goal is a simple one, gentlemen; the replacement of the computer. A ship that can navigate space without a computer on board can be constructed in one fifth the time and at one tenth the expense of a computer-laden ship. We could build fleets five times, ten times, as great as Deneb could if we could but eliminate the computer.

"And I see something even beyond this. It may be fantastic now; a mere dream; but in the future I see the manned missile!"

There was an instant murmur from the audience.

The general drove on. "At the present time, our chief bottleneck is the fact that missiles are limited in intelligence. The computer controlling them can only be so large, and for that reason they can meet the changing nature of anti-missile defenses in an unsatisfactory way. Few missiles, if any, accomplish their goal and missile warfare is coming to a dead end; for the enemy, fortunately, as well as for ourselves.

"On the other hand, a missile with a man or two within, controlling flight by graphitics, would be lighter, more mobile, more intelligent. It would give us a lead that might well mean the margin of victory. Besides which, gentlemen, the exigencies of war compel us to remember one thing. A man is much more dispensable than a computer. Manned missiles could be launched in numbers and under circumstances that no good general would care to undertake as far as computer-directed missilies are concerned——"

He said much more but Technician Aub did not wait.

Technician Aub, in the privacy of his quarters, labored long over the note he was leaving behind. It read finally as follows:

"When I began the study of what is now called graphitics, it was no more than a hobby. I saw no more in it than an interesting amusement, an exercise of mind.

"When Project Number began, I thought that others were wiser than I; that graphitics might be put to practical use as a benefit to mankind, to aid in the production of really practical mass-transference devices perhaps. But now I see it is to be used only for death and destruction.

"I cannot face the responsibility involved in having invented graphitics."

He then deliberately turned the focus of a protein-depolarizer on himself and fell instantly and painlessly dead.

They stood over the grave of the little Technician while tribute was paid to the greatness of his discovery.

Programmer Shuman bowed his head along with the rest of them, but remained unmoved. The Technician had done his share and was no longer needed, after all. He might have started graphitics, but now that it had started, it would carry on by itself overwhelmingly, triumphantly, until manned missiles were possible with who knew what else.

Nine times seven, thought Shuman with deep satisfaction, is sixty-three, and I don't need a computer to tell me so. The computer is in my own head.

And it was amazing the feeling of power that gave him.

Questions for discussion

1. Why did Aub kill himself? In what way were his feelings similar to the feelings of some of the nuclear physicists of our times?
2. Any good science-fiction story is based upon certain assumptions of future happenings. What are the assumptions in this story?
3. In learning to depend upon computers, what present-day skills and knowledge have the people of this story forgotten?

4. This story is a *satire*. In a satire, an author criticizes certain kinds of human behavior or attitudes. In this story, generals are satirized because they are more concerned with the exigencies of war than with the advance of science. Thus, the general approves of graphitics only after the war is over; he does not want to be sidetracked from the practical problems of war. Asimov also satirizes Brant, the politician, Loesser, the mathematician, and Shuman, the programmer. How is each of these people satirized?

   In addition, Asimov satirizes certain general failings of the human race. For example, he satirizes man's inability to live in peace by depicting a future society that is at war with another planet in outer space and that concentrates upon the methods of war even more than we do. Asimov also satirizes the following tendencies of man. How does he satirize each one?

   a. The tendency to avoid physical and mental effort.
   b. Man's predisposition to permit machines to work for him.
   c. Man's conservative bent, which prevents his accepting new ideas readily.

5. An ironical situation is one in which the outcome is the opposite of what one normally would expect it to be. For example, the entire intent of Project Number—to liberate men from machines by means of human computation—is ironical, unexpected, since the problem we are concerned with today is the opposite—freeing people from the job of computing. Explain what is ironical about each of the following:

   a. The idea that the human mind duplicates the processes of the computer.
   b. The idea that the workings of the computer are virtually incomprehensible.
   c. The precedence people in the story give computers over the human mind.
   d. A futuristic manned missile.
   e. The dispensability of man and the indispensability of the computer.

6. Asimov uses both satire and irony to develop the theme of the story. By ridiculing certain kinds of human behavior and certain kinds of prevalent attitudes, and by portraying situations that are the opposite of what one might expect them to be, Asimov addresses modern man. What is the message or main idea that underlies the story?

Vocabulary growth

CONTEXT. Reread the context of the following sentences on the pages indicated, and work out a meaning for each italicized word. Check your estimate of these words with the dictionary.

a. Page 133, "He smoked Denebian tobacco with the air of one whose patriotism was so *notorious,* he could be allowed such liberties."
b. Page 137, ". . . the congressman rose and his deep voice automatically took on some of the *cadences* he used in public debate. . . ."
c. Page 138, "As the human brain takes over, more of our energy can be directed into peacetime *pursuits* and the *impingement* of war on the ordinary man will be less."
d. Page 139, "Communications devices become less *massive* and more efficient constantly."

For composition

1. How is your imagination working? Write a statement of what life will be like 100 years from now. What will people have learned? What will they have forgotten?
2. The writer seems to say that there will always be war. Do you agree? Disagree? Write a defense of your opinion, giving facts and reasons.
3. Go to the library and find what material you can on one of the following subjects. Then write a report on it.

a. Hydroponics   c. Machines That Learn
b. New Uses for Computers   d. Machines That Make Machines

The Parsley Garden

WILLIAM SAROYAN

When a boy is humiliated, he wants to get even. There are many ways to get even, as you will discover.

ONE day in August Al Condraj was wandering through Woolworth's without a penny to spend when he saw a small hammer that was not a toy but a real hammer and he was possessed with a longing to have it. He believed it was just what he needed by which to break the monotony and with which to make something. He had gathered some first-class nails from Foley's Packing House where the boxmakers worked and where they had carelessly dropped at least fifteen cents' worth. He had gladly gone to the trouble of gathering them together because it had seemed to him that a nail, as such, was not something to be wasted. He had the nails, perhaps a half pound of them, at least two hundred of them, in a paper bag in the apple box in which he kept his junk at home.

Now, with the ten-cent hammer he believed he could make something out of box wood and the nails, although he had no idea what. Some sort of a table perhaps, or a small bench.

At any rate he took the hammer and slipped it into the pocket of his overalls, but just as he did so a man took him firmly by the arm without a word and pushed him to the back of the store into a small office. Another man, an older one, was seated behind a desk in the office, working with papers. The younger man, the one who had captured him, was excited and his forehead was covered with sweat.

"Well," he said, "here's one more of them."

The man behind the desk got to his feet and looked Al Condraj up and down.

"What's *he* swiped?"

145

"A hammer." The young man looked at Al with hatred. "Hand it over," he said.

The boy brought the hammer out of his pocket and handed it to the young man, who said, "I ought to hit you over the head with it, that's what I ought to do."

He turned to the older man, the boss, the manager of the store, and he said, "What do you want me to do with him?"

"Leave him with me," the older man said.

The younger man stepped out of the office, and the older man sat down and went back to work. Al Condraj stood in the office fifteen minutes before the older man looked at him again.

"Well," he said.

Al didn't know what to say. The man wasn't looking at him, he was looking at the door.

Finally Al said, "I didn't mean to steal it. I just need it and I haven't got any money."

"Just because you haven't got any money doesn't mean you've got a right to steal things," the man said. "Now, does it?"

"No, sir."

"Well, what am I going to do with you? Turn you over to the police?"

Al didn't say anything, but he certainly didn't want to be turned over to the police. He hated the man, but at the same time he realized somebody else could be a lot tougher than he was being.

"If I let you go, will you promise never to steal from this store again?"

"Yes, sir."

"All right," the man said. "Go out this way and don't come back to this store until you've got some money to spend."

He opened a door to the hall that led to the alley, and Al Condraj hurried down the hall and out into the alley.

The first thing he did when he was free was laugh, but he knew he had been humiliated, and he was deeply ashamed. It was not in his nature to take things that did not belong to him. He hated the young man who had caught him and he hated the manager of the store who had made him stand in silence in the office so long. He hadn't liked it at all when the young man had said he ought to hit him over the head with the hammer.

He should have had the courage to look him straight in the eye and say, "You and who else?"

Of course he *had* stolen the hammer and he had been caught, but it seemed to him he oughtn't to have been so humiliated.

After he had walked three blocks he decided he didn't want to go home just yet, so he turned around and started walking back to town. He almost believed he meant to go back and say something to the young man who had caught him. And then he wasn't sure he didn't mean to go back and steal the hammer again, and this time *not* get caught. As long as he had been made to feel like a thief anyway, the least he ought to get out of it was the hammer.

Outside the store he lost his nerve, though. He stood in the street, looking in, for at least ten minutes.

Then, crushed and confused and now bitterly ashamed of himself, first for having stolen something, then for having been caught, then for having been humiliated, then for not having guts enough to go back and do the job right, he began walking home again, his mind so troubled that he didn't greet his pal Pete Wawchek when they came face to face outside Graf's Hardware.

When he got home he was too ashamed to go inside and examine his junk, so he had a long drink of water from the faucet in the back yard. The faucet was used by his mother to water the stuff she planted every year: okra, bell peppers, tomatoes, cucumbers, onions, garlic, mint, eggplants and parsley.

His mother called the whole business the parsley garden, and every night in the summer she would bring chairs out of the house and put them around the table she had had Ondro, the neighborhood handyman, make for her for fifteen cents, and she would sit at the table and enjoy the cool of the garden and the smell of the things she had planted and tended.

Sometimes she would even make a salad and moisten the flat old-country bread and slice some white cheese, and she and he would have supper in the parsley garden. After supper she would attach the water hose to the faucet and water her plants and the place would be cooler than ever and it would smell real good, real fresh and cool and green, all the different growing things making a green-garden smell out of themselves and the air and the water.

After the long drink of water he sat down where the parsley itself was growing and he pulled a handful of it out and slowly ate it.

Then he went inside and told his mother what had happened. He even told her what he had *thought* of doing after he had been turned loose: to go back and steal the hammer again.

"I don't want you to steal," his mother said in broken English. "Here is ten cents. You go back to that man and you give him this money and you bring it home, that hammer."

"No," Al Condraj said. "I won't take your money for something I don't really need. I just thought I ought to have a hammer, so I could make something if I felt like it. I've got a lot of nails and some box wood, but I haven't got a hammer."

"Go buy it, that hammer," his mother said.

"No," Al said.

"All right," his mother said. "Shut up."

That's what she always said when she didn't know what else to say.

Al went out and sat on the steps. His humiliation was beginning to really hurt now. He decided to wander off along the railroad tracks to Foley's because he needed to think about it some more. At Foley's he watched Johnny Gale nailing boxes for ten minutes, but Johnny was too busy to notice him or talk to him, although one day at Sunday school, two or three years ago, Johnny had greeted him and said, "How's the boy?" Johnny worked with a boxmaker's hatchet and everybody in Fresno said he was the fastest boxmaker in town. He was the closest thing to a machine any packing house ever saw. Foley himself was proud of Johnny Gale.

Al Condraj finally set out for home because he didn't want to get in the way. He didn't want somebody working hard to notice that he was being watched and maybe say to him, "Go on, beat it." He didn't want Johnny Gale to do something like that. He didn't want to invite another humiliation.

On the way home he looked for money but all he found was the usual pieces of broken glass and rusty nails, the things that were always cutting his bare feet every summer.

When he got home his mother had made a salad and set the table, so he sat down to eat, but when he put the food in his mouth he just didn't care for it. He got up and went into the three-room house and got his apple box out of the corner of his room and went through his junk. It was all there, the same as yesterday.

He wandered off back to town and stood in front of the closed store, hating the young man who had caught him, and then he went along to the Hippodrome and looked at the display photographs from the two movies that were being shown that day.

Then he went along to the public library to have a look at all the books again, but he didn't like any of them, so he wandered around town some more, and then around half-past eight he went home and went to bed.

His mother had already gone to bed because she had to be up at five to go to work at Inderrieden's, packing figs. Some days there would be work all day, some days there would be only half a day of it, but whatever his mother earned during the summer had to keep them the whole year.

He didn't sleep much that night because he couldn't get over what had happened, and he went over six or seven ways by which to adjust the matter. He went so far as to believe it would be necessary to kill the young man who had caught him. He also believed it would be necessary for him to steal systematically and successfully the rest of his life. It was a hot night and he couldn't sleep.

Finally, his mother got up and walked barefooted to the kitchen for a drink of water and on the way back she said to him softly, "Shut up."

When she got up at five in the morning he was out of the house, but that had happened many times before. He was a restless boy, and he kept moving all the time every summer. He was making mistakes and paying for them, and he had just tried stealing and had been caught at it and he was troubled. She fixed her breakfast, packed her lunch and hurried off to work, hoping it would be a full day.

It was a full day, and then there was overtime, and although she had no more lunch she decided to work on for the extra money, anyway. Almost all the other packers were staying on, too, and her neighbor across the alley, Leeza Ahboot, who worked beside her, said, "Let us work until the work stops, then we'll go home and fix a supper between us and eat it in your parsley garden where it's so cool. It's a hot day and there's no sense not making an extra fifty or sixty cents."

When the two women reached the garden it was almost nine o'clock, but still daylight, and she saw her son nailing pieces of box wood together, making something with a hammer. It looked like a bench. He had already watered the garden and tidied up the rest of the yard, and the place seemed very nice, and her son seemed very serious and busy. She and Leeza went straight to work for their supper, picking bell peppers and tomatoes and cucumbers and a great deal of parsley for the salad.

Then Leeza went to her house for some bread which she had baked the night before, and some white cheese, and in a few minutes they were having supper together and talking pleasantly about the successful day they had had. After supper, they made Turkish coffee over an open fire in the yard. They drank the coffee and smoked a cigarette apiece, and told one another stories about their experiences in the old country and here in Fresno, and then they looked into their cups at the grounds to see if any good fortune was indicated, and there was: health and work and supper out of doors in the summer and enough money for the rest of the year.

Al Condraj worked and overheard some of the things they said, and then Leeza went home to go to bed, and his mother said, "Where you get it, that hammer, Al?"

"I got it at the store."

"How you get it? You steal it?"

Al Condraj finished the bench and sat on it. "No," he said. "I didn't steal it."

"How you get it?"

"I worked at the store for it," Al said.

"The store where you steal it yesterday?"

"Yes."

"Who give you job?"

"The boss."

"What you do?"

"I carried different stuff to the different counters."

"Well, that's good," the woman said. "How long you work for that little hammer?"

"I worked all day," Al said. "Mr. Clemmer gave me the hammer after I'd worked one hour, but I went right on working. The fellow who caught me yesterday showed me what to do, and we worked together. We didn't talk, but at the end of the day he took me to Mr. Clemmer's office and he told Mr. Clemmer that I'd worked hard all day and ought to be paid at least a dollar."

"That's good," the woman said.

"So Mr. Clemmer put a silver dollar on his desk for me, and then the fellow who caught me yesterday told him the store needed a boy like me every day, for a dollar a day, and Mr. Clemmer said I could have the job."

"That's good," the woman said. "You can make it a little money for yourself."

"I left the dollar on Mr. Clemmer's desk," Al Condraj said, "and I told them both I didn't want the job."

"Why you say that?" the woman said. "Dollar a day for eleven-year-old boy good money. Why you not take job?"

"Because I hate the both of them," the boy said. "I would never work for people like that. I just looked at them and picked up my hammer and walked out. I came home and I made this bench."

"All right," his mother said. "Shut up."

His mother went inside and went to bed, but Al Condraj sat on the bench he had made and smelled the parsley garden and didn't feel humiliated any more.

But nothing could stop him from hating the two men, even though he knew they hadn't done anything they shouldn't have done.

Questions for discussion

1. Why did Al refuse the dollar and the job that Mr. Clemmer offered him? What is your opinion of this refusal?

2. How did Mr. Clemmer feel about Al when he was caught stealing? What did the young man think of Al at this time? What did the men think of Al at the close of the story? Which of the two men had changed his opinion of Al?

3. What was Al's feeling toward the men after he had been caught? Why did he hate Mr. Clemmer?

4. What was Al's feeling toward these two men at the close of the story? Why do you suppose he still felt this way? Was this feeling just and reasonable?

5. Why did Al refuse the money his mother offered him?

6. The author emphasizes over and over again that Al felt humiliated. That is, his pride had been hurt. Why did Al feel ashamed?

7. What possible courses of action did Al consider as "ways by which to adjust the matter"? Were you surprised that he decided to work for the hammer? It must have hurt his pride to have to go back and ask the man for a job. Why did he do so? Was it because he wanted the hammer so much?

8. What kind of a person was Al's mother? Why do you suppose that she did not insist that Al go back and take the job? Was money important to her? What else was more important to her than money?
9. Why is the story entitled "The Parsley Garden"? Look back at the paragraphs in which the garden is mentioned. What does the parsley garden do for Leeza and Al's mother? What effect does it have on Al himself?
10. This is a story about an eleven-year-old boy, but the author hopes to make the reader see himself in the boy's thoughts and actions. He stands for all of us. The loss of self-respect and its recovery are experiences that all of us have had. What is the main idea, or theme, of this story?

Vocabulary growth

WORDS ARE INTERESTING. If you look in the dictionary, you will see that *humble, humility,* and *humiliate* all come from a Latin word meaning "low," akin to *humus,* or earth. What connection do you see between "earth" and the meaning of *humiliate:* "to lower the pride or dignity of"?

WORD FORMATION. Thousands of English words are built up by the addition of suffixes to base words. For example, in the story above, the words *systematically* and *successfully* appear. You can see the base words *system* and *success.* You can also see the suffixes *-atic, -al, -ly,* and *-ful.* How many words can you build on the following base words? You may add prefixes too.

| act | add | fix |
| form | time | grade |

For composition

1. For Al and his mother, the parsley garden was a refuge. For Walter Mitty (page 47), his imagination was a refuge. Write a short composition in which you compare and contrast the way these refuges were used. Who do you think had a better purpose, Al and his mother, or Walter Mitty? Why?
2. What happens when you get caught doing something wrong? Did you hate those who caught you? Did you plan to "get even"? Did you "get even"? Write a short narrative describing the experience and your reaction to it.

3. It has often been said that the way to gain an enemy is to do a person a favor. On the other hand, it often appears that you like a person whom you have helped in some way. Do these observations check with your experience? Write your own opinion, supported by instances from your experience.

4. The story makes clear why Al stole the hammer. He suffered painful anguish. He had lost his self-respect and felt humiliated, but he took steps to set the matter right. He was fair and honest in his judgment about the two men. Yet, at the end of the story, he had not stopped hating them. Al was a young boy facing new and agonizing experiences. It is not surprising that he had not yet learned that forgiving is the next step. That is an agonizing experience, too, but forgiving is a better feeling than hating. Forgiving is one aspect of love. Perhaps you might write two paragraphs: one showing a person who seems to have forgiveness in his heart; the other showing a person whose anger and unhappiness is making his life miserable. Show how attitudes of both will radiate to others and affect them, too.

5. Shoplifting is reported to be so widespread today that merchants lose millions of dollars each year. Then, higher prices must be charged. Taxes must be raised so that the police force can be enlarged. Insurance rates are increased because the risks are greater. The cost of living for all people then rises. Both customers and employees enrich themselves by this kind of theft, at the expense of all—even themselves. They too must pay the higher costs of living. Do you have any ideas about ways to help decrease this problem? Do some people engage in it just as a prank to outwit the owner? Have you ever been the victim of a "rip-off"? Write a dialogue between two persons with differing viewpoints: one approves of this kind of stealing; the other doesn't. Each is trying to convince the other that his way of life is the only one that makes sense.

The Piece of String

GUY DE MAUPASSANT

Where rumor is concerned, mountains are sometimes made of mole-hills. But who would suppose that a little piece of string...

ALONG all the roads around Goderville the peasants and their wives were coming toward the burgh because it was market day. The men were proceeding with slow steps, the whole body bent forward at each movement of their long twisted legs, deformed by their hard work, by the weight on the plow which, at the same time, raised the left shoulder and swerved the figure, by the reaping of the wheat which made the knees spread to make a firm "purchase," by all the slow and painful labors of the country. Their blouses, blue, "stiff-starched," shining as if varnished, ornamented with a little design in white at the neck and wrists, puffed about their bony bodies, seemed like balloons ready to carry them off. From each of them a head, two arms, and two feet protruded.

Some led a cow or a calf by a cord, and their wives, walking be-hind the animal, whipped its haunches with a leafy branch to hasten its progress. They carried large baskets on their arms from which, in some cases, chickens and, in others, ducks thrust out their heads. And they walked with a quicker, livelier step than their husbands. Their spare straight figures were wrapped in a scanty little shawl, pinned over their flat bosoms, and their heads were enveloped in a white cloth glued to the hair and surmounted by a cap.

Then a wagon passed at the jerky trot of a nag, shaking strangely, two men seated side by side and a woman in the bottom of the vehicle, the latter holding on to the sides to lessen the hard jolts.

154

In the public square of Goderville there was a crowd, a throng of human beings and animals mixed together. The horns of the cattle, the tall hats with long nap of the rich peasants, and the head-gear of the peasant women rose above the surface of the assembly. And the clamorous, shrill, screaming voices made a continuous and savage din which sometimes was dominated by the robust lungs of some countryman's laugh, or the long lowing of a cow tied to the wall of a house.

All that smacked of the stable, the dairy and the dirt heap, hay and sweat, giving forth that unpleasant odor, human and animal, peculiar to the people of the field.

Maître[1] Hauchecome, of Breaute, had just arrived at Goderville, and he was directing his steps toward the public square, when he perceived upon the ground a little piece of string. Maître Hauche-come, economical like a true Norman, thought that everything useful ought to be picked up, and he bent painfully, for he suffered from rheumatism. He took the bit of thin cord from the ground and began to roll it carefully when he noticed Maître Malandain, the harness-maker, on the threshold of his door, looking at him. They had here-tofore had business together on the subject of a halter, and they were on bad terms, being both good haters. Maître Hauchecome was seized with a sort of shame to be seen thus by his enemy, pick-ing a bit of string out of the dirt. He concealed his "find" quickly under his blouse, then in his trousers' pocket; then he pretended to be still looking on the ground for something which he did not find, and he went toward the market, his head forward, bent double by his pains.

He was soon lost in the noisy and slowly moving crowd, which was busy with interminable bargainings. The peasants milked, went and came, perplexed, always in fear of being cheated, not daring to decide, watching the vender's eye, ever trying to find the trick in the man and the flaw in the beast.

The women, having placed their great baskets at their feet, had taken out the poultry which lay upon the ground, tied together by the feet, with terrified eyes and scarlet crests.

They heard offers, stated their prices with a dry air and impassive

---

[1] *Maître*: Among French peasants and villagers, the word *maître* indicates an owner, a landlord, or a proprietor. The word *monsieur* is used for a gentleman of higher social rank, such as the mayor of a village.

face, or perhaps, suddenly deciding on some proposed reduction, shouted to the customer who was slowly going away: "All right, Maître Authirne, I'll give it to you for that."

Then little by little the square was deserted, and the Angelus ringing at noon, those who had stayed too long, scattered to their shops.

At Jourdain's the great room was full of people eating, as the big court was full of vehicles of all kinds, carts, gigs, wagons, dump carts, yellow with dirt, mended and patched, raising their shafts to the sky like two arms, or perhaps with their shafts in the ground and their backs in the air.

Just opposite the diners seated at the table, the immense fireplace, filled with bright flames, cast a lively heat on the backs of the row on the right. Three spits were turning on which were chickens, pigeons, and legs of mutton; and an appetizing odor of roast beef and gravy dripping over the nicely browned skin rose from the hearth, increased the jovialness, and made everybody's mouth water.

All the aristocracy of the plow ate there at Maître Jourdain's, tavern keeper and horse dealer, a rascal who had money.

The dishes were passed and emptied, as were the jugs of yellow cider. Everyone told his affairs, his purchases, and sales. They discussed the crops. The weather was favorable for the green things but not for the wheat.

Suddenly the drum beat in the court, before the house. Everybody rose except a few indifferent persons, and ran to the door, or to the windows, their mouths still full and napkins in their hands.

After the public crier had ceased his drum-beating, he called out in a jerky voice, speaking his phrases irregularly:

"It is hereby made known to the inhabitants of Goderville, and in general to all persons present at the market, that there was lost this morning, on the road to Benzeville, between nine and ten o'clock, a black leather pocketbook containing five hundred francs and some business papers. The finder is requested to return same with all haste to the mayor's office or to Maître Fortune Houlbreque of Manneville; there will be twenty francs reward."

Then the man went away. The heavy roll of the drum and the crier's voice were again heard at a distance.

Then they began to talk of this event, discussing the chances that Maître Houlbreque had of finding or not finding his pocketbook.

And the meal concluded. They were finishing their coffee when a chief of the gendarmes appeared upon the threshold.

He inquired:

"Is Maître Hauchecome, of Breaute, here?"

Maître Hauchecome, seated at the other end of the table replied: "Here I am."

And the officer resumed:

"Maître Hauchecome, will you have the goodness to accompany me to the mayor's office? The mayor would like to talk to you."

The peasant, surprised and disturbed, swallowed at a draught his tiny glass of brandy, rose, and, even more bent than in the morning, for the first steps after each rest were especially difficult, set out, repeating: "Here I am, here I am."

The mayor was awaiting him, seated on an armchair. He was the notary of the vicinity, a stout, serious man, with pompous phrases.

"Maître Hauchecome," said he, "you were seen this morning to pick up, on the road to Benzeville, the pocketbook lost by Maître Houlbreque, of Manneville."

The countryman, astounded, looked at the mayor, already terrified by this suspicion resting on him without his knowing why.

"Me? Me? Me pick up the pocketbook?"

"Yes, you, yourself."

"Word of honor, I never heard of it."

"But you were seen."

"I was seen, me? Who says he saw me?"

"Monsieur Malandain, the harness-maker."

The old man remembered, understood, and flushed with anger.

"Ah, he saw me, the clodhopper, he saw me pick up this string, here, M'sieu' the Mayor." And rummaging in his pocket he drew out the little piece of string.

But the mayor, incredulous, shook his head.

"You will not make me believe, Maître Hauchecome, that Monsieur Malandain, who is a man worthy of credence, mistook this cord for a pocketbook."

The peasant, furious, lifted his hand, spat at one side to attest his honor, repeating:

"It is nevertheless the truth of the good God, the sacred truth, M'sieu' the Mayor. I repeat it on my soul and my salvation."

The mayor resumed:

"After picking up the object, you stood like a stilt, looking a long while in the mud to see if any piece of money had fallen out."

The good old man choked with indignation and fear.

"How anyone can tell—how anyone can tell—such lies to take away an honest man's reputation! How can anyone—"

There was no use in his protesting; nobody believed him. He was confronted with Monsieur Malandain, who repeated and maintained his affirmation. They abused each other for an hour. At his own request, Maître Hauchecome was searched, nothing was found on him.

Finally the mayor, very much perplexed, discharged him with the warning that he would consult the public prosecutor and ask for further orders.

The news had spread. As he left the mayor's office, the old man was surrounded and questioned with a serious or bantering curiosity, in which there was no indignation. He began to tell the story of the string. No one believed him. They laughed at him.

He went along, stopping his friends, beginning endlessly his statements and his protestations, showing his pockets turned inside out, to prove that he had nothing.

They said:

"Old rascal, get out!"

And he grew angry, becoming exasperated, hot, and distressed at not being believed, not knowing what to do and always repeating himself.

Night came. He must depart. He started on his way with three neighbors to whom he pointed out the place where he had picked up the bit of string; and all along the road he spoke of his adventure.

In the evening he took a turn in the village of Breaute, in order to tell it to everybody. He only met with incredulity.

It made him ill at night.

The next day about one o'clock in the afternoon, Marius Paumelle, a hired man in the employ of Maître Breton, husbandman at Ymanville, returned the pocketbook and its contents belonging to Maître Houlbreque af Manneville.

This man claimed to have found the object in the road; but not knowing how to read, he had carried it to the house and given it to his employer.

The news spread through the neighborhood. Maître Hauchecome was informed of it. He immediately went the circuit and began to recount his story completed by the happy climax. He was in triumph.

"What grieved me so much was not the thing itself, as the lying. There is nothing so shameful as to be placed under a cloud on account of a lie."

He talked of his adventure all day long, he told it on the highway to people who were passing by, in the wineshop to people who were drinking there, and to persons coming out of church the following Sunday. He stopped strangers to tell them about it. He was calm now, and yet something disturbed him without his knowing exactly what it was. People had the air of joking while they listened. They did not seem convinced. He seemed to feel that remarks were being made behind his back.

On Tuesday of the next week he went to the market at Goderville, urged solely by the necessity he felt of discussing the case.

Malandain, standing at his door, began to laugh on seeing him pass. Why?

He approached a farmer from Crequetot, who did not let him finish, and giving him a thump in the stomach said to his face:

"You big rascal."

Then he turned his back on him.

Maître Hauchecome was confused; why was he called a big rascal?

When he was seated at the table in Jourdain's tavern, he commenced to explain "the affair."

A horse dealer from Monvilliers called to him:

"Come, come, old sharper, that's an old trick; I know all about your piece of string!"

Hauchecome stammered:

"But since the pocketbook was found."

But the other man replied:

"Shut up, papa, there is one that finds, and there is one that reports. At any rate you are mixed with it."

The peasant stood choking. He understood. They accused him of having had the pocketbook returned by a confederate, by an accomplice.

He tried to protest. All the table began to laugh.

He could not finish his dinner and went away, in the midst of jeers.

He went home ashamed and indignant, choking with anger and confusion, the more dejected that he was capable with his Norman cunning of doing what they had accused him of, and even boasting of it as of a good turn. His innocence to him, in a confused way, was impossible to prove, as his sharpness was known. And he was stricken to the heart by the injustice of the suspicion.

Then he began to recount the adventures again, prolonging his history every day, adding each time new reasons, more energetic protestations, more solemn oaths which he imagined and prepared in his hours of solitude, his whole mind given up to the story of the string. He was believed so much the less as his defense was more complicated and his arguing more subtle.

"Those are lying excuses," they said behind his back.

He felt it, consumed his heart over it, and wore himself out with useless efforts. He wasted away before their very eyes.

The wags now made him tell about the string to amuse them, as they make a soldier who has been on a campaign tell about his battles. His mind, touched to the depth, began to weaken.

Toward the end of December he took to his bed.

He died in the first days of January, and in the delirium of his death struggles he kept claiming his innocence, reiterating:

"A piece of string, a piece of string—look—here it is, M'sieu' the Mayor."

Questions for discussion

1. In what ways was Hauchecome a typical Norman? What did his picking up the piece of string reveal about him?
2. Why did he behave as he did when he noticed that Malandain was watching him? Was his behavior true to life? Explain.
3. The incident about the pocketbook took on the proportions that it did, not because of the accusation against Hauchecome, but because of his insistence of his innocence. Explain the irony of the situation after the pocketbook was found. Why do you think Hauchecome felt as he did? Was it only because of the way others acted or because of something in himself? Explain.
4. How would you state the idea behind this story?

5. De Maupassant uses vivid description to create a picture of life among the Norman peasants. Point out several examples of this. How important is this setting to what happens in the story?
6. Reread page 160, beginning with the third paragraph: "Then he began . . ." through the line, " 'Those are lying excuses,' they said behind his back." The author wrote this story in France in the late nineteenth century. Do the words likewise describe persons in high positions in the government of our country today? Have citizens been misled by rumor and gossip? Or, have enough facts been given them now, so that they may separate falsehood from fact? Have any suffered the fate of Maître Hauchecome?

Vocabulary growth

WORD BUILDING. There is quite a family of words built on the root *cred-* of the Latin word *credere*, which means "to believe."

creed	credence
credible, incredible	credulous, incredulous
credibly, incredibly	credulity, incredulity
credibility, incredibility	

Look up these words in the dictionary. Practice using them in sentences, with the proper distinctions indicated by the dictionary.

For composition

1. Everyone is aware of some acts or thoughts of which he is ashamed. Write a well-organized paragraph on this subject, beginning, "I'm feeling a little guilty . . ."
2. Have you ever felt that you or someone you know had been accused unfairly? How was the matter cleared up? Was the person's reputation damaged? Write an account of an actual or imaginary incident based on this idea.
3. Write a short sketch in which you show how an insignificant detail can sometimes lead to complications.

A Visit to Grandmother

WILLIAM MELVIN KELLEY

Sometimes people react differently to the same set of circumstances...

CHIG knew something was wrong the instant his father kissed her. He had always known his father to be the warmest of men, a man so kind that when people ventured timidly into his office, it took only a few words from him to make them relax, and even laugh. Doctor Charles Dunford cared about people.

But when he had bent to kiss the old lady's black face, something new and almost ugly had come into his eyes: fear, uncertainty, sadness, and perhaps even hatred.

Ten days before in New York, Chig's father had decided suddenly he wanted to go to Nashville to attend his college class reunion, twenty years out. Both Chig's brother and sister, Peter and Connie, were packing for camp and besides were too young for such an affair. But Chig was seventeen, had nothing to do that summer, and his father asked if he would like to go along. His father had given him additional reasons: "All my running buddies got their diplomas and were snapped up by them crafty young gals, and had kids within a year—now all those kids, some of them gals, are your age."

The reunion had lasted a week. As they packed for home, his father, in a far too offhand way, had suggested they visit Chig's grandmother. "We this close. We might as well drop in on her and my brothers."

So, instead of going north, they had gone farther south, had

162

just entered her house. And Chig had a suspicion now that the reunion had been only an excuse to drive south, that his father had been heading to this house all the time.

His father had never talked much about his family, with the exception of his brother, GL, who seemed part con man, part practical joker, and part Don Juan; he had spoken of GL with the kind of indulgence he would have shown a cute, but ill-behaved and potentially dangerous, five-year-old.

Chig's father had left home when he was fifteen. When asked why, he would answer: "I wanted to go to school. They didn't have a Negro high school at home, so I went up to Knoxville and lived with a cousin and went to school."

They had been met at the door by Aunt Rose, GL's wife, and ushered into the living room. The old lady had looked up from her seat by the window. Aunt Rose stood between the visitors.

The old lady eyed his father. "Rose, who that? Rose?" She squinted. She looked like a doll, made of black straw, the wrinkles in her face running in one direction like the head of a broom. Her hair was white and coarse and grew out straight from her head. Her eyes were brown—the whites, too, seemed light brown—and were hidden behind thick glasses, which remained somehow on a tiny nose. "That Hiram?" That was another of his father's brothers. "No, it ain't Hiram; too big for Hiram." She turned then to Chig. "Now that man, he look like Eleanor, Charles's wife, but Charles wouldn't never send my grandson to see me. I never even hear from Charles." She stopped again.

"It Charles, Mama. That who it is." Aunt Rose, between them, led them closer. "It Charles come all the way from New York to see you, and brung little Charles with him."

The old lady stared up at them. "Charles? Rose, that really Charles?" She turned away, and reached for a handkerchief in the pocket of her clean, ironed, flowered housecoat, and wiped her eyes. "God have mercy. Charles." She spread her arms up to him, and he bent down and kissed her cheek. That was when Chig saw his father, grimacing. She hugged him; Chig watched the muscles in her arms as they tightened around his father's neck. She half rose out of her chair. "How are you, son?"

Chig could not hear his father's answer.

She let him go, and fell back into her chair, grabbing the arms.

Her hands were as dark as the wood, and seemed to become part of it. "Now, who that standing there? Who that man?"

"That's one of your grandsons, Mama." His father's voice cracked. "Charles Dunford, junior. You saw him once, when he was a baby, in Chicago. He's grown now."

"I can see that, boy!" She looked at Chig squarely. "Come here, son, and kiss me once." He did. "What they call you? Charles too?"

"No ma'am, they call me Chig."

She smiled. She had all her teeth, but they were too perfect to be her own. "That's good. Can't have two boys answering to Charles in the same house. Won't nobody at all come. So you that little boy. You don't remember me, do you. I used to take you to church in Chicago, and you'd get up and hop in time to the music. You studying to be a preacher?"

"No, ma'am. I don't think so. I might be a lawyer."

"You'll be an honest one, won't you?"

"I'll try."

"Trying ain't enough! You be honest, you hear? Promise me. You be honest like your daddy."

"All right. I promise."

"Good. Rose, where's GL at? Where's that thief? He gone again?"

"I don't know, Mama." Aunt Rose looked embarrassed. "He say he was going by his liquor store. He'll be back."

"Well, then where's Hiram? You call up those boys, and get them over here—now! You got enough to eat? Let me go see." She started to get up. Chig reached out his hand. She shook him off. "What they tell you about me, Chig? They tell you I'm all laid up? Don't believe it. They don't know nothing about old ladies. When I want help, I'll let you know. Only time I'll need help getting anywheres is when I dies and they lift me into the ground."

She was standing now, her back and shoulders straight. She came only to Chig's chest. She squinted up at him. "You eat much? Your daddy ate like two men."

"Yes, ma'am."

"That's good. That means you ain't nervous. Your mama, she ain't nervous. I remember that. In Chicago, she'd sit down by a window all afternoon and never say nothing, just knit." She smiled. "Let me see what we got to eat."

"I'll do that, Mama." Aunt Rose spoke softly. "You haven't seen Charles in a long time. You sit and talk."

The old lady squinted at her. "You can do the cooking if you promise it ain't because you think I can't."

Aunt Rose chuckled. "I know you can do it, Mama."

"All right. I'll just sit and talk a spell." She sat again and arranged her skirt around her short legs.

Chig did most of the talking, told all about himself before she asked. His father only spoke when he was spoken to, and then, only one word at a time, as if by coming back home, he had become a small boy again, sitting in the parlor while his mother spoke with her guests.

When Uncle Hiram and Mae, his wife, came they sat down to eat. Chig did not have to ask about Uncle GL's absence; Aunt Rose volunteered an explanation: "Can't never tell where the man is at. One Thursday morning he left here and next thing we knew, he was calling from Chicago, saying he went up to see Joe Louis fight. He'll be here though; he ain't as young and foot-loose as he used to be." Chig's father had mentioned driving down that GL was about five years older than he was, nearly fifty.

Uncle Hiram was somewhat smaller than Chig's father; his short-cropped kinky hair was half gray, half black. One spot, just off his forehead, was totally white. Later, Chig found out it had been that way since he was twenty. Mae (Chig could not bring himself to call her Aunt) was a good deal younger than Hiram, pretty enough so that Chig would have looked at her twice on the street. She was a honey-colored woman, with long eyelashes. She was wearing a white sheath.

At dinner, Chig and his father sat on one side, opposite Uncle Hiram and Mae; his grandmother and Aunt Rose sat at the ends. The food was good; there was a lot and Chig ate a lot. All through the meal, they talked about the family as it had been thirty years before, and particularly about the young GL. Mae and Chig asked questions; the old lady answered; Aunt Rose directed the discussion, steering the old lady onto the best stories; Chig's father laughed from time to time; Uncle Hiram ate.

"Why don't you tell them about the horse, Mama?" Aunt Rose,

over Chig's weak protest, was spooning mashed potatoes onto his plate. "There now, Chig."

"I'm trying to think." The old lady was holding her fork halfway to her mouth, looking at them over her glasses. "Oh, you talking about that crazy horse GL brung home that time."

"That's right, Mama." Aunt Rose nodded and slid another slice of white meat on Chig's plate.

Mae started to giggle. "Oh, I've heard this. This is funny, Chig."

The old lady put down her fork and began: Well, GL went out of the house one day with an old, no-good chair I wanted him to take over to the church for a bazaar, and he met up with this man who'd just brung in some horses from out West. Now, I reckon you can expect one swindler to be in every town, but you don't—rightly think there'll be two, and God forbid they should ever meet—but they did, GL and his chair, this man and his horses. Well, I wished I'd-a been there; there must-a been some mighty high-powered talking going on. That man with his horses, he told GL them horses was half-Arab, half-Indian, and GL told that man the chair was an antique he'd stole from some rich white folks. So they swapped. Well, I was a-looking out the window and seen GL dragging this animal to the house. It looked pretty gentle and its eyes was most closed and its feet was shuffling.

"GL, where'd you get that thing?" I says.

"I swapped him for that old chair, Mama," he says. "And made myself a bargain. This is even better than Papa's horse."

Well, I'm a-looking at this horse and noticing how he be looking more and more wide awake every minute, sort of warming up like a teakettle until, I swears to you, that horse is blowing steam out its nose.

"Come on, Mama," GL says, "come on and I'll take you for a ride." Now George, my husband, God rest his tired soul, he'd brung home this white folks' buggy which had a busted wheel and fixed it and was to take it back that day and GL says: "Come on, Mama, we'll use this fine buggy and take us a ride."

"GL," I says, "no, we ain't. Them white folks'll burn us alive if we use their buggy. You just take that horse right on back." You see, I was sure that boy'd come by that animal ungainly.

"Mama, I can't take him back," GL says.

"Why not?" I says.

"Because I don't rightly know where that man is at," GL says.

"Oh," I says. "Well, then I reckon we stuck with it." And I turned around to go back into the house because it was getting late, near dinner time, and I was cooking for ten.

"Mama," GL says to my back. "Mama, ain't you coming for a ride with me?"

"Go on, boy. You ain't getting me inside kicking range of that animal." I was eying that beast and it was boiling hotter all the time. I reckon maybe that man had drugged it. "That horse is wild, GL," I says.

"No, he ain't. He ain't. That man say he is buggy and saddle broke and as sweet as the inside of a apple."

My oldest girl, Essie, had-a come out on the porch and she says: "Go on, Mama. I'll cook. You ain't been out the house in weeks."

"Sure, come on, Mama," GL says. "There ain't nothing to be fidgety about. This horse is gentle as a rose petal." And just then that animal snorts so hard it sets up a little dust storm around its feet.

"Yes, Mama," Essie says, "you can see he gentle." Well, I looked at Essie and then at that horse because I didn't think we could be looking at the same animal. I should-a figured how Essie's eyes ain't never been so good.

"Come on, Mama," GL says.

"All right," I says. So I stood on the porch and watched GL hitching that horse up to the white folks' buggy. For a while there, the animal was pretty quiet, pawing a little, but not much. And I was feeling a little better about riding with GL behind that crazy-looking horse. I could see how GL was happy I was going with him. He was scurrying around that animal buckling buckles and strapping straps, all the time smiling, and that made me feel good.

Then he was finished, and I must say, that horse looked mighty fine hitched to that buggy and I knew anybody what climbed up there would look pretty good too. GL came around and stood at the bottom of the steps, and he took off his hat and bowed and said: "Madam," and reached out his hand to me and I was feeling real elegant like a fine lady. He helped me up to the seat and then got up beside me and we moved out down our alley. And I remember how colored folks come out on their porches and shook their heads, saying: "Lord now, will you look at Eva Dunford, the fine lady! Don't she look good sitting up there!" And I pretended not to hear and sat up straight and proud.

We rode on through the center of town, up Market Street, and all the way out where Hiram is living now, which in them days was all woods, there not being even a farm in sight and that's when that horse must-a first realized he weren't at all broke or tame or maybe thought he was back out West again, and started to gallop.

"GL," I says, "now you ain't joking with your mama, is you? Because if you is, I'll strap you purple if I live through this."

Well, GL was pulling on the reins with all his meager strength, and yelling, "Whoa, you. Say now, whoa!" He turned to me just long enough to say, "I ain't fooling with you, Mama. Honest!"

I reckon that animal weren't too satisfied with the road, because it made a sharp right turn just then, down into a gully and struck out across a hilly meadow. "Mama," GL yells. "Mama, do something!"

I didn't know what to do, but I figured I had to do something so I stood up, hopped down onto the horse's back and pulled it to a stop. Don't ask me how I did that: I reckon it was that I was a mother and my baby asked me to do something, is all.

Well, we walked that animal all the way home; sometimes I had to club it over the nose with my fist to make it come, but we made it, GL and me. "You remember how tired we was, Charles?"

"I wasn't here at the time." Chig turned to his father and found his face completely blank, without even a trace of a smile or a laugh.

"Well, of course you was, son. That happened in . . . in . . . it was a hot summer that year and—"

"I left here in June of that year. You wrote me about it."

The old lady stared past Chig at him. They all turned to him; Uncle Hiram looked up from his plate.

"Then you don't remember how we all laughed?"

"No, I don't, Mama. And I probably wouldn't have laughed. I don't think it was funny." They were staring into each other's eyes.

"Why not, Charles?"

"Because in the first place, the horse was gained by fraud. And in the second place, both of you might have been seriously injured or even killed." He broke off their stare and spoke to himself more than to any of them: "And if I'd done it, you would've beaten me good for it."

"Pardon?" The old lady had not heard him; only Chig had heard.

Chig's father sat up straight as if preparing to debate. "I said that if I had done it, if I had done just exactly what GL did, you would have beaten me good for it, Mama." He was looking at her again.

"Why you say that, son?" She was leaning toward him.

"Don't you know? Tell the truth. It can't hurt me now." His voice cracked, but only once. "If GL and I did something wrong, you'd beat me first and then be too damn tired to beat him. At dinner, he'd always get seconds and I wouldn't. You'd do things with him, like ride in that buggy, but if I wanted you to do something with me, you were always too busy." He paused and considered whether to say what he finally did say: "I cried when I left here. Nobody loved me, Mama. I cried all the way up to Knoxville. That was the last time I ever cried in my life."

"Oh, Charles." She started to get up, to come around the table to him.

He stopped her. "It's too late."

"But you don't understand."

"What don't I understand? I understood then; I understand now."

Tears now traveled down the lines in her face, but when she spoke, her voice was clear. "I thought you knew. I had ten children. I had to give all of them what they needed most." She nodded. "I paid more mind to GL. I had to. GL could-a ended up swinging if I hadn't. But you was smarter. You was more growed up than GL when you was five and he was ten, and I tried to show you that by letting you do what you wanted to do."

"That's not true, Mama. You know it. GL was light-skinned and had good hair and looked almost white and you loved him for that."

"Charles, no. No, son. I didn't love any one of you more than any other."

"That can't be true." His father was standing now, his fists clenched tight. "Admit it, Mama . . . please!" Chig looked at him, shocked; the man was actually crying.

"It may not-a been right what I done, but I ain't no liar." Chig knew she did not really understand what had happened, what he wanted of her. "I'm not lying to you, Charles."

Chig's father had gone pale. He spoke very softly. "You're about thirty years too late, Mama." He bolted from the table. Silverware and dishes rang and jumped. Chig heard him hurrying up to their room.

They sat in silence for awhile and then heard a key in the front door. A man with a new, lacquered straw hat came in. He was wearing brown and white two-tone shoes with very pointed toes and a white summer suit. "Say now! Man! I heard my brother was in town. Where he at? Where that rascal?"

He stood in the doorway, smiling broadly, an engaging, open, friendly smile, the innocent smile of a five-year-old.

Questions for discussion

1. Early in the story, before the family sits down to dinner, it becomes clear that there has been a rift between Dr. Dunford and his mother. Point out sentences that prove this.
2. An elderly woman may be forgetful, but Chig's grandmother remembers many things very well. What details show that she has fond memories of Chig and his parents?
3. What does the grandmother's anecdote about the chair-horse swapping incident reveal about the kind of person GL was when he was young? What does the last sentence in the story reveal about the kind of person he is now?
4. Chig's father gives several reasons for not enjoying the anecdote the grandmother tells. Which reason is the significant one? How does this reveal the cause of the long-standing rift between his mother and himself?
5. What was the grandmother's explanation of her behavior toward her sons, Charles and GL? Do you think she was right to act as she did? How did her treatment of the boys lead to the rift between her and Charles?
6. What value did Charles, his mother, and GL place on honesty?
7. What did Dr. Dunford's reaction—leaving the dinner table—reveal about his feelings?
8. What did Chig learn about his father during the visit?

Vocabulary growth

CONTEXT. Although this story has a complex theme, the author has used a simple vocabulary. An exception is the sentence on page 163: "...he had spoken of GL with the kind of *indulgence* he would have shown a cute, but ill-behaved and *potentially* dangerous, five-year-old." By examining the context of this sentence, what meanings do you get for the italicized words?

For composition

1. Write a statement of the theme of this story. Often such a statement requires only one careful sentence. Because this story is quite complex, you may need several sentences. Try to limit yourself to three.
2. Near the end of the story, on page 170, Chig's father says, "You're about thirty years too late, Mama." Imagine that Chig's father had said instead, "*I'm* about thirty years too late, Mama." Write a well-organized paragraph in which you describe how this would change the character of Chig's father.
3. We usually want to blame others when things go wrong. Describe a humorous or serious incident in which you or someone you know acted in this way. Tell what happened as a result. You might call this composition "It's All Your Fault."
4. Admitting a small mistake may be easy; admitting a large mistake is difficult. Write a well thought-out paragraph in which you give reasons why you admire (or do not admire) a person who admits a mistake.

THE
SUM
OF THE
PARTS

The Sum of the Parts

The preceding sections concentrated on the main elements that make up a short story—plot, character, setting, and theme. This enabled you to study and appreciate the craft of the short story writer more easily. Clearly, however, these elements are interdependent. The fusion of these elements creates the total unity of impression, the overall impact of the story.

In this final section, you must rely to a greater extent on your own initiative. You must put to work the knowledge you have acquired thus far in your study of the short story. In considering each story that follows, you should ask yourself such questions as:

1. Does this plot show originality? Is it convincing and true to life? How well has the author handled the conflict in the story? Is the climax effective?

2. Are the characters, especially the central character, portrayed skillfully and convincingly? What makes the central character an interesting individual? What does this character tell me about myself and other people?

3. Could the story have occurred without this particular setting? Does the setting contribute effectively to the atmosphere and mood? Does the setting affect the characters in any important way?

4. What is the theme of this story? Is it a significant or illuminating one? How does the theme contribute to an understanding of myself and others?

In considering these and other questions that may arise as you read, you will be closer to appreciating the purpose and craft of these writers; and you will have a deeper understanding of the stories themselves.

"The Lost Brooch" by the Russian writer, Anton Chekhov, is related to "The Piece of String," which appeared in the previous section. In both stories, a person is unfairly accused. Chekhov, however, creates complications and a climax that are surprising and quite unlike those of de Maupassant.

Crises occur in all homes. In "Spring Victory" by Jesse Stuart, you will see how a young boy grows up quickly when he is confronted with responsibility during a long, hard winter in the hills of Kentucky.

Molly Morgan and her brothers could hardly wait until their father came home from one of his trips. There were presents, surprises, and fascinating stories of his travels. Changes come into everyone's life, however, and sometimes changes are hard to face.

"One Ordinary Day, with Peanuts" by Shirley Jackson seems to be about ordinary people. Yet something extraordinary seems to be going on with Mr. and Mrs. Johnson. See if you can determine what it is.

Finally, in "The Guest" by Albert Camus, you will meet two unforgetable characters. Each is faced with a painfully difficult decision. Each choice clearly calls for great courage and for sacrifice. You will experience a moment of truth in the lives of Daru, the educated Frenchman, and his guest, the desert Arab, in faraway Algeria.

The Lost Brooch

ANTON CHEKHOV

An article of value is lost. The finger of suspicion points from one person to another. People react to suspicion in surprising ways, as you will discover.

In many Russian stories the same character may have several names. A daughter of a man whose name is Peter may be called Petrovna (meaning daughter of Peter), but she may have, in addition, first names which have been given her at birth or when she was christened. If she is married, her husband's last name also becomes a part of her name. The same person may also have nicknames which you will not recognize as quickly as you would recognize the nickname Jim for James. In this story Theodosia Vasilevny, Madame Kushkina, and Fenya are all names for the same person. Nicolai Sergeitch is her husband. Kushkin is his last name, but his wife is called Madame Kushkina, the *a* is added to indicate the feminine form of her husband's last name.

MASHENKA Pavletsky, a young girl who had just finished her studies at boarding school, returning home from a walk, to the house of the Kushkins, where she was living as a governess, came upon an extraordinary commotion. The doorman, Michael, who let her in, was agitated and red as a lobster. A commotion could be heard from upstairs.

"The mistress is probably having one of her spells," Mashenka thought, "or she has been quarreling with her husband."

In the reception room and in the hall she ran into some of the maids. One servant was crying. Then Mashenka saw the master himself run out of her room. This Nicolai Sergeitch, though not yet old, had a flabby face and a big bald spot. He was red in the face. He shuddered. Taking no notice of the governess, he went past her and throwing up his hands, exclaimed, "Oh, how ghastly this is! How tactless! How stupid, absurd! It's abominable!"

177

Mashenka stepped into her room and there, for the first time in her life, she experienced in all of its acuteness the feeling which is so familiar to all timid people in a subordinate position, living on the bread of the rich and powerful. They were making a search of her room. The mistress, Theodosia Vasilevny, a plump, broad-shouldered woman with heavy black eyebrows under her cap, uncouth, with a slight growth of mustache, with red hands and face, and in her manners resembling a rude country cook, was standing at her table and putting back into her workbag balls of wool, scraps, and slips of paper. Evidently the appearance of the governess took her by surprise, as, looking up and catching sight of her white, astonished face, she became somewhat embarrassed and stammered, "Pardon, I . . . accidentally spilled . . . I caught my sleeve . . ."

And still mumbling something, Madame Kushkina gave a swish to her train and went out. Mashenka looked around her room with amazement, and understanding nothing, not knowing what to think, shrugged her shoulders and turned cold with fear. What was Theodosia Vasilevny looking for in her bag? If, as she said, she had really caught her sleeve in it and spilled it, then why had Nicolai Sergeitch dashed out of her room looking so red and excited? Why was one of the table drawers partly open? The money box, in which the governess kept coins and old stamps locked up, was unfastened. They had opened it, but they had not been able to lock it, although they had covered the whole lock with scratches. The bookstand, the top of the table, the bed—all bore fresh traces of the search. And the basket with the linen, too. The linen was neatly folded, but not in that order in which Mashenka had left it on going out of the house. This meant that it was really a search, but what was the object of it? What had happened? Mashenka recalled the agitation of the doorman, the commotion, which was still going on, the crying servant; didn't all this have some connection with the search that had just taken place in her room? Wasn't she involved in some terrible affair? Mashenka turned pale, and, cold all over, she sank down on the linen basket.

A servant came into the room.

"Liza, don't you know that they . . . have been searching in my room?" asked the governess.

"A brooch of the mistress worth two thousand rubles has been lost."

"Yes, but why search me?"

"They searched everybody, Miss. They went through everything of mine, too. They stripped us all stark naked and searched us. And there I was, Miss, as before God. I never even went near her toilet table, let alone touching the brooch. And I shall tell that to the police, too."

"But . . . why search me?" continued the governess, unable to understand.

"Someone stole the brooch, I tell you. . . . The mistress herself searched everybody with her own hands. They even searched Michael, the doorman, himself. A downright scandal! Nicolai Sergeitch just looks on, cackling like a hen. But there's no need for you to be upset about this, Miss. They didn't find anything in your room! As long as you didn't take the brooch there's nothing for you to be afraid of."

"But this is vile, Liza . . . insulting," said Mashenka, choking with indignation. "This is baseness, meanness! What right had she to suspect me and to ransack my things?"

"You are living amongst strangers, Miss," sighed Liza. "Although you are a young lady, yet . . . it's as if you were a servant. . . . This isn't like being at home with papa and mama."

Mashenka threw herself down on the bed and began to sob bitterly. Never before had such an outrage been perpetrated against her, never had she been so deeply insulted as now. . . . They had suspected her, a well-bred, sensitive girl, the daughter of a professor, of stealing; they had searched her like a woman of the streets! It would be impossible, seemingly, to conceive of any insult greater than that. And to this feeling of outrage was added another heavy fear: what might happen now? All sorts of absurd ideas came into her mind. If they were capable of suspecting her of stealing, then that meant that they might arrest her, strip her stark naked and search her, and then lead her through the street under guard, imprison her in a dark, cold cell with mice and vermin, in just the sort of place they put Princess Tarakanova. Who would intercede for her? Her people lived far away in the provinces; they hadn't the money to come to her. She was alone in the great city as in a great field, without relatives, without acquaintances. They could do with her what they wished.

"I shall run to all the judges and lawyers," thought Mashenka shuddering. "I shall explain to them, I shall take oath. . . . They will prove that I cannot be the thief."

Mashenka recalled that in her room in the basket, under the sheets, were lying some sweets, that, following an old habit established at boarding school, she had put into her pocket at dinner and had carried off to her room with her. The thought that this little secret of hers was already known to her master and mistress threw her into a fever, and the result of all this, the fear, the shame, the insult, was that her heart began to palpitate violently and made itself felt in her temples, her hands, and deep within her.

"Dinner is served!" They were calling Mashenka. Should she go down or not? Mashenka smoothed her hair, wiped her face with a wet towel, and went into the dining room. There dinner was already begun. At one end of the table sat Theodosia Vasilevny, pompous, with a grave, stupid face; at the other end was Nicolai Sergeitch. At the sides sat the guests and the children. Two footmen in frock coats and white gloves served the dinner. Everybody knew that there had been a commotion in the house, that the mistress was upset, and all kept silent. Nothing was heard but their chewing and the clatter of the spoons against the plates.

The mistress herself opened the conversation.

"What have we for the third course?" she asked the footman in a dull, martyred voice.

"Sturgeon *a la russe,*" answered the footman.

"I ordered that, Fenya," Nicolai Sergeitch made haste to say. "I was hungry for fish. If you don't like it, my dear, then don't have them serve it. You see I . . . among the rest . . ."

Theodosia Vasilevny did not like dishes that she had not ordered herself, and now her eyes filled with tears.

"There, there, let's not get upset," said Mamikov, her family doctor, in a sirupy voice as he lightly patted her hand and smiled sweetly. "We are nervous enough without that. Let's forget about the brooch. One's health is more precious than two thousand rubles."

"I don't care about the miserable two thousand!" answered the mistress, and a big tear ran down her cheek. "The fact itself fills me with indignation! I have never put up with stealing in my house. I am not sorry, I am not sorry about anything. But to steal in my house—that is such ungratefulness! To repay me in such a way for my kindness!"

Everyone looked at his plate, but it seemed to Mashenka that after what the mistress said everyone was staring at her. Suddenly a lump came into her throat; she began to cry and pressed her handkerchief to her face.

"Pardon . . ." she stammered, "I cannot. My head aches. I am going."

And she rose from the table, awkwardly banging her chair and more disconcerted than ever went out.

"God knows," said Nicolai Sergeitch, "there was no need to make a search in her room. How ridiculous that was, really!"

"I do not say that she took the brooch," said Theodosia Vasilevny, "but you can vouch for her, I suppose? I confess, I put little trust in these learned paupers."

"Really, Fenya, it is beside the point. Excuse me, Fenya, but according to law you haven't the right to search anyone."

"I don't know anything about your laws. I only know that my brooch is gone, that is all. And I'm going to find that brooch," and she hit her fork against her plate, her eyes flashing with anger. "And you go ahead and eat and don't interfere with my affairs."

Nicolai Sergeitch meekly dropped his eyes and sighed. Meanwhile, Mashenka, having reached her room, threw herself on the bed. She was no longer frightened or ashamed, but a violent desire obsessed her to slap the face of this hard, this arrogant, stupid, smug woman.

As she lay there, breathing hard into the pillow, she dreamed how sweet it would be to go right now and buy the most costly brooch and fling it into the face of this stupid and unreasonable woman. If God would only let Theodosia Vasilevny be brought to ruin, so that she would have to go begging and might understand all the horror of poverty and of not being one's own master, and if the outraged Mashenka might only offer her charity. Oh, if she might only fall heir to a large fortune, buy a carriage, and ride dashingly past her windows that she might envy her.

But all this was daydreaming; in reality there was only one thing to do, to go away as quickly as possible, not to remain here even a single hour. True, it was terrible to give up her place, to go back to her people who had nothing, but what could she do? Mashenka couldn't look at her mistress again, nor at her little room; she was stifled here, full of horror. Theodosia Vasilevny, daft on the subject of diseases and of her would-be aristocracy, was so repulsive to her that it seemed as if everything in the world became gross and ugly because of the fact that this woman was in existence. Mashenka jumped up from the bed and began to pack.

"May I come in?" asked Nicolai Sergeitch at the door; he had come to the door noiselessly and spoke in a soft, gentle voice. "May I?"

"Come in." He came in and remained standing at the door. His eyes looked dim and his little red nose shone. He had been drinking beer after dinner, and this was evidenced in his gait and in his weak flabby hands.

"What does this mean?" he asked pointing to the basket.

"I am packing. I am sorry, Nicolai Sergeitch, but I can't stay in your house any longer. This search has offended me deeply!"

"I understand. Only there's no need of doing this. Why? Your room was searched, but you . . . what difference does that make to you? You will lose nothing because of that."

Mashenka was silent and went on packing. Nicolai Sergeitch kept worrying his mustache as if trying to think what else to say and continued in a wheedling voice:

"I understand, of course, but you must be forbearing. You know my wife is excitable, flighty; you mustn't judge her harshly."

Mashenka said nothing.

"If you are so offended," continued Nicolai Sergeitch, "well, then . . . I am ready to apologize before you. I am sorry."

Mashenka made no answer but only bent lower over her trunk. This hollow-cheeked, spineless creature was of no significance whatever in the house. He played the miserable part of a weakling and somebody always in the way even for the servants; and his apology, likewise, meant nothing.

"M-m- . . . you say nothing? This isn't enough for you? In that case I apologize for my wife. In the name of my wife. . . . She didn't behave with much tact, I admit like a gentleman."

Nicolai Sergeitch walked about, sighed, and went on: "That means you want to keep on gnawing me here, beneath my heart. . . . You want my conscience to torment me."

"I know, Nicolai Sergeitch, you are not to blame," said Mashenka, looking straight into his face with her big, tear-stained eyes. "Why then do you fret yourself?"

"Of course, but for all that . . . don't go away . . . I beg you."

Mashenka shook her head in sign of negation. Nicolai Sergeitch remained standing at the window and began drumming on the window with his finger tips.

"For me such misunderstandings are simply torture," he said. "How about my getting down on my knees before you, eh, how would that be? Your pride has been offended, and here you are crying and getting ready to go away; but here I am with some pride, too, and you have no mercy on it. Or do you want me to tell you what I shall not tell even in confession? Listen, you want me to confess to what I shall not confess to a soul even in the face of death?"

Mashenka did not answer.

"I took my wife's brooch!" said Nicolai Sergeitch quickly. "Are you satisfied now? Does that make it all right? Yes, I . . . took it. . . . Only, of course, I count on your discretion. For God's sake, not a word to anyone, not half a hint!"

Mashenka, amazed and startled, went on packing; she caught up her things, crumpled them, and without any kind of order stuffed them into the trunk and the basket. Now, after the outspoken confession made by Nicolai Sergeitch, she could not remain a minute longer, and she no longer understood how she had been able to live in this house before.

"And it's no wonder . . ." continued Nicolai Sergeitch after a long silence. "The usual story. I need money, and she doesn't give me any. This house and all these things belonged to my father. All this is mine, and the brooch belonged to my mother, and . . . everything is mine. But she has seized everything, taken possession of everything. . . . I can't go to court with her . . . you agree. I beg you earnestly, forgive me . . . and stay. *Tout comprendre, tout pardonner.*[1] Will you stay?"

"No," said Mashenka with decision, beginning to tremble. "Let me alone, I beg you."

"Well, God be with you," sighed Nicolai Sergeitch, sitting down on a stool near the trunk.

"I confess, I like those people who can still be offended, who can feel scorn, and so on. I could sit here a hundred years and look at your indignant face. . . . So then, you won't stay? I understand. . . . It has to be so . . . yes, of course. It is easy for you, but for me—tsk, tsk. . . . And not a step out of this cellar. I might go to

[1] *Tout comprendre, tout pardonner:* To understand all is to pardon all.

one of our estates, but there are these scoundrels of my wife everywhere . . . agronomists, stewards, devil take them. They mortgage and remortgage. . . . You mustn't catch the fish, keep off the grass —don't break the trees."

"Nicolai Sergeitch!" Theodosia Vasilevny's voice was heard from the drawing room. "Agnia, call the master."

"So you won't stay?" asked Nicolai Sergeitch, rising hastily and moving toward the door. "You might just as well stay. In the evenings I could drop in to see you . . . we could talk, eh? Will you stay? If you go, in the whole house there won't be one human face. Oh, this is awful!"

The pallid, hollow-cheeked face of Nicolai Sergeitch implored her, but Mashenka shook her head, and with a wave of the hand he went out.

In half an hour she was already on her way.

Questions for discussion

1. Was Mashenka actually accused of stealing the brooch? Was she singled out as being more suspicious than any of the others? Why was she so outraged by the search? Why did she decide to leave?
2. Did Mashenka do the right thing by leaving? What else might she have done?
3. What Mashenka did is contrasted with what she would have liked to have done, as expressed in her daydream. Which was the wiser and more mature reaction—the daydream or the abrupt departure?
4. Did the ending of the story satisfy you? Why, or why not? Would it have been a better story if Mashenka had confronted Madame Kushkina and criticized her actions? What details in the story make such an action impossible?
5. Why didn't Mashenka go directly to Madame Kushkina's and reveal at once the name of the real thief? What would she have gained by doing this?
6. What kind of things seem important to Madame Kushkina? Does her husband share these interests?
7. FORESHADOWING. There are several instances of planted clues which explain Nicolai Sergeitch's surprising actions. At our first sight of him, he rushes past Mashenka without speaking. Why? What has upset him? As the dinner begins, Nicolai apologizes for ordering the fish. How does this foreshadow the revelation he makes to Mashenka?

What is Nicolai's reaction to his wife's search for the brooch? What does this point to later in the story?

8. Do you feel sorry for Nicolai Sergeitch, or do you feel that he deserves little sympathy? Explain.

9. Why does Nicolai confess to Mashenka? Why does he want her to stay? Does his confession to her make him the gentleman that he claims to be?

Vocabulary growth

FIGURES OF SPEECH. A figure of speech is a literary device used to arouse a vivid picture in the imagination of the reader. The *simile* and the *metaphor* are very frequently used. Both indicate comparisons. The simile uses *as* or *like* to state the comparison. The vivid effect arises out of the fact that the two things compared are really unlike except in the one respect used in the comparison. "Michael—was agitated and *red as a lobster.*" "Nicolai Sergeitch—*cackling like a hen*—" "She was alone in the city *as in a great field.*" These are similies. The metaphor states a comparison or likeness without making use of the word *like* or *as*. "—you want to keep on *gnawing* me here, beneath my heart. . . . You want my conscience to torment me." Was Mashenka really gnawing Nicolai Sergeitch? A rat or some such horrible creature gnaws, but here, the author compares this sort of animal behavior to a human's actions. Make a list of all similes and metaphors that you can find in this story.

For composition

Anton Chekhov died in Russia in 1904, approximately fifty years after the death of Edgar Allan Poe in the United States. Chekhov was not greatly concerned with the strong, single emotional effect which Poe emphasized. Nor did he work out plots as dramatic as those of Guy de Maupassant, who was writing in France at the same time that Chekhov was writing. The Russian writer focused his attention upon character. His stories are simply and realistically told. His characters are like the people he observed in real life around him. "The Lost Brooch" has several fine studies of characters. The following suggestions may help you to gain a better understanding of these characters.

1. Reread Mashenka's daydream on page 181. Write a daydream for Nicolai Sergeitch which comes to him when he first realizes that Mashenka has gone and that he is now all alone with his arrogant wife.

2. Imagine that Mashenka kept a diary. Write the entry that she made on the evening of that terrible day.

3. The story is written from an omniscient (all-knowing) point of view with the author inside and outside the minds of the characters. How would the story sound if written in the first person? Try writing an account of Mashenka's arrival home at the opening of the story. Write it in the first person from Nicolai's point of view. You might begin, "I could stand it no longer. My wife was impossible, insulting everyone, searching everything. I rushed out of Mashenka's room . . ."

Spring Victory

JESSE STUART

Some people in distress just give up. Others cry for help. And others react as the family in this story did.

"**I** don't know what to do," Mom said. "We've just enough bread for three more days. We don't have much of anything else to eat with our bread. This is a terrible winter and your father down sick."

Mom sat on a hickory-split-bottomed chair. She put the bottom in the chair last spring. I went to the woods after the sap got up and peeled the green hickory bark from the small hickory sapling. Mom took a case knife and scraped the green from the slats of bark and wove them across the bottom of a chair that Pa wanted to throw away.

"If your father was only well," Mom said and looked at the blazing forestick. "I'll have to think of something. You children run along and play. Leave me alone to think."

Sophie and I crossed the floorless dog-trot between the two big log-pens of our house. We called this dog-trot the "entry." We kept our stovewood and firewood stacked in the entry. This was a place where the rain, snow and sleet couldn't touch the wood. It was easy to walk out of the kitchen and carry an arm load of the stovewood for the kitchen stove when Mom was getting a meal. It was easy for me to carry firewood from the big stack in the entry to the fireplace where Mom was looking into the fire and dreaming now.

"There's not any place for us to run and play," Sophie said. "The only place we have to run and play is in the entry. And the cold wind blows through here."

"You are right," I said. "But Mom wants us to get away from her for a little while. Mom is worried."

Sophie stood by the firewood pile. She put her small white hand

187

upon a big oak backlog that had part of the dead bark slipped from it. Sophie's long blond hair was lifted from her shoulders by a puff of wind. The cold wind brought tears to her eyes. Beyond the entry we saw the pine-tops upon the mountainside sagging with snow. We couldn't see any briar thickets on the high hill slopes. They were snowed under. The garden fence posts barely stuck out of the snow. Four paths led away from our house—one to the barn, one to the smokehouse, one to the well and one to the hollow back of our house where Mom and I hauled wood with our horse. The big logs that Fred pulled with a long chain around them made a path through the deep snow from the dark hollow under the pines to our wood-yard.

"This snow has been on the ground since last November," Sophie said. "That was 1917. Now it is January, 1918. You are ten years old and I am thirteen years old."

We stood in the entry by the woodpile and talked until we got cold, then Sophie opened the door and we walked into the room. We hurried to the big bright fire to warm our cold hands. Mom was staring into the fireplace with her eagle-gray eyes. She looked steadily toward the fire. She was holding James on her lap. Mary was sitting in a small rocking chair beside her. Pa turned over in bed and asked for water.

Mom got up from the rocking chair with James in her arms. She walked toward Pa's bed. Mom poured a glass of water from a pitcher that was on a stand at the head of Pa's bed.

"Do you feel any better, Mick?" Mom said.

"Nope, I don't, Sal," he said. "I feel weak as water. I'll tell you that flu is bad stuff. I got up too soon and took a back-set."

Pa took the glass of water and drank. Mom stood and watched him with James in her arms.

"Is the firewood holding out?" Pa asked as he handed Mom the empty glass.

"Yes, it is," Mom said. "We have plenty of wood."

"How about food for the family and for the livestock?"

"We're getting along all right," Mom said. "Don't worry, Mick. We'll take care of everything. You get well just as soon as you can. You won't get well if you keep on worrying."

"I can't keep from worrying," Pa said. "Here I'm down sick and can't get out of bed. Crops failed us last year and we don't have bread for the children. And I've never seen such snow on the ground. This is a dark winter to me."

"It's a dark winter for all of us," Mom said. "But remember the snow will leave the hills one of these days and the sun will shine on blue violets under the last year's leaves."

Mom put the water glass back on the standtable beside the water pitcher. She walked back to her rocking chair. The firelight glowed over the room and tiny shadows flickered on the newspaper-papered walls.

"Son, we are not whipped yet," Mom said to me. "Your Pa is asleep now. I'll tell you what we are going to do."

I walked over beside Mom's chair. Sophie stood beside her too.

"Sophie can do the cooking," Mom said. "Can't you bake bread and cook potatoes, Sophie?"

"Yes, Mom."

"And you can use an ax well for a boy ten years old," Mom said.

"It's easy for me to chop with my pole-ax."

"Then you take your ax and go to the hills," Mom said, pointing from the front window to the steep snow-covered bluff east of our house. "You can find all kinds of tough-butted white oaks on the bluff over there. Cut them down, trim them and scoot them over the hill. We're going to make baskets out of them."

I kept my pole-ax in the entry by the firewood pile, where it would not be snowed under. As I walked out of the front room I pulled my toboggan cap low over my ears. I wrapped my overalls close around my legs so the snow wouldn't get around my feet. I picked up my pole-ax and walked down the path toward the barn. The cold whistling January wind stung my face. Fred nickered to me as I passed the barn. The creek was frozen over and the snow had covered the ice save for a hole that I had chopped so the cow and horse could get water.

I passed the water-hole and the empty hog pen. I started up the steep bluff toward the white-oak trees. The snow came to my waist. I held to bushes and pulled up the hills—breaking a tiny path through the waist-deep snow. Finally, I reached the white-oak grove and stood beneath a shaggy-topped white-oak sapling. The dead last year's leaves were still clinging to its boughs. These clusters of dead leaves were weighted with snow. When the sharp bit of my pole-ax hit the frozen white-oak wood, a loud ring struck the distant frozen hill across the valley. The sounds came back to my ears. Snow rained on me from the top of the white-oak sapling. I felled the white oak down the bluff toward the barn. I trimmed its branches and cut its top away. I slid the sapling over the bluff toward the barn. I cut twelve white-oak saplings, and trimmed and topped them and slid them over the bluff toward the barn.

It was easier for me to get down the bluff than it had been to climb it. The white-oak saplings had made a path through the deep snow. I followed this broken path toward the barn. I carried the white-oak saplings from the barn to the entry. I carried one at a time on my shoulder; the green, white-oak timber was heavy. After I'd carried them to the entry I went into the house to see what Mom wanted me to do next.

"After you warm yourself," Mom said, "I want you to take a handsaw and saw these white-oak saplings into six-foot lengths. After you saw them into lengths, I want you to split the lengths into four quarters and bring them to me."

By the time that Mom had given me instructions, I was warm enough to go to work again. I sawed the poles into six-foot lengths and split them with my pole-ax. I carried them into our front room and stacked them in a pile of small green fence rails. Mom looked the pile over and picked up one of the cuts and started to work. She used a butcher knife, a drawing knife and a case knife. She split the lengths again and again and ripped long splits from each length. She split one length into coarser splits to make ribs for the baskets. Another length she split into basket handles.

"I'm going to make feed baskets," Mom said. "People will always need feed baskets. I'm going to make them in three different sizes. I'm going to make peck baskets. Men will want peck baskets to carry eggs to town on Saturdays. They'll want them to carry salt, sugar and coffee from the store where they have a long way to walk. I'm going to make a half-bushel basket for it will be about the right size to carry corn to the mules, nubbins to the cows and ears of corn to the fattening hogs. And I'm going to make bushel feed baskets."

Sophie got supper that night and I fed Fred and fed and milked Gypsy. I found two more hens under our chicken-roost on the snow. They were frozen stiff as boards. I felt of their craws and I could feel only a few grains of corn. I didn't tell Mom about the chickens. I buried them in the snow. Every day a chicken, guinea or a turkey froze to death. Some days as many as six fowls would freeze to death. I found sparrows frozen to death around the barn. When I put hay down for Gypsy and gave her corn nubbins in a feed box I milked cold milk from her into the bucket. There was an icy stillness in the January night air and millions of bright stars shivered in a cold blue sky.

By the time that Sophie had steaming-hot corn bread baked, and I had done the feeding, the milking and carried in firewood and stovewood for the night, Mom had made two baskets. Sophie had crossed the entry from the kitchen to tell Mom that supper was ready, and I was putting my kindling wood in the corner to start the morning fire when Mom held up a basket to us.

"Look, children," she said. "I'm not quite as good as I used to be when I helped Pap make baskets. I need practice."

"Mom, that's a pretty basket," I said.

"Supper is ready," Sophie said.

We crossed the entry for supper. The starlight from the winter skies couldn't shine in at our entry. Mom carried a pine torch to light our way to the kitchen. Sophie led James across the entry and Mary held to Mom's skirt. The hot steaming corn bread was sweet to our taste. We had milk and bread and hot boiled potatoes.

"Tomorrow," Mom said, "I want you to saddle Fred and ride to Greenwood with four baskets. I'll have two more made by morning. Sell the peck basket for thirty-five cents. Sell the half-bushel basket for sixty cents. Sell the two bushel baskets for a dollar apiece. That will be two dollars and ninety-five cents if you sell all the baskets."

"I'll do it, Mom, just as soon as I get the feeding done," I said.

I went to bed that night and dreamed of riding Fred to town. I dreamed that my baskets sold. I dreamed that men wanted more baskets and I came home with my pockets filled with money and a load of corn meal, flour, lard and candy on Fred's back—all that he could carry.

I awoke and built a fire in the front room to warm it for Mom. She slept in a bed with Sophie and Mary just across from Pa's bed—in the other corner of the room. I slept upstairs with James. After I'd built the fire in the front room, I crossed the entry with a pine torch. It was yet before daylight on the short winter day. I put a fire in the stove and took my milk bucket and feed basket and started toward the barn. I fed Fred corn in his box and threw down hay from the loft. I forked hay to Gypsy's manger and gave her corn nubbins to eat while I milked her.

When I finished my work, Mom had cooked our breakfast. She made griddle cakes for us and we ate sorghum molasses with hot griddle cakes. After breakfast while Mom was feeding Pa, I put the saddle on Fred and bridled him. I rode to our front door. Mom came out with four baskets. She carried two in each hand.

"Watch old Fred," Mom said. "Do be careful. If the snow balls on his feet, get off his back and find you a sharp-edged rock or a sharp stick and knock the snowballs from his feet. If he falls with you and hurts you—what are we going to do then?"

Mom looked serious when she spoke to me. I wasn't afraid of Fred falling with me. I was glad to get on my way. I wasn't afraid. I wanted to ride Fred to town. It was the first time in my life that I had ever been allowed to ride to town to sell anything.

"You get a sack of meal if you sell a basket," Mom said. "It will cost you fifty cents. If you sell all your baskets, get a sack of flour too. That's a dollar. That will make a dollar and a half. You'll have a dollar and forty-five cents left. Get a quarter's worth of salt, a quarter's worth of sugar and a small bucket of lard. If you have a penny left, bring it home to me; I've got a use for every penny."

I tied the basket handles together and put two baskets on each side of me behind the saddle. I pulled my toboggan cap low over my ears and rode Fred up the hollow toward Greenup. My feet were warm in my wool socks and brogan shoes. The cold wind hit my face as I rode away in the winter morning mists. Mom stood in the door and watched me out of sight. I rode up the dark hollow where frost filled the air and where the rough sides of the black-oak trees that stood on the rocky bluffs were white with frost and looked like shadowy ghosts. The frozen snow crunched beneath Fred's big feet.

As I rode over the hill toward the town, a man was feeding his cattle.

"Would you like to buy a basket, Mister?" I asked.

"How do you sell them, Sonnie?" he asked.

"Thirty-five cents for the peck basket," I said. "Sixty cents for the half-bushel basket and a dollar apiece for the bushel baskets."

"I'll take both of the bushel baskets," he said as he pulled his billfold from his pocket and reached me two one-dollar bills. I untied the baskets from the saddle and gave them to him. Two dollars in my pocket and two baskets to sell. The next log shack I passed, I climbed down from my saddle and knocked at the door. A man came to the door.

"Do you want to buy a basket, Mister?" I asked.

"Sonnie, it's cold weather to sell baskets, isn't it?" he said. "You're out awfully early too. What time did you start this morning?"

"Daylight."

As we talked, the man stepped out into the yard and looked at my baskets. He asked me the price and I told him.

"I'll take both your baskets," he said. "These are well-made baskets and I need feed baskets. I'll take a couple of bushel baskets if you'll make them for me."

"I'll bring 'em to you in two days from now," I said, "if I live and Mom lives."

"Does your mother make these baskets?"

"Yes."

"She certainly put them together well," he said. "I've made baskets and I know a basket."

I said good-by to the tall beardy-faced man. I felt good to take Pa's place and go to town. I felt like I was helping run the place. I got off Fred's back twice and knocked the balls of snow from his feet with a stick. I rode to town and got my meal and flour. I put a sack of flour in one end of a coffee sack and a sack of meal in the other and balanced it across Fred's broad back—tied the coffee sack to a ring in my saddle. I carried the sugar, salt and lard in another sack in front of my saddle. Slowly, I went over the hill home.

When I rode back home, Mom came out the front door to meet me. I showed her my meal, flour, sugar, salt and lard. Mom's face brightened with a smile. She stood beside the horse and held the bridle reins when I climbed from the saddle a little stiff with cold.

"And here's twenty-five cents left," I said as I pulled my mitten from my right hand and pulled a quarter from my pocket.

"We'll make it," Mom said. "The winter is dark now but after a while spring will come. Violets are budding under the dead leaves beneath the snow right now!"

When I went to the woods to haul wood for the fireplace and the kitchen stove, Mom put on Pa's clothes and went with me. Pa's boots fit tightly on Mom's legs. Mom's long slender body fit well in Pa's corduroy pants. His coat was not too broad for Mom's shoulders.

I tied Fred to a tree by his bridle rein. Then Mom and I took the double-bitted ax and the crosscut saw down to a tall dead oak. I cut a notch part of the way into the dead tree the way I wanted it to fall. Mom took the ax and finished chopping the notch. We got down on our knees together and pulled the long crosscut saw through the hard dead oak tree. After we sawed awhile, we heard a crack and the tree bent earthward and hit the snow-covered hill below with a slash. The snow dashed in a white powdery cloud high into the air. I took the ax and trimmed the knots from the tree while Mom led Fred up to the tree, hooked the snaking chain around the log and fastened the trace chains to the singletree.

"He's ready," Mom said.

I climbed on Fred's back and reined him with the bridle reins down the path. Clouds of snow blew from under Fred's feet as he moved the big dead log toward the woodyard. Mom followed with the ax in her ungloved hand and the crosscut saw across her shoulder. When Fred got to the woodyard, he stopped. I got off his back— unhitched the traces and took him to the barn. I came back to the woodyard. All afternoon Mom got down on her knees in the snow on one side of the log and I got down on the other side of the big dead log. We dragged the crosscut saw across the bone-dry seasoned oak log. We cut stovewood lengths and firewood lengths until we finished the log. Then we split the wood lengths with our axes. I used my pole-ax on the stovewood lengths for the cookstove. Mom used the double-bitted ax and split the longer firewood lengths. After we split the lengths into finer wood, I carried it and stacked it in the entry where it was safe from rain, sleet and snow.

"When your Pa gets well again," Mom said, "I won't have so much work to do. He always took care of the wood getting."

Mom would sit up on the long winter evenings when the wind blew around the house and weave baskets. Sophie would often help her with the white-oak splits after she had washed the supper dishes. Sophie would take the case knife and smooth the splinters from the splits. I would take the drawing knife and rip off long splits from the white-oak sapling lengths. It was fun for us to do this around the winter fire while we laughed and talked and parched corn in a skillet. Mary parched the corn while Sophie and I helped Mom. Pa lay in bed—his face pale on the white pillow in the dim flicker of the pine torch above our mantel and the leaping blazes from the forestick.

Sometimes Pa talked to us about spring and when he would be plowing again. He told us he'd never plant the swamps in the hollow
again and have the craw-dads to cut down the young corn soon as it
sprouted from the furrow. One day when Mom worked steadily all
day and Sophie and I helped her in the evening, she made twelve
baskets.

"It's one of the biggest day's work I've ever done in my life,"
Mom said. "If I could make twelve baskets one day with another,
your Pa wouldn't have to worry about spring and plowing."

"Mom wanted me to be careful about the horse falling," I
thought. "She told me to keep the snow knocked from his feet so it
wouldn't ball and throw him when I rode him to Greenwood—Mom
doesn't know what she would do without me—well, she'd better
watch about making twelve baskets one day with another. What
would we do if Mom would get sick?"

As I walked toward the barn over the frozen snow, I had these
thoughts about my mother.

Every weekday, I took baskets to Greenwood. I sold them almost
any place I stopped. When I sold all my baskets one day, I learned
to take orders for the next day. There was a ready sale for the baskets
my mother made. And I learned to be a good salesman for a boy of
ten. After I'd go to Greenup in the morning and sell baskets and
bring back the things Mom told me to get, I'd climb the bluff above
the hog pen and cut the bushy-topped white-oak saplings and slide
them over the bluff to the barn. Then I'd carry them to the entry
and saw them into lengths with a handsaw, split them into quarters
and carry them into the house for Mom.

When our feed ran out, Mom sent me to Broughton's to see about
feed.

"I think John Broughton's got corn and I know he's got fodder
to sell," Mom said. "You get the saddle on Fred and ride out there
and see. Don't pay over twenty cents a shock for fodder. Offer him
fifteen cents at first and if he won't take that, then offer him twenty
cents. We have to have feed for Fred and Gypsy. Offer him ninety
cents a barrel for corn and don't give him over a dollar a barrel."

When I rode away to Broughton's to see about feed, I left Mom
at home making baskets. I rode down the hollow and turned up the
left fork of Ragweed Hollow. The snow was nearly to Fred's neck in

places. I found my way to Broughton's barn where Mr. Broughton was feeding his cows.

"I'll take fifteen cents a shock for thirty shocks of fodder," Mr. Broughton said. "That's all I have to sell. That ought to winter your horse and cow until grass gets here this spring. I won't take ninety cents a barrel for my corn. I'll take a dollar a barrel for it and put it in your corncrib. I can let you have ten barrels of corn."

"All right, Mr. Broughton," I said. "I'll pay you for the corn and fodder right now if you'll promise me you'll deliver the fodder while you're bringing the corn."

Mr. Broughton's eyes looked big when I told him I'd pay him now. I know he wondered where I got the money. He knew Pa was sick, for he had been around home a couple of times to see him and talked to him far into the night. I paid Mr. Broughton a ten-dollar bill, four one-dollar bills, and I gave him a half-dollar, and then I rode toward home. The next day we had feed in our barn to last until the hills got green again.

"How's the feed holding out?" Pa asked.

"Mick, we've got plenty of feed."

"That feed's lasting the longest of any feed yet."

"We've got enough to last until the pastures get green."

Pa would curve his thin lips in a smile. He would lie on the bed and ask questions about the horse, cow and the chickens.

Often when I walked along the creek I found rabbits dead—frozen hard as an icicle. I found dead quails. I found dead possums. Maybe they had starved to death for something to eat. I found still life wherever I went. The weather had been so cold and all life had shrunk to the bone, perished for food or had frozen to death.

The snow didn't show any signs of melting. All we did at home was get wood, feed the horse and cow, cook, eat, sleep and make baskets. I took four, six, eight and often ten baskets away each day to Greenup. People called me the "Basket Boy." I brought back meal, flour, lard and groceries. Every day I brought back a piece of dry goods for Mom. She'd write down on paper what she wanted and I'd bring it back. Each day I brought back some money to Mom. I never spent all that I got for the baskets. Mom planned the spending so I'd bring the money home.

"A body needs a little money about the house," Mom said. "We never know what time we might need it. I've got to keep a little ahead to buy medicine for your Pa. He's liable to get worse any time. It's hard to tell. He's had a long lingering spell this winter and his face is awful white. His jawbones look like they'll come through the skin any minute, his face is so thin."

As the winter days dragged on toward spring and the great sheets of snow remained on the steep hill slopes, Mom did not go to the woodyard and help me cut wood like she had. I cut the wood with my pole-ax. Mom sat in her chair before the fire and wove baskets. She seldom got up for anything. Pa talked more to Mom now than he had ever talked. She propped him up in bed with his pillow behind his back and he watched her weave baskets. He talked to her about when the snow would leave and the ground would show—dark with melted snow-water running down over the hills leaping like fish in the sunlight.

"Go to Greenwood and get the Doctor," Mom said one day. "Get on Fred and hurry to town!"

"Is Pa worse?" I asked.

"Don't ask questions but hurry," Mom said.

I rode Fred over the snow fast as I could go. I got Doctor Morris out of bed. He rode his horse and we raced back over the snow in the winter moonlight and starlight. When we got to the house, I saw a light from the front window. Sophie met me at the front door and told me that we'd have to sit by a fire in the kitchen stove. Doctor Morris went into the house.

It was some time before daylight when I heard a baby cry.

"I hear a baby crying, Sophie," I said.

"Yes, didn't you know?"

"But I never would have thought that."

"Come in the front room, you children," Doctor Morris said as he looked in at the kitchen door. "You will be very happy when you see the big fine brother I have brought you."

Sophie and I ran into the room to see our brother. We had a lamp in our front room now. I could understand why Mom had me to buy it. I could understand about the cloth she had me to get. I thought of these things as I looked at Mom lying on the bed with the quilts turned down enough for us to see our brother. We stood beside the bed watching the quilts shake when he kicked. And he cried like he was mad at everybody. There was a smile on Mom's lips.

It was March and the sun had shone brightly for three days. The snow melted and the snow-water ran in tiny streams down the small drains on the steep bluffs.

When Pop saw the dark hills again he sat up in bed. There was more color in his face now. Each day he looked at the hills and talked to Mom. Soon as Mom got up from the bed, Pa was up walking about. Color was coming back rapidly to his face. Flesh was coming back to his skeleton body. Sophie did the cooking and I did the feeding. I got the wood. Mom had paid all of our bills and she had a little money left after she paid Doctor Morris.

"All our debts are paid, Mick," Mom said. "The hard winter is over. Violets are in bloom and pasture grass is coming back to the pastures."

Mom stood in the late March wind with our tiny brother wrapped in a blanket in her arms. She kicked the dead leaves away with the toe of her shoe from a clump of blooming violets. I walked ahead of Pa and cut stalks and sprouts with a grubbing hoe. Pa rested between the handles of the plow and looked at Mom standing at the edge of the field with the early buds of spring about her.

Questions for discussion

1. The boy tells the story. Is he the main character, or is his mother? Support your answer by referring to the story.
2. The author makes it clear that this was a very severe winter. Point out the details he uses to make this clear.
3. Does it seem reasonable that Mom could make such fine quality baskets? What clues at the beginning point up her skill and experience?
4. Were you surprised to learn about the birth of the baby? Look back and find the clues that point to this event.
5. What is the significance in the story of Mom's saying to Pa, ". . . the sun will shine on blue violets under the last year's leaves "? Where else do the blue violets come into the story?
6. POINT OF VIEW. The story is told in the first person, but it is told objectively. That is, you are told what the characters said and did, but you are not told how they *felt* about their situation. Nevertheless, you know how they must have felt.
   a. What do you think Mom's feeling was at the beginning of the story? What do you think her feelings were when the boy came back from selling the first baskets? What were her feelings at the end of the story?

b. What do you think Pa's feelings were at the start of the story? At the close of the story (see last paragraph)? Why do you think "Pa talked more to Mom now than he had ever talked"?

c. Can you find two places in which the boy says something about his feelings? Do you know how he felt about the heavy winter work?

7. The conflict in the story is external; the family must survive the hard winter. At what point does it seem clear that the family will triumph?

Vocabulary growth

VARIANT MEANINGS. The word *dog-trot* is used here to refer to the space between two buildings. To people of the Kentucky hills, a *dog-trot* is any space where dogs can exercise and still not be at large. What other meaning does dog-trot have?

"She put her small white hand upon a big oak backlog. . . ." What is a *backlog*? You may have to consult the dictionary and find out. What is a *backlog* of orders in business? What is the connection between the two kinds of backlogs? Which meaning do you think arose first?

For composition

1. What thoughts were going through the minds of the characters in this story? Take one of the following situations and write a paragraph that tells how the characters *felt* about the situation:

a. "If your father was only well," Mom said. . . . "You children run along and play. Leave me alone to think."

b. "I passed the water-hole and the empty hog pen."

c. "Pa rested between the handles of the plow and looked at Mom standing at the edge of the field with the early buds of spring about her."

Molly Morgan

JOHN STEINBECK

As Molly Morgan sits through the ordeal of her first interview for her first job, her mind keeps recalling memories of the past. Through these flashbacks, you will learn many things about her family that have an important bearing on the rest of the story. The story is realistic: there is happiness; there is sadness—and there is Molly Morgan.

MOLLY Morgan got off the train in Salinas and waited three quarters of an hour for the bus. The big automobile was empty except for the driver and Molly.

"I've never been to the Pastures of Heaven, you know," she said. "Is it far from the main road?"

"About three miles," said the driver.

"Will there be a car to take me into the valley?"

"No, not unless you're met."

"But how do people get in there?"

The driver ran over the flattened body of a jack rabbit with apparent satisfaction. "I only hit 'em when they're dead," he apologized. "In the dark, when they get caught in the lights, I try to miss 'em."

"Yes, but how am I going to get into the Pastures of Heaven?"

"I dunno. Walk, I guess. Most people walk if they ain't met."

When he set her down at the entrance to the dirt sideroad, Molly Morgan grimly picked up her suitcase and marched toward the draw in the hills. An old Ford truck squeaked up beside her.

"Goin' into the valley, ma'am?"

"Oh—yes, yes, I am."

"Well, get in, then. Needn't be scared. I'm Pat Humbert. I got a place in the Pastures."

Molly surveyed the grimy man and acknowledged his introduction. "I'm the new schoolteacher, I mean, I think I am. Do you know where Mr. Whiteside lives?"

"Sure, I go right by there. He's clerk of the board. I'm on the school board myself, you know. We wondered what you'd look like." Then he grew embarrassed at what he had said, and flushed under his coating of dirt. " 'Course I mean what you'd *be* like. Last teacher we had gave a good deal of trouble. She was all right, but she was sick —I mean, sick and nervous. Finally quit because she was sick."

Molly picked at the fingertips of her gloves. "My letter says I'm to call on Mr. Whiteside. Is he all right? I don't mean that. I mean— is he—what kind of a man is he?"

"Oh, you'll get along with him all right. He's a fine old man. Born in that house he lives in. Been to college, too. He's a good man. Been clerk of the board for over twenty years."

When he put her down in front of the big old house of John Whiteside, she was really frightened. "Now it's coming," she said to herself. "But there's nothing to be afraid of. He can't do anything to me." Molly was only nineteen. She felt that this moment of inter- view for her first job was a tremendous inch in her whole exist- ence.

The walk up to the door did not reassure her, for the path lay between tight little flower beds hedged in with clipped box, seem- ingly planted with the admonition, "Now grow and multiply, but don't grow too high, nor multiply too greatly, and above all things, keep out of this path!" There was a hand on those flowers, a guiding and a correcting hand. The large white house was very dignified. Venetian blinds of yellow wood were tilted down to keep out the noon sun. Halfway up the path she came in sight of the entrance. There was a veranda as broad and warm and welcoming as an embrace. Through her mind flew the thought, "Surely you can tell the hospitality of a house by its entrance. Suppose it had a little door and no porch." But in spite of the welcoming of the wide steps and the big doorway, her timidities clung to her when she rang the bell. The big door opened, and a large, comfortable woman stood smiling at Molly.

"I hope you're not selling something," said Mrs. Whiteside. "I never want to buy anything and I always do, and then I'm mad."

Molly laughed. She felt suddenly very happy. Until that moment she hadn't known how frightened she really was. "Oh, no," she cried. "I'm the new schoolteacher. My letter says I'm to interview Mr. Whiteside. Can I see him?"

"Well, it's noon, and he's just finishing his dinner. Did you have dinner?"

"Oh, of course. I mean, no."

Mrs. Whiteside chuckled and stood aside for her to enter. "Well, I'm glad you're sure." She led Molly into a large dining room, lined with mahogany, glass-fronted dish closets. The square table was littered with the dishes of a meal. "Why, John must have finished and gone. Sit down, young woman. I'll bring back the roast."

"Oh, no. Really, thank you, no, I'll just talk to Mr. Whiteside and then go along."

"Sit down. You'll need nourishment to face John."

"Is—is he very stern, with new teachers, I mean?"

"Well," said Mrs. Whiteside. "That depends. If they haven't had their dinner, he's a regular bear. He shouts at them. But when they've just got up from the table, he's only just fierce."

Molly laughed happily. "You have children," she said. "Oh, you've raised lots of children—and you like them."

Mrs. Whiteside scowled. "One child raised me. Raised me right through the roof. It was too hard on me. He's out raising cows now, poor devils. I don't think I raised him very high."

When Molly had finished eating, Mrs. Whiteside threw open a side door and called, "John, here's someone to see you." She pushed Molly through the doorway into a room that was a kind of a library, for big bookcases were loaded with thick, old, comfortable books, all filigreed in gold. And it was a kind of a sitting room. There was a fireplace of brick with a mantel of little red tile bricks and the most extraordinary vases on the mantel. Hung on a nail over the mantel, slung really, like a rifle on a shoulder strap, was a huge meerschaum pipe in the Jaeger fashion. Big leather chairs with leather tassels hanging to them, stood about the fireplace, all of them patent rocking chairs with the kind of springs that chant when you rock them. And lastly, the room was a kind of an office, for there was an old-fashioned roll-top desk, and behind it sat John Whiteside. When he looked up, Molly saw that he had at once the kindest and the sternest eyes she had ever seen, and the whitest hair, too. Real blue-white, silky hair, a great duster of it.

"I am Mary Morgan," she began formally.

"Oh, yes, Miss Morgan, I've been expecting you. Won't you sit down?"

She sat in one of the big rockers, and the springs cried with sweet pain. "I love these chairs," she said. "We used to have one when I was a little girl." Then she felt silly. "I've come to interview you about this position. My letter said to do that."

"Don't be so tense, Miss Morgan. I've interviewed every teacher we've had for years. And," he said, smiling, "I still don't know how to go about it."

"Oh—I'm glad, Mr. Whiteside. I never asked for a job before. I was really afraid of it."

"Well, Miss Mary Morgan, as near as I can figure, the purpose of this interview is to give me a little knowledge of your past and of the kind of person you are. I'm supposed to know something about you when you've finished. And now that you know my purpose, I suppose you'll be self-conscious and anxious to give a good impression. Maybe if you just tell me a little about yourself, everything'll be all right. Just a few words about the kind of girl you are, and where you came from."

Molly nodded quickly. "Yes, I'll try to do that, Mr. Whiteside," and she dropped her mind back into the past.

There was the old, squalid, unpainted house with its wide back porch and the round washtubs leaning against the rail. High in the great willow tree her two brothers, Joe and Tom, crashed about crying, "Now I'm an eagle." "I'm a parrot." "Now I'm an old chicken." "Watch me!"

The screen door on the back porch opened, and their mother leaned tiredly out. Her hair would not lie smoothly no matter how much she combed it. Thick strings of it hung down beside her face. Her eyes were always a little red, and her hands and wrists painfully cracked. "Tom, Joe," she called. "You'll get hurt up there. Don't worry me so, boys! Don't you love your mother at all?" The voices in the tree were hushed. The shrieking spirits of the eagle and the old chicken were drenched in self-reproach. Molly sat in the dust, wrapping a rag around a stick and doing her best to imagine it a tall lady in a dress. "Molly, come in and stay with your mother. I'm so tired today."

Molly stood up the stick in the deep dust. "You, miss," she whispered fiercely. "You'll get whipped on your bare bottom when I come back." Then she obediently went into the house.

Her mother sat in a straight chair in the kitchen. "Draw up, Molly. Just sit with me for a little while. Love me, Molly! Love your mother a little bit. You are mother's good little girl, aren't you?" Molly squirmed on her chair. "Don't you love your mother, Molly?"

The little girl was very miserable. She knew her mother would cry in a moment, and then she would be compelled to stroke the stringy hair. Both she and her brothers knew they should love their mother. She did everything for them. They were ashamed that they hated to be near her, but they couldn't help it. When she called to them and they were not in sight, they pretended not to hear, and crept away, talking in whispers.

"Well, to begin with, we were very poor," Molly said to John Whiteside. "I guess we were really poverty-stricken. I had two brothers a little older than I. My father was a traveling salesman, but even so, my mother had to work. She worked terribly hard for us."

About once in every six months a great event occurred. In the morning the mother crept silently out of the bedroom. Her hair was brushed as smoothly as it could be; her eyes sparkled, and she looked happy and almost pretty. She whispered, "Quiet, children! Your father's home."

Molly and her brothers sneaked out of the house, but even in the yard they talked in excited whispers. The news traveled quickly about the neighborhood. Soon the yard was filled with whispering children. "They say their father's home." "Is your father really home?" "Where's he been this time?" By noon there were a dozen children in the yard, standing in expectant little groups, cautioning one another to be quiet.

About noon the screen door on the porch sprang open and whacked against the wall. Their father leaped out. "Hi," he yelled. "Hi, kids!" Molly and her brothers flung themselves upon him and hugged his legs, while he plucked them off and hurled them into the air like kittens.

Mrs. Morgan fluttered about, clucking with excitement, "Children, children. Don't muss your father's clothes."

The neighbor children threw handsprings and wrestled and shrieked with joy. It was better than any holiday.

"Wait till you see," their father cried. "Wait till you see what I brought you. It's a secret now." And when the hysteria had quieted a little he carried his suitcase out on the porch and opened it. There were presents such as no one had ever seen, mechanical toys unknown before—tin bugs that crawled, and astounding steam shovels that worked in sand. There were superb glass marbles with bears and dogs right in their centers. He had something for everyone, several things for everyone. It was all the great holidays packed into one.

Usually it was midafternoon before the children became calm enough not to shriek occasionally. But eventually George Morgan sat on the steps, and they all gathered about while he told his adventures. This time he had been to Mexico while there was a revolution. Again he had gone to Honolulu, had seen the volcano and had himself ridden on a surfboard. Always there were cities and people, strange people; always adventures and a hundred funny incidents, funnier than anything they had ever heard. It couldn't all be told at one time. After school they had to gather to hear more and more. Throughout the world George Morgan tramped, collecting glorious adventures.

"As far as my home life went," Miss Morgan said, "I guess I almost didn't have any father. He was able to get home very seldom from his business trips."
John Whiteside nodded gravely.
Molly's hands rustled in her lap and her eyes were dim.

One time he brought a dumpy, woolly puppy in a box, and it wet on the floor immediately.
"What kind of a dog is it?" Tom asked in his most sophisticated manner.
Their father laughed loudly. He was so young! He looked twenty years younger than their mother. "It's a dollar and a half dog," he explained. "You get an awful lot of kinds of dog for a dollar and a half. It's like this. . . . Suppose you go into a candy store and say, 'I want a nickel's worth of peppermints and gumdrops and licorice and raspberry chews.' Well, I went in and said, 'Give me a dollar and a half's worth of mixed dog.' That's the kind it is. It's Molly's dog, and she has to name it."

"I'm going to name it George," said Molly.

Her father bowed strangely to her, and said, "Thank you, Molly." They all noticed that he wasn't laughing at her, either.

Molly got up very early the next morning and took George about the yard to show him the secrets. She opened the hoard where two pennies and a gold policeman's button were buried. She hooked his little front paws over the back fence so he could look down the street at the schoolhouse. Lastly she climbed into the willow tree, carrying George under one arm. Tom came out of the house and sauntered under the tree. "Look out you don't drop him," Tom called, and just at that moment the puppy squirmed out of her arms and fell. He landed on the hard ground with a disgusting little thump. One leg bent out at a crazy angle, and the puppy screamed long, horrible screams, with sobs between breaths. Molly scrambled out of the tree, dull and stunned by the accident. Tom was standing over the puppy, his face white and twisted with pain, and George, the puppy, screamed on and on.

"We can't let him," Tom cried. "We can't let him." He ran to the woodpile and brought back a hatchet. Molly was too stupefied to look away, but Tom closed his eyes and struck. The screams stopped suddenly. Tom threw the hatchet from him and leaped over the back fence. Molly saw him running away as though he were being chased.

At that moment Joe and her father came out of the back door. Molly remembered how haggard and thin and gray her father's face was when he looked at the puppy. It was something in her father's face that started Molly to crying. "I dropped him out of the tree, and he hurt himself, and Tom hit him, and then Tom ran away." Her voice sounded sulky. Her father hugged Molly's head against his hip.

"Poor Tom!" he said. "Molly, you must remember never to say anything to Tom about it, and never to look at him as though you remembered." He threw a gunny sack over the puppy. "We must have a funeral," he said. "Did I ever tell you about the Chinese funeral I went to, about the colored paper they throw in the air, and the little fat roast pigs on the grave?" Joe edged in closer, and even Molly's eyes took on a gleam of interest. "Well, it was this way. . . ."

Molly looked up at John Whiteside and saw that he seemed to be studying a piece of paper on his desk. "When I was twelve years old, my father was killed in an accident," she said.

The great visits usually lasted about two weeks. Always there came an afternoon when George Morgan walked out into the town and did not come back until late at night. The mother made the children go to bed early, but they could hear him come home, stumbling a little against the furniture, and they could hear his voice through the wall. These were the only times when his voice was sad and discouraged. Lying with held breaths, in their beds, the children knew what that meant. In the morning he would be gone, and their hearts would be gone with him.

They had endless discussions about what he was doing. Their father was a glad argonaut, a silver knight. Virtue and Courage and Beauty—he wore a coat of them. "Sometime," the boys said, "sometime when we're big, we'll go with him and see all those things."

"I'll go, too," Molly insisted.

"Oh, you're a girl. You couldn't go, you know."

"But he'd let me go, you know he would. Sometime he'll take me with him. You see if he doesn't."

When he was gone their mother grew plaintive again, and her eyes reddened. Querulously she demanded their love, as though it were a package they could put in her hand.

One time their father went away, and he never came back. He had never sent any money, nor had he ever written to them, but this time he just disappeared for good. For two years they waited, and then their mother said he must be dead. The children shuddered at the thought, but they refused to believe it, because no one so beautiful and fine as their father could be dead. Some place in the world he was having adventures. There was some good reason why he couldn't come back to them. Some day when the reason was gone, he would come. Some morning he would be there with finer presents and better stories than ever before. But their mother said he must have had an accident. He must be dead. Their mother was distracted. She read those advertisements which offered to help her make money at home. The children made paper flowers and shamefacedly tried to sell them.

The boys tried to develop magazine routes, and the whole family nearly starved. Finally, when they couldn't stand it any longer, the boys ran away and joined the navy. After that Molly saw them as seldom as she had seen her father, and they were so changed, so hard and boisterous, that she didn't even care, for her brothers were strangers to her.

"I went through high school, and then I went to San Jose and entered Teachers' College. I worked for my board and room at the home of Mrs. Allen Morit. Before I finished school my mother died, so I guess I'm a kind of an orphan, you see."

"I'm sorry," John Whiteside murmured gently.

Molly flushed. "That wasn't a bid for sympathy, Mr. Whiteside. You said you wanted to know about me. Everyone has to be an orphan some time."

Molly worked for her board and room. She did the work of a full time servant, only she received no pay. Money for clothes had to be accumulated by working in a store during summer vacation. Mrs. Morit trained her girls. "I can take a green girl, not worth a cent," she often said, "and when that girl's worked for me six months, she can get fifty dollars a month. Lots of women know it, and they just snap up my girls. This is the first schoolgirl I've tried, but even she shows a lot of improvement. She reads too much though. I always say a servant should be asleep by ten o'clock, or else she can't do her work right."

Mrs. Morit's method was one of constant criticism and nagging, carried on in a just, firm tone. "Now, Molly, I don't want to find fault, but if you don't wipe the silver drier than that, it'll have streaks."—"The butter knife goes this way, Molly. Then you can put the tumbler here."

"'I always give a reason for everything," she told her friends.

In the evening, after the dishes were washed, Molly sat on her bed and studied, and when the light was off, she lay on her bed and thought of her father. It was ridiculous to do it, she knew. It was a waste of time. Her father came up to the door, wearing a cutaway coat, and striped trousers and a top hat. He carried a huge bouquet of red roses in his hand. "I couldn't come before, Molly. Get on your coat quickly. First we're going down to get that evening dress in the window of Prussia's, but we'll have to hurry. I have tickets for the train to New York tonight. Hurry up, Molly! Don't stand there gawping." It was silly. Her father was dead. No, she didn't really believe he was dead. Somewhere in the world he lived beautifully, and sometime he would come back.

Molly told one of her friends at school, "I don't really believe it, you see, but I don't disbelieve it. If I ever knew he was dead, why it would be awful. I don't know what I'd do then. I don't want to think about *knowing* he's dead."

When her mother died, she felt little besides shame. Her mother had wanted so much to be loved, and she hadn't known how to draw love. Her importunities had bothered the children and driven them away.

"Well, that's about all," Molly finished. "I got my diploma, and then I was sent down here."

"It was about the easiest interview I ever had," John Whiteside said.

"Do you think I'll get the position, then?"

The old man gave a quick, twinkly glance at the big meerschaum hanging over the mantel.

"That's his friend," Molly thought. "He has secrets with that pipe."

"Yes, I think you'll get the job. I think you have it already. Now, Miss Morgan, where are you going to live? You must find board and room some place."

Before she knew she was going to say it, she had blurted, "I want to live here."

John Whiteside opened his eyes in astonishment. "But we never take boarders, Miss Morgan."

"Oh, I'm sorry I said that. I just like it so much here, you see."

He called, "Willa," and when his wife stood in the half-open door, "This young lady wants to board with us. She's the new teacher."

Mrs. Whiteside frowned. "Couldn't think of it. We never take boarders. She's too pretty to be around that fool of a Bill. What would happen to those cows of his? It'd be a lot of trouble. You can sleep in the third bedroom upstairs," she said to Molly. "It doesn't catch much sun anyway."

Life changed its face. All of a sudden Molly found she was a queen. From the first day the children of the school adored her, for she understood them, and what was more, she let them understand her. It took her some time to realize that she had become an important person. If two men got to arguing at the store about a point of history or literature or mathematics, and the argument deadlocked, it ended up, "Take it to the teacher! If she doesn't know, she'll find it." Molly was very proud to be able to decide such questions. At parties she had to help with the decorations and to plan refreshments. "I think we'll put pine boughs around everywhere. They're pretty, and they smell so good. They smell like a party." She was supposed to know everything and to help with everything, and she loved it.

At the Whiteside home she slaved in the kitchen under the mutterings of Willa. At the end of six months, Mrs. Whiteside grumbled to her husband, "Now if Bill only had any sense. But then," she continued, "if *she* has any sense—" and there she left it.

At night Molly wrote letters to the few friends she had made in Teachers' College, letters full of little stories about her neighbors, and full of joy. She must attend every party because of the social prestige of her position. On Saturdays she ran about the hills and brought back ferns and wild flowers to plant about the house.

Bill Whiteside took one look at Molly and scuttled back to his cows. It was a long time before he found the courage to talk to her very much. He was a big, simple young man who had neither his father's balance nor his mother's humor. Eventually, however, he trailed after Molly and looked after her from distances.

One evening, with a kind of feeling of thanksgiving for her happiness, Molly told Bill about her father. They were sitting in canvas chairs on the wide veranda, waiting for the moon. She told him about the visits, and then about the disappearance. "Do you see what I have, Bill?" she cried. "My lovely father is some place. He's mine. You think he's living, don't you, Bill?"

"Might be," said Bill. "From what you say, he was a kind of an irresponsible cuss, though. Excuse me, Molly. Still, if he's alive, it's funny he never wrote."

Molly felt cold. It was just the kind of reasoning she had successfully avoided for so long. "Of course," she said stiffly, "I know that. I have to do some work now, Bill."

High up on a hill that edged the valley of the Pastures of Heaven, there was an old cabin which commanded a view of the whole country and of all the roads in the vicinity. It was said that the bandit Vasquez had built the cabin and lived in it for a year while the posses went crashing through the country looking for him. It was a landmark. All the people of the valley had been to see it at one time or another. Nearly everyone asked Molly whether she had been there yet. "No," she said, "but I will go up some day. I'll go some Saturday. I know where the trail to it is," One morning she dressed in her new hiking boots and corduroy skirt. Bill sidled up and offered to accompany her. "No," she said. "You have work to do. I can't take you away from it."

"Work be hanged!" said Bill.

"Well, I'd rather go alone. I don't want to hurt your feelings, but I just want to go alone, Bill." She was sorry not to let him accompany her, but his remark about her father had frightened her. "I want to have an adventure," she said to herself. "If Bill comes along, it won't be an adventure at all. It'll just be a trip." It took her an hour and a half to climb up the steep trail under the oaks. The leaves on the ground were as slippery as glass, and the sun was hot. The good smell of ferns and dank moss and yerba buena filled the air. When Molly came at last to the ridge crest, she was damp and winded. The cabin stood in a small clearing in the brush, a little square wooden room with no windows. Its doorless entrance was a black shadow. The place was quiet, the kind of humming quiet that flies and bees and crickets make. The whole hillside sang softly in the sun. Molly approached on tiptoe. Her heart was beating violently. "Now I'm having an adventure," she whispered. "Now I'm right in the middle of an adventure at Vasquez' cabin. She peered in at the doorway and saw a lizard scuttle out of sight. A cobweb fell across her forehead and seemed to try to restrain her. There was nothing at all in the cabin, nothing but the dirt floor and the rotting wooden walls, and the dry, deserted smell of the earth that has long been covered from the sun. Molly was filled with excitement. "At night he sat in there. Sometimes when he heard noises like men creeping up on him, he went out of the door like the ghost of a shadow, and just melted into the darkness." She looked down on the valley of the Pastures of Heaven. The orchards lay in dark green squares; the grain was yellow, and the hills behind, a light brown washed with lavender. Among the farms the roads twisted and curled, avoiding a field, looping around a huge tree, half circling a hill flank. Over the whole valley was stretched a veil of heat shimmer. "Unreal," Molly whispered, "fantastic. It's a story, a real story, and I'm having an adventure." A breeze rose out of the valley like the sigh of a sleeper, and then subsided.

"In the daytime that young Vasquez looked down on the valley just as I'm looking. He stood right here, and looked at the roads down there. He wore a purple vest braided with gold, and the trousers on his slim legs widened at the bottom like the mouths of trumpets. His spur rowels were wrapped with silk ribbons to keep them from clinking. Sometimes he saw the posses riding by on the road below. Lucky for him the men bent over their horses' necks, and didn't look up at the hilltops. Vasquez laughed, but he was afraid, too. Sometimes he sang. His songs were soft and sad because he knew he couldn't live very long."

Molly sat down on the slope and rested her chin in her cupped hands. Young Vasquez was standing beside her, and Vasquez had her father's gay face, his shining eyes as he came on the porch shouting, "Hi, Kids!" This was the kind of adventure her father had. Molly shook herself and stood up. "Now I want to go back to the first and think it all over again."

In the late afternoon Mrs. Whiteside sent Bill out to look for Molly. "She might have turned an ankle, you know." But Molly emerged from the trail just as Bill approached it from the road.

"We were beginning to wonder if you'd got lost," he said. "Did you go up to the cabin?"

"Yes."

"Funny old box, isn't it? Just an old woodshed. There are a dozen just like it down here. You'd be surprised, though, how many people go up there to look at it. The funny part is, nobody's sure Vasquez was ever there."

"Oh, I think he must have been there."

"What makes you think that?"

"I don't know."

Bill became serious. "Everybody thinks Vasquez was a kind of a hero, when really he was just a thief. He started in stealing sheep and horses and ended up robbing stages. He had to kill a few people to do it. It seems to me, Molly, we ought to teach people to hate robbers, not worship them."

"Of course, Bill," she said wearily. "You're perfectly right. Would you mind not talking for a little while, Bill? I guess I'm a little tired, and nervous, too."

The year wheeled around. Pussywillows had their kittens, and wild flowers covered the hills. Molly found herself wanted and needed in the valley. She even attended school board meetings. There had been a time when those secret and august conferences were held behind closed doors, a mystery and a terror to everyone. Now that Molly was asked to step into John Whiteside's sitting room, she found that the board discussed crops, told stories, and circulated mild gossip.

Bert Munroe had been elected early in the fall, and by the spring-time he was the most energetic member. He it was who planned dances at the schoolhouse, who insisted upon having plays and picnics. He even offered prizes for the best report cards in the school. The board was coming to rely pretty much on Bert Munroe.

One evening Molly came down late from her room. As always, when the board was meeting, Mrs. Whiteside sat in the dining room. "I don't think I'll go in to the meeting," Molly said. "Let them have one time to themselves. Sometimes I feel that they would tell other kinds of stories if I weren't there."

"You go on in, Molly! They can't hold a board meeting without you. They're so used to you, they'd be lost. Besides. I'm not at all sure I want them to tell those other stories."

Obediently Molly knocked on the door and went into the sitting room. Bert Munroe paused politely in the story he was narrating. "I was just telling about my new farm hand, Miss Morgan. I'll start over again, 'cause it's kind of funny. You see, I needed a hay hand, and I picked this fellow up under the Salinas River bridge. He was pretty drunk, but he wanted a job. Now I've got him, I find he isn't worth a cent as a hand, but I can't get rid of him. That son of a gun has been every place. You ought to hear him tell about the places he's been. My kids wouldn't let me get rid of him if I wanted to. Why he can take the littlest thing he's seen and make a fine story out of it. My kids just sit around with their ears spread, listening to him. Well, about twice a month he walks into Salinas and goes on a bust. He's one of those dirty, periodic drunks. The Salinas cops always call me up when they find him in a gutter, and I have to drive in to get him. And you know, when he comes out of it, he's always got some kind of present in his pocket for my kid Manny. There's nothing you can do with a man like that. He disarms you. I don't get a dollar's worth of work a month out of him."

Molly felt a sick dread rising in her. The men were laughing at the story. "You're too soft, Bert. You can't afford to keep an enter-tainer on the place. I'd sure get rid of him quick."

Molly stood up. She was dreadfully afraid someone would ask the man's name. "I'm not feeling very well tonight," she said. "If you gentlemen will excuse me, I think I'll go to bed." The men stood up while she left the room. In her bed she buried her head in the pillow. "It's crazy," she said to herself. "There isn't a chance in the world. I'm forgetting all about it right now." But she found to her dismay that she was crying.

The next few weeks were agonizing to Molly. She was reluctant to leave the house. Walking to and from school she watched the road ahead of her. "If I see any kind of a stranger I'll run away. But that's foolish. I'm being a fool." Only in her own room did she feel safe. Her terror was making her lose color, was taking the glint out of her eyes.

"Molly, you ought to go to bed," Mrs. Whiteside insisted. "Don't be a little idiot. Do I have to smack you the way I do Bill to make you go to bed?" But Molly would not go to bed. She thought too many things when she was in bed.

The next time the board met, Bert Munroe did not appear. Molly felt reassured and almost happy at his absence.

"You're feeling better, aren't you, Miss Morgan?"

"Oh, yes. It was only a little thing, a kind of a cold. If I'd gone to bed I might have been really sick."

The meeting was an hour gone before Bert Munroe came in. "Sorry to be late," he apologized. "The same old thing happened. My so-called hay hand was asleep in the street in Salinas. What a mess! He's out in the car sleeping it off now. I'll have to hose the car out tomorrow."

Molly's throat closed with terror. For a second she thought she was going to faint. "Excuse me, I must go," she cried, and ran out of the room. She walked into the dark hallway and steadied herself against the wall. Then slowly and automatically she marched out of the front door and down the steps. The night was filled with whispers. Out in the road she could see the black mass that was Bert Munroe's car. She was surprised at the way her footsteps plodded down the path of their own volition. "Now I'm killing myself," she said. "Now I'm throwing everything away. I wonder why." The gate was under her hand, and her hand flexed to open it. Then a tiny breeze sprang up and brought to her nose the sharp foulness of vomit. She heard a blubbering, drunken snore. Instantly something whirled in her head. Molly spun around and ran frantically back to the house. In her room she locked the door and sat stiffly down, panting with the effort of her run. It seemed hours before she heard the men go out of the house, calling their good-nights. Then Bert's motor started, and the sound of it died away down the road. Now that she was ready to go she felt paralyzed.

John Whiteside was writing at his desk when Molly entered the sitting room. He looked up questioningly at her. "You aren't well, Miss Morgan. You need a doctor."

She planted herself woodenly beside the desk. "Could you get a substitute teacher for me?" she asked.

"Of course I could. You pile right into bed and I'll call a doctor."

"It isn't that, Mr. Whiteside. I want to go away tonight."

"What are you talking about? You aren't well."

"I told you my father was dead. I don't know whether he's dead or not. I'm afraid—I want to go away tonight."

He stared intently at her. "Tell me what you mean," he said softly.

"If I should see that drunken man of Mr. Munroe's—" she paused, suddenly terrified at what she was about to say.

John Whiteside nodded very slowly.

"No," she cried. "I don't think that. I'm sure I don't."

"I'd like to do something, Molly."

"I don't want to go, I love it here—But I'm afraid. It's so important to me."

John Whiteside stood up and came close to her and put his arm about her shoulders. "I don't think I understand, quite," he said. "I don't think I want to understand. That isn't necessary." He seemed to be talking to himself. "It wouldn't be quite courteous—to understand."

"Once I'm away I'll be able not to believe it," Molly whimpered.

He gave her shoulders one quick squeeze with his encircling arm. "You run upstairs and pack your things, Molly," he said. "I'll get out the car and drive you right in to Salinas now."

Questions for discussion

1. Can you justify Molly's decision to run away? Was it a responsible thing to do? Was it realistic? Why did she decide to go? Molly rejected her father. Did she also condemn him?

2. Study the Vocabulary Growth section first. It will help you answer these questions:

   a. Did the Morgan children have *illusions* about their father? Did
       they have *illusions* about their mother? Explain.
   b. Did the father try to *delude* his children? Did he really enjoy his
       children? Cite evidence from the story.
   c. Did the father *elude* his responsibilities to his family? Support
       your answer with evidence from the story.
   d. At what point did *disillusionment* come to Molly?
3. Why was Molly so attracted to Mr. and Mrs. Whiteside? What did
   they provide for her that she had missed before?
4. Compassion is the quality of real and sympathetic feeling for another
   person who is in trouble. Is there an example of compassion in this
   story? Support your view with evidence from the story.
5. Do you think that the account of Vasquez belongs in the story?
   To what other character in the story is Vasquez similar? What is
   Molly's feeling about Vasquez? Why do you think the author put
   the account of Vasquez into the story?
6. Daydreaming may be good or bad, depending upon why a person
   indulges in it. What effect did daydreaming have on Molly?
7. How did you feel about the unhappy ending of this story? Was it
   reasonable in terms of what we know about Molly and about Mr.
   Whiteside? Does a story have to have a happy ending in order to be
   satisfying?
8. By what means does the author portray Molly's mother and father?
   Does he portray them *directly* by telling about them? Does he portray
   them *indirectly* by showing how other people react to them? by what
   the mother and father say and do? Give examples.
9. By what means does the author portray Molly? Give examples.

Vocabulary growth

For centuries, Latin was the language educated people read and wrote
in. Many of our words are built upon Latin roots. The word *ludicrous*,
for example, is based upon a Latin word meaning "to play." You can
find the root -*lud*- in many words:

   a. *delusion, delude*—To *delude* is to deceive.
   b. *elusion, elude*—To *elude* is to avoid slyly, to escape from.
   c. *allusion, allude*—To *allude* to something means to refer to it,
       to point it out.
   d. *illusion* (the verb is not often used)—An *illusion* is a deceptive
       image or deceptive vision. A mirage in the desert is an illusion.
   e. *disillusion,* or *disillusionment*—To *disillusion* is to free from a
       deception.

For composition

1. What did Molly write in her diary that night when she was alone in Salinas? Pretend that you are Molly on that night. Make an entry in your diary, describing what you have seen and felt in the course of the day, and what you are feeling this night.
2. Have you ever been disillusioned with someone important in your life? Write a paragraph showing how you felt at the awful moment of discovery.
3. Have you ever had an important interview for a job, or for any other reason? Write a paragraph describing your feelings at the time.
4. Molly found herself in a number of situations in which she might have acted with *heroism*, or with *cowardice*. Write a brief paper in which you attempt to show clearly the difference between these two words.

One Ordinary Day, with Peanuts

SHIRLEY JACKSON

*You will have fun reading this story. Somewhere along the way you
will decide that something very odd is going on here, and that the story
expresses a serious idea. Suppose that you didn't have to go to work. Suppose that you had enough money to do what you wanted. Suppose. . . .*

Mr. John Philip Johnson shut his front door behind him and
came down his front steps in the bright morning with a feeling
that all was well with the world on this best of all days, and wasn't
the sun warm and good, and didn't his shoes feel comfortable after
the resoling, and he knew that he had undoubtedly chosen the precise
very tie which belonged with the day and the sun and his comfortable
feet, and, after all, wasn't the world just a wonderful place? In spite
of the fact that he was a small man, and the tie was perhaps a shade
vivid, Mr. Johnson irradiated this feeling of well-being as he came
down the steps and onto the dirty sidewalk, and he smiled at people
who passed him, and some of them even smiled back. He stopped at
the newsstand on the corner and bought his paper, saying "Good
morning" with real conviction to the man who sold him the paper
and the two or three other people who were lucky enough to be
buying papers when Mr. Johnson skipped up. He remembered to fill
his pockets with candy and peanuts, and then he set out to get himself uptown. He stopped in a flower shop and bought a carnation for
his buttonhole, and stopped almost immediately afterward to give the
carnation to a small child in a carriage, who looked at him dumbly,
and then smiled, and Mr. Johnson smiled, and the child's mother
looked at Mr. Johnson for a minute and then smiled too.

When he had gone several blocks uptown, Mr. Johnson cut across
the avenue and went along a side street, chosen at random; he did
not follow the same route every morning, but preferred to pursue

his eventful way in wide detours, more like a puppy than a man intent upon business. It happened this morning that halfway down the block a moving van was parked, and the furniture from an upstairs apartment stood half on the sidewalk, half on the steps, while an amused group of people loitered, examining the scratches on the tables and the worn spots on the chairs, and a harassed woman, trying to watch a young child and the movers and the furniture all at the same time, gave the clear impression of endeavoring to shelter her private life from the people staring at her belongings. Mr. Johnson stopped, and for a moment joined the crowd, and then he came forward and, touching his hat civilly, said, "Perhaps I can keep an eye on your little boy for you?"

The woman turned and glared at him distrustfully, and Mr. Johnson added hastily, "We'll sit right here on the steps." He beckoned to the little boy, who hesitated and then responded agreeably to Mr. Johnson's genial smile. Mr. Johnson brought out a handful of peanuts from his pocket and sat on the steps with the boy, who at first refused the peanuts on the grounds that his mother did not allow him to accept food from strangers; Mr. Johnson said that probably his mother had not intended peanuts to be included, since elephants at the circus ate them, and the boy considered, and then agreed solemnly. They sat on the steps cracking peanuts in a comradely fashion, and Mr. Johnson said, "So you're moving?"

"Yep," said the boy.

"Where you going?"

"Vermont."

"Nice place. Plenty of snow there. Maple sugar, too; you like maple sugar?"

"Sure."

"Plenty of maple sugar in Vermont. You going to live on a farm?"

"Going to live with Grandpa."

"Grandpa like peanuts?"

"Sure."

"Ought to take him some," said Mr. Johnson, reaching into his pocket. "Just you and Mommy going?"

"Yep."

"Tell you what," Mr. Johnson said. "You take some peanuts to eat on the train."

The boy's mother, after glancing at them frequently, had seemingly decided that Mr. Johnson was trustworthy, because she had devoted herself wholeheartedly to seeing that the movers did not—what movers rarely do, but every housewife believes they will—crack a leg from her good table, or set a kitchen chair down on a lamp. Most of the furniture was loaded by now, and she was deep in that nervous stage when she knew there was something she had forgotten to pack—hidden away in the back of a closet somewhere, or left at a neighbor's and forgotten, or on the clothesline—and was trying to remember under stress what it was.

"This all, lady?" the chief mover said, completing her dismay.

Uncertainly, she nodded.

"Want to go on the truck with the furniture, sonny?" the mover asked the boy, and laughed. The boy laughed too and said to Mr. Johnson, "I guess I'll have a good time at Vermont."

"Fine time," said Mr. Johnson, and stood up. "Have one more peanut before you go," he said to the boy.

The boy's mother said to Mr. Johnson, "Thank you so much; it was a great help to me."

"Nothing at all," said Mr. Johnson gallantly. "Where in Vermont are you going?"

The mother looked at the little boy accusingly, as though he had given away a secret of some importance, and said unwillingly, "Greenwich."

"Lovely town," said Mr. Johnson. He took out a card, and wrote a name on the back. "Very good friend of mine lives in Greenwich," he said. "Call on him for anything you need. His wife makes the best doughnuts in town," he added soberly to the little boy.

"Swell," said the little boy.

"Goodbye," said Mr. Johnson.

He went on, stepping happily with his new-shod feet, feeling the warm sun on his back and on the top of his head. Halfway down the block he met a stray dog and fed him a peanut.

At the corner, where another wide avenue faced him, Mr. Johnson decided to go on uptown again. Moving with comparative laziness, he was passed on either side by people hurrying and frowning, and people brushed past him going the other way, clattering along to get somewhere quickly. Mr. Johnson stopped on every corner and waited patiently for the light to change, and he stepped out of the way of anyone who seemed to be in any particular hurry, but one young lady came too fast for him, and crashed wildly into him when he stooped to pat a kitten which had run out onto the sidewalk from an apartment house and was now unable to get back through the rushing feet.

"Excuse me," said the young lady, trying frantically to pick up Mr. Johnson and hurry on at the same time, "terribly sorry."

The kitten, regardless now of danger, raced back to its home. "Perfectly all right," said Mr. Johnson, adjusting himself carefully. "You seem to be in a hurry."

"Of course I'm in a hurry," said the young lady. "I'm late."

She was extremely cross and the frown between her eyes seemed well on its way to becoming permanent. She had obviously awakened late, because she had not spent any extra time in making herself look pretty, and her dress was plain and unadorned with collar or brooch, and her lipstick was noticeably crooked. She tried to brush past Mr. Johnson, but, risking her suspicious displeasure, he took her arm and said, "Please wait."

"Look," she said ominously, "I ran into you and your lawyer can see my lawyer and I will gladly pay all damages and all inconveniences suffered therefrom but please this minute let me go because *I am late.*"

"Late for what?" said Mr. Johnson; he tried his winning smile on her but it did no more than keep her, he suspected, from knocking him down again.

"Late for work," she said between her teeth. "Late for my employment. I have a job and if I am late I lose exactly so much an hour and I cannot really afford what your pleasant conversation is costing me, be it *ever* so pleasant."

"I'll pay for it," said Mr. Johnson. Now these were magic words, not necessarily because they were true, or because she seriously expected Mr. Johnson to pay for anything, but because Mr. Johnson's flat statement, obviously innocent of irony, could not be, coming from Mr. Johnson, anything but the statement of a responsible and truthful and respectable man.

"What *do* you mean?" she asked.

"I said that since I am obviously responsible for your being late I shall certainly pay for it."

"Don't be silly," she said, and for the first time the frown disappeared. "*I* wouldn't expect you to pay for anything—a few minutes ago I was offering to pay *you*. Anyway," she added, almost smiling, "it *was* my fault."

"What happens if you don't go to work?"

She stared. "I don't get paid."

"Precisely," said Mr. Johnson.

"What do you mean, precisely? If I don't show up at the office exactly twenty minutes ago I lose a dollar and twenty cents an hour, or two cents a minute or . . ." she thought. ". . . Almost a dime for the time I've spent talking to you."

Mr. Johnson laughed, and finally she laughed, too. "You're late already," he pointed out. "Will you give me another four cents worth?"

"I don't understand why."

"You'll see," Mr. Johnson promised. He led her over to the side of the walk, next to the buildings, and said, "Stand here," and went out into the rush of people going both ways. Selecting and considering, as one who must make a choice involving perhaps whole years of lives, he estimated the people going by. Once he almost moved, and then at the last minute thought better of it and drew back. Finally, from half a block away, he saw what he wanted, and moved out into the center of the traffic to intercept a young man, who was hurrying, and dressed as though he had awakened late, and frowning.

"Oof," said the young man, because Mr. Johnson had thought of no better way to intercept anyone than the one the young woman had unwittingly used upon him. "Where do you think you're going?" the young man demanded from the sidewalk.

"I want to speak to you," said Mr. Johnson ominously.

The young man got up nervously, dusting himself and eying Mr. Johnson. "What for?" he said. "What'd *I* do?"

"That's what bothers me most about people nowadays," Mr. Johnson complained broadly to the people passing. "No matter whether they've done anything or not, they always figure someone's after them. About what you're going to do," he told the young man.

"Listen," said the young man, trying to brush past him, "I'm late, and I don't have any time to listen. Here's a dime, now get going."

"Thank you," said Mr. Johnson, pocketing the dime. "Look," he said, "what happens if you stop running?"

"I'm late," said the young man, still trying to get past Mr. Johnson, who was unexpectedly clinging.

"How much you make an hour?" Mr. Johnson demanded.

"A communist, are you?" said the young man. "Now will you please let me—"

"No," said Mr. Johnson insistently, "*how* much?"

"Dollar fifty," said the young man. "And *now* will you—"

"You like adventure?"

The young man stared, and, staring, found himself caught and held by Mr. Johnson's genial smile; he almost smiled back and then repressed it and made an effort to tear away. "I got to *hurry*," he said.

"Mystery? Like surprises? Unusual and exciting events?"

"You selling something?"

"Sure," said Mr. Johnson. "You want to take a chance?"

The young man hesitated, looked longingly up the avenue toward what might have been his destination and then, when Mr. Johnson said "I'll pay for it" with his own peculiar convincing emphasis, turned and said, "Well, okay. But I got to *see* it first, what I'm buying."

Mr. Johnson, breathing hard, led the young man over to the side where the girl was standing; she had been watching with interest Mr. Johnson's capture of the young man and now, smiling timidly, she looked at Mr. Johnson as though prepared to be surprised at nothing.

Mr. Johnson reached into his pocket and took out his wallet. "Here," he said, and handed a bill to the girl. "This about equals your day's pay."

"But no," she said, surprised in spite of herself. "I mean, I *couldn't.*"

"Please do not interrupt," Mr. Johnson told her. "And *here*," he said to the young man, "this will take care of *you*." The young man accepted the bill dazedly, but said, "Probably counterfeit" to the young woman out of the side of his mouth. "Now," Mr. Johnson went on, disregarding the young man, "what is your name, miss?"

"Kent," she said helplessly. "Mildred Kent."

"Fine," said Mr. Johnson. "And you, sir?"

"Arthur Adams," said the young man stiffly.

"Splendid," said Mr. Johnson. "Now, Miss Kent, I would like you to meet Mr. Adams. Mr. Adams, Miss Kent."

Miss Kent stared, wet her lips nervously, made a gesture as though she might run, and said, "How do you do?"

Mr. Adams straightened his shoulders, scowled at Mr. Johnson, made a gesture as though he might run, and said, "How do you do?"

"Now *this*," said Mr. Johnson, taking several bills from his wallet, "should be enough for the day for both of you. I would suggest, perhaps, Coney Island—although I personally am not fond of the place—or perhaps a nice lunch somewhere, and dancing, or a matinee, or even a movie, although take care to choose a really *good* one; there are *so* many bad movies these days. You might," he said, struck with an inspiration, "visit the Bronx Zoo, or the Planetarium. Anywhere, as a matter of fact," he concluded, "that you would like to go. Have a nice time."

As he started to move away Arthur Adams, breaking from his dumbfounded stare, said, "But see here, mister, you *can't* do this. Why—how do you know—I mean, *we* don't even know—I mean, how do you know we won't just take the money and not do what you said?"

"You've taken the money," Mr. Johnson said. "You don't have to follow any of my suggestions. You may know something you prefer to do—perhaps a museum, or something."

"But suppose I just run away with it and leave her here?"

"I know you won't," said Mr. Johnson gently, "because you remembered to ask *me* that. Goodbye," he added, and went on.

As he stepped up the street, conscious of the sun on his head and his good shoes, he heard from somewhere behind him the young man saying, "Look, you know you don't *have* to if you don't want to," and the girl saying, "But unless *you* don't want to . . . " Mr. Johnson smiled to himself and then thought that he had better hurry along; when he wanted to he could move very quickly, and before the young woman had gotten around to saying, "Well, I will if *you* will," Mr. Johnson was several blocks away and had already stopped twice, once to help a lady lift several large packages into a taxi and once to hand a peanut to a seagull. By this time he was in an area of large stores and many more people and he was buffeted constantly from either side by people hurrying and cross and late and sullen. Once he offered a peanut to a man who asked him for a dime, and once he offered a peanut to a bus driver who had stopped his bus at an intersection and had opened the window next to his seat and put out his head as though longing for fresh air and the comparative quiet of the traffic. The man wanting a dime took the peanut because Mr. Johnson had wrapped a dollar bill around it, but the bus driver took the peanut and asked ironically, "You want a transfer, Jack?"

On a busy corner Mr. Johnson encountered two young people— for one minute he thought they might be Mildred Kent and Arthur Adams—who were eagerly scanning a newspaper, their backs pressed against a storefront to avoid the people passing, their heads bent together. Mr. Johnson, whose curiosity was insatiable, leaned onto the storefront next to them and peeked over the man's shoulder; they were scanning the "Apartments Vacant" columns.

Mr. Johnson remembered the street where the woman and her little boy were going to Vermont and he tapped the man on the shoulder and said amiably, "Try down on West Seventeen. About the middle of the block, people moved out this morning."

"Say, what do you—" said the man, and then, seeing Mr. Johnson clearly, "Well, thanks. Where did you say?"

"West Seventeen," said Mr. Johnson. "About the middle of the block." He smiled again and said, "Good luck."

"Thanks," said the man.

"Thanks," said the girl, as they moved off.

"Goodbye," said Mr. Johnson.

He lunched alone in a pleasant restaurant, where the food was rich, and only Mr. Johnson's excellent digestion could encompass two of their whipped-cream-and-chocolate-and-rum-cake pastries for dessert. He had three cups of coffee, tipped the waiter largely, and went out into the street again into the wonderful sunlight, his shoes still comfortable and fresh on his feet. Outside he found a beggar staring into the windows of the restaurant he had left and, carefully looking through the money in his pocket, Mr. Johnson approached the beggar and pressed some coins and a couple of bills into his hand. "It's the price of the veal cutlet lunch plus tip," said Mr. Johnson. "Goodbye."

After his lunch he rested; he walked into the nearest park and fed peanuts to the pigeons. It was late afternoon by the time he was ready to start back downtown, and he had refereed two checker games and watched a small boy and girl whose mother had fallen asleep and awakened with surprise and fear which turned to amusement when she saw Mr. Johnson. He had given away almost all of his candy, and had fed all the rest of his peanuts to the pigeons, and it was time to go home. Although the late afternoon sun was pleasant, and his shoes were still entirely comfortable, he decided to take a taxi downtown.

He had a difficult time catching a taxi, because he gave up the first three or four empty ones to people who seemed to need them more; finally, however, he stood alone on the corner and—almost like netting a frisky fish—he hailed desperately until he succeeded in catching a cab which had been proceeding with haste uptown and seemed to draw in toward Mr. Johnson against its own will.

"Mister," the cab driver said as Mr. Johnson climbed in, "I figured you was an omen, like. I wasn't going to pick you up at all."

"Kind of you," said Mr. Johnson ambiguously.

"If I'd of let you go it would of cost me ten bucks," said the driver.

"Really?" said Mr. Johnson.

"Yeah," said the driver. "Guy just got out of the cab, he turned around and give me ten bucks, said take this and bet it in a hurry on a horse named Vulcan, right away."

"Vulcan?" said Mr. Johnson, horrified. "A fire sign on a Wednesday?"

"What?" said the driver. "Anyway, I said to myself if I got no fare between here and there I'd bet the ten, but if anyone looked like they needed the cab I'd take it as a omen and I'd take the ten home to the wife."

"You were very right," said Mr. Johnson heartily. "This is Wednesday, you would have lost your money. Monday, yes, or even Saturday. But never never never a fire sign on a Wednesday. Sunday would have been good, now."

"Vulcan don't run on Sunday," said the driver.

"You wait till another day," said Mr. Johnson. "Down this street, please, driver. I'll get off on the next corner."

"He *told* me Vulcan, though," said the driver.

"I'll tell you," said Mr. Johnson, hesitating with the door of the cab half open. "You take that ten dollars and I'll give you another ten dollars to go with it, and you go right ahead and bet that money on any Thursday on any horse that has a name indicating . . . let me see, Thursday . . . well, grain. Or any growing food."

"Grain?" said the driver. "You mean a horse named, like, Wheat or something?"

"Certainly," said Mr. Johnson. "Or, as a matter of fact, to make it even easier, any horse whose name includes the letters C, R, L. Perfectly simple."

"Tall corn?" said the driver, a light in his eye. "You mean a horse named, like, Tall Corn?"

"Absolutely," said Mr. Johnson. "Here's your money."

"Tall Corn," said the driver. "Thank *you*, mister."

"Goodbye," said Mr. Johnson.

He was on his own corner and went straight up to his apartment. He let himself in and called "Hello?" and Mrs. Johnson answered from the kitchen, "Hello, dear, aren't you early?"

"Took a taxi home," Mr. Johnson said. "I remembered the cheesecake, too. What's for dinner?"

Mrs. Johnson came out of the kitchen and kissed him; she was a comfortable woman, and smiling as Mr. Johnson smiled. "Hard day?" she asked.

"Not very," said Mr. Johnson, hanging his coat in the closet. "How about you?"

"So-so," she said. She stood in the kitchen doorway while he settled into his easy chair and took off his good shoes and took out the paper he had bought that morning. "Here and there," she said.

"I didn't do so badly," Mr. Johnson said. "Couple young people."

"Fine," she said. "I had a little nap this afternoon, took it easy most of the day. Went into a department store this morning and accused the woman next to me of shoplifting, and had the store detective pick her up. Sent three dogs to the pound—*you* know, the usual thing. Oh, and listen," she added, remembering.

"What?" asked Mr. Johnson.

"Well," she said, "I got onto a bus and asked the driver for a transfer, and when he helped someone else first I said that he was impertinent, and quarreled with him. And then I said why wasn't he in the army, and I said it loud enough for everyone to hear, and I took his number and I turned in a complaint. Probably got him fired."

"Fine," said Mr. Johnson. "But you do look tired. Want to change over tomorrow?"

"I *would* like to," she said. "I could do with a change."

"Right," said Mr. Johnson. "What's for dinner?"

"Veal cutlet."

"Had it for lunch," said Mr. Johnson.

Questions for discussion

1. What is the meaning of Mr. Johnson's question on page 227, "Want to change over tomorrow?" What had Mrs. Johnson been doing all day? The changeover takes place at once. How can you tell?
2. What is the significance of Mr. Johnson's saying, "Fine. But you look tired."? Why would he say that the disagreeable things his wife had been doing were fine? What is the scheme or plan upon which the two have been working?
3. When Mr. Johnson says, "But you do look tired . . . ," what does he mean? Did he get tired from the kinds of things he had been doing? What is the author saying here?
4. This story is a *fantasy*; that is, it is not presented as an account of real people meeting real problems. It is all based on an assumption that certain conditions are true. It reports what *might* happen if certain conditions existed. Examine the things that Mr. and Mrs. Johnson did. Were any of them impossible for the average person to do? What would the average person have to do to himself in order to spend a day as Mr. Johnson did? What is the author saying here?
5. The beggar and the man who wanted a dime accepted Mr. Johnson's help. What was the first reaction of the boy? of the bus driver? of the young couple looking for an apartment? What is the author saying here about the way people in a big city treat strangers?
6. The incident of Miss Kent and Mr. Adams has a special meaning. What is the author saying here about people in general? "If only people weren't always. . . ."
7. Refer to the Glossary for an explanation of *irony*. What touch of irony is there in the title of this story? In what way was Mr. Johnson's day "ordinary"? In what way was it not?
8. What is the theme of the story? Your class may not agree. There may be no one right answer, but you should be able to support your own answer by referring to incidents in the story. Write a paragraph in which you state your idea of the theme, with supporting evidence. Read this paragraph aloud to the class, as part of the discussion.

Vocabulary growth

CONTEXT. On page 221 you read, "Now these were magic words, not necessarily because they were true, or because she seriously expected

Mr. Johnson to pay for anything, but because Mr. Johnson's flat statement, obviously *innocent* of *irony*, could not be, coming from Mr. Johnson, anything but the statement of a responsible and truthful and respectable man."

   a. What does *innocent* mean here?

   b. Why was the statement not *ironical?*

   c. Under what circumstances could such a statement be *ironical?*

WORDS ARE INTERESTING. *Innocent* has an interesting background. With the aid of your dictionary, find out the background of this word. What base word appears in *innocent?* What other English words also have this base word?

For composition

1. If you liked "One Ordinary Day, with Peanuts," you will like Shirley Jackson's other stories, such as "Charles," "The Lottery," and "Strangers in Town." In "One Ordinary Day," just as in many other of her stories, the author seems to be saying, "Suppose the rules were different? What if people had to obey this kind of rule? Then, how would they behave?" You might try to write a short, short story, or a simple narrative based on this kind of assumption. For example:

   a. For one day, no one can accept money for anything.

   b. For one day, there is a news blackout. There are no newspapers, no radio, and no television.

   c. For one day, everyone goes barefoot.

   d. For one month, John Andrews can decide what the weather will be.

The Guest

ALBERT CAMUS

In 1962, Algeria became one of the independent countries of
northern Africa. The action of this story takes place in the years preceding, while the territory was still governed by France.

Daru felt himself a part of the region where he was born: bleak
mountainous highlands, a scorching sun, and windblown shifting sands
in the vast distance below.

Though born to French parents, Daru felt a kinship with the native
desert Arabs. He well knew that should he ever, in peril of his life, need
food or water, shelter or protection, while journeying through the desert, the
hospitality of their tents would be offered without question. Should a hostile
enemy be in pursuit, his host would protect him as long as he remained
a guest. And were he himself an enemy, the code of the desert would be
respected. The traveler might tarry, sharing the food and protection of
his host. In this spirit of brotherhood, he must, in turn, depart never to
bring shame or harm to those whose hospitality he had received.

Daru and his guest both understand the code of the desert nomad.
Both also are subject to the law of the French government. A crisis
arises. Each of these men must choose a course of action. Many readers
have been amazed at the decisions.

THE schoolmaster was watching the two men climb toward him.
One was on horseback, the other on foot. They had not yet tackled
the abrupt rise leading to the schoolhouse built on the hillside. They
were toiling onward, making slow progress in the snow, among the
stones, on the vast expanse of the high, deserted plateau. From time
to time the horse stumbled. Without hearing anything yet, he could
see the breath issuing from the horse's nostrils. One of the men, at
least, knew the region. They were following the trail although it had
disappeared days ago under a layer of dirty white snow. The schoolmaster calculated that it would take them half an hour to get onto
the hill. It was cold; he went back into the school to get a sweater.

230

He crossed the empty, frigid classroom. On the blackboard the four rivers of France, drawn with four different colored chalks, had been flowing toward their estuaries for the past three days. Snow had suddenly fallen in mid-October after eight months of drought without the transition of rain, and the twenty pupils, more or less, who lived in the villages scattered over the plateau had stopped coming. With fair weather they would return. Daru now heated only the single room that was his lodging, adjoining the classroom and giving also onto the plateau to the east. Like the class windows, his window looked to the south too. On that side the school was a few kilometers from the point where the plateau began to slope toward the south. In clear weather could be seen the purple mass of the mountain range where the gap opened onto the desert.

Somewhat warmed, Daru returned to the window from which he had first seen the two men. They were no longer visible. Hence they must have tackled the rise. The sky was not so dark, for the snow had stopped falling during the night. The morning had opened with a dirty light which had scarcely become brighter as the ceiling of clouds lifted. At two in the afternoon it seemed as if the day were merely beginning. But still this was better than those three days when the thick snow was falling admidst unbroken darkness with little gusts of wind that rattled the double door of the classroom. Then Daru had spent long hours in his room, leaving it only to go to the shed and feed the chickens or get some coal. Fortunately the delivery truck from Tadjid, the nearest village to the north, had brought his supplies two days before the blizzard. It would return in forty-eight hours.

Besides, he had enough to resist a siege, for the little room was cluttered with bags of wheat that the administration left as a stock to distribute to those of his pupils whose families had suffered from the drought. Actually they had all been victims because they were all poor. Every day Daru would distribute a ration to the children. They had missed it, he knew, during these bad days. Possibly one of the fathers or big brothers would come this afternoon and he could supply them with grain. It was just a matter of carrying them over to the next harvest. Now shiploads of wheat were arriving from France and the worst was over. But it would be hard to forget that poverty, that army of ragged ghosts wandering in the sunlight, the plateaus burned to a cinder month after month, the earth shriveled up little by little, literally scorched, every stone bursting into dust under one's foot. The sheep had died then by thousands and even a few men, here and there, sometimes without anyone's knowing.

In contrast with such poverty, he who lived almost like a monk in his remote schoolhouse, nonetheless satisfied with the little he had and with the rough life, had felt like a lord with his white-washed walls, his narrow couch, his unpainted shelves, his well, and his weekly provision of water and food. And suddenly this snow, without warning, without the foretaste of rain. This is the way the region was, cruel to live in, even without men—who didn't help matters either. But Daru had been born here. Everywhere else, he felt exiled.

He stepped out onto the terrace in front of the schoolhouse. The two men were now halfway up the slope. He recognized the horseman as Balducci, the old gendarme he had known for a long time. Balducci was holding on the end of a rope an Arab who was walking behind him with hands bound and head lowered. The gendarme waved a greeting to which Daru did not reply, lost as he was in contemplation of the Arab dressed in a faded blue jellaba, his feet in sandals but covered with socks of heavy raw wool, his head surmounted by a narrow, short *chèche*. They were approaching. Balducci was holding back his horse in order not to hurt the Arab, and the group was advancing slowly.

Within earshot, Balducci shouted: "One hour to do the three kilometers from El Ameur!" Daru did not answer. Short and square in his thick sweater, he watched them climb. Not once had the Arab raised his head. "Hello," said Daru when they got up onto the terrace. "Come in and warm up." Balducci painfully got down from his horse without letting go the rope. From under his bristling mustache he smiled at the schoolmaster. His little dark eyes, deep-set under a tanned forehead, and his mouth surrounded with wrinkles made him look attentive and studious. Daru took the bridle, led the horse to the shed, and came back to the two men, who were now waiting for him in the school. He led them into his room. "I am going to heat up the classroom," he said. "We'll be more comfortable there." When he entered the room again, Balducci was on the couch. He had undone the rope tying him to the Arab, who had squatted near the stove. His hands still bound, the *chèche* pushed back on his head, he was looking toward the window. At first Daru noticed only his huge lips, fat, smooth, almost Negroid; yet his nose was straight, his eyes were dark and full of fever. The *chèche* revealed an obstinate forehead and, under the weathered skin now rather discolored by the cold, the whole face had a restless and rebellious look that struck Daru when the Arab, turning his face toward him, looked him straight in the eyes. "Go into the other room," said the schoolmaster, "and I'll make you some mint tea." "Thanks," Balducci said. "What a chore! How I long for retirement." And addressing his prisoner in Arabic: "Come on, you." The Arab got up and, slowly, holding his bound wrists in front of him, went into the classroom.

With the tea, Daru brought a chair. But Balducci was already enthroned on the nearest pupil's desk and the Arab had squatted against the teacher's platform facing the stove, which stood between the desk and the window. When he held out the glass of tea to the prisoner, Daru hesitated at the sight of his bound hands. "He might perhaps be untied." "Sure," said Balducci. "That was for the trip." He started to get to his feet. But Daru, setting the glass on the floor, had knelt beside the Arab. Without saying anything, the Arab watched him with his feverish eyes. Once his hands were free, he rubbed his swollen wrists against each other, took the glass of tea, and sucked up the burning liquid in swift little sips.

"Good," said Daru. "And where are you headed?"

Balducci withdrew his mustache from the tea. "Here, son."

"Odd pupils! And you're spending the night?"

"No. I'm going back to El Ameur. And you will deliver this fellow to Tinguit. He is expected at police headquarters."

Balducci was looking at Daru with a friendly little smile.

"What's this story?" asked the schoolmaster. "Are you pulling my leg?"

"No, son. Those are the orders."

"The orders? I'm not . . ." Daru hesitated, not wanting to hurt the old Corsican. "I mean, that's not my job."

"What! What's the meaning of that? In wartime people do all kinds of jobs."

"Then I'll wait for the declaration of war!"

Balducci nodded.

"O.K. But the orders exist and they concern you too. Things are brewing, it appears. There is talk of a forthcoming revolt. We are mobilized, in a way."

Daru still had his obstinate look.

"Listen, son," Balducci said. "I like you and you must understand. There's only a dozen of us at El Ameur to patrol throughout the whole territory of a small department and I must get back in a hurry. I was told to hand this guy over to you and return without delay. He couldn't be kept there. His village was beginning to stir; they wanted to take him back. You must take him to Tinguit tomorrow before the day is over. Twenty kilometers shouldn't faze a husky fellow like you. After that, all will be over. You'll come back to your pupils and your comfortable life."

Behind the wall the horse could be heard snorting and pawing the earth. Daru was looking out the window. Decidedly, the weather was clearing and the light was increasing over the snowy plateau. When all the snow was melted, the sun would take over again and once more would burn the fields of stone. For days, still, the unchanging sky would shed its dry light on the solitary expanse where nothing had any connection with man.

"After all," he said, turning around toward Balducci, "what did he do?" And, before the gendarme had opened his mouth, he asked: "Does he speak French?"

"No, not a word. We had been looking for him for a month, but they were hiding him. He killed his cousin."

"Is he against us?"

"I don't think so. But you can never be sure."

"Why did he kill?"

"A family squabble, I think. One owed the other grain, it seems. It's not at all clear. In short, he killed his cousin with a billhook. You know, like a sheep, *kreezk!*"

Balducci made the gesture of drawing a blade across his throat and the Arab, his attention attracted, watched him with a sort of anxiety. Daru felt a sudden wrath against the man, against all men with their rotten spite, their tireless hates, their blood lust.

But the kettle was singing on the stove. He served Balducci more tea, hesitated, then served the Arab again, who, a second time, drank avidly. His raised arms made the jellaba fall open and the schoolmaster saw his thin, muscular chest.

"Thanks, kid," Balducci said. "And now, I'm off."

He got up and went toward the Arab, taking a small rope from his pocket.

"What are you doing?" Daru asked dryly.

Balducci, disconcerted, showed him the rope.

"Don't bother."

The old gendarme hesitated. "It's up to you. Of course, you are armed?"

"I have my shotgun."

"Where?"

"In the trunk."

"You ought to have it near your bed."

"Why? I have nothing to fear."

"You're crazy, son. If there's an uprising, no one is safe, we're all in the same boat."

"I'll defend myself. I'll have time to see them coming."

Balducci began to laugh, then suddenly the mustache covered the white teeth.

"You'll have time? O.K. That's just what I was saying. You have always been a little cracked. That's why I like you, my son was like that."

At the same time he took out his revolver and put it on the desk.

"Keep it; I don't need two weapons from here to El Ameur."

The revolver shone against the black paint of the table. When the gendarme turned toward him, the schoolmaster caught the smell of leather and horseflesh.

"Listen, Balducci," Daru said suddenly, "every bit of this disgusts me, and first of all your fellow here. But I won't hand him over. Fight, yes, if I have to. But not that."

The old gendarme stood in front of him and looked at him severely.

"You're being a fool," he said slowly. "I don't like it either. You don't get used to putting a rope on a man even after years of it, and you're even ashamed—yes, ashamed. But you can't let them have their way."

"I won't hand him over," Daru said again.

"It's an order, son, and I repeat it."

"That's right. Repeat to them what I've said to you: I won't hand him over."

Balducci made a visible effort to reflect. He looked at the Arab and at Daru. At last he decided.

"No, I won't tell them anything. If you want to drop us, go ahead; I'll not denounce you. I have an order to deliver the prisoner and I'm doing so. And now you'll just sign this paper for me."

"There's no need. I'll not deny that you left him with me."

"Don't be mean with me. I know you'll tell the truth. You're from hereabouts and you are a man. But you must sign, that's the rule."

Daru opened his drawer, took out a little square bottle of purple ink, the red wooden penholder with the "sergeant-major" pen he used for making models of penmanship, and signed. The gendarme carefully folded the paper and put it into his wallet. Then he moved toward the door.

"I'll see you off," Daru said.

"No," said Balducci. "There's no use being polite. You insulted me."

He looked at the Arab, motionless in the same spot, sniffed peevishly, and turned away toward the door. "Good-by, son," he said. The door shut behind him. Balducci appeared suddenly outside the window and then disappeared. His footsteps were muffled by the snow. The horse stirred on the other side of the wall and several chickens fluttered in fright. A moment later Balducci reappeared outside the window leading the horse by the bridle. He walked toward the little rise without turning around and disappeared from sight with the horse following him. A big stone could be heard bouncing down. Daru walked back toward the prisoner, who, without stirring, never took his eyes off him. "Wait," the schoolmaster said in Arabic and went toward the bedroom. As he was going through the door, he had a second thought, went to the desk, took the revolver, and stuck it in his pocket. Then, without looking back, he went into his room.

For some time he lay on his couch watching the sky gradually close over, listening to the silence. It was this silence that had seemed painful to him during the first days here, after the war. He had requested a post in the little town at the base of the foothills separating the upper plateaus from the desert. There, rocky walls, green and black to the north, pink and lavender to the south, marked the frontier of eternal summer. He had been named to a post farther north, on the plateau itself. In the beginning, the solitude and the silence had been hard for him on these wastelands peopled only by stones. Occasionally, furrows suggested cultivation, but they had been dug to uncover a certain kind of stone good for building. The only plowing here was to harvest rocks. Elsewhere a thin layer of soil accumulated in the hollows would be scraped out to enrich paltry village gardens. This is the way it was: bare rock covered three quarters of the region. Towns sprang up, flourished, then disappeared; men came by, loved one another or fought bitterly, then died. No one in this desert, neither he nor his guest, mattered. And yet, outside this desert neither of them, Daru knew, could have really lived.

When he got up, no noise came from the classroom. He was amazed at the unmixed joy he derived from the mere thought that the Arab might have fled and that he would be alone with no decision to make. But the prisoner was there. He had merely stretched out between the stove and the desk. With eyes open, he was staring at the ceiling. In that position, his thick lips were particularly noticeable, giving him a pouting look. "Come," said Daru. The Arab got up and followed him. In the bedroom, the schoolmaster pointed to a chair near the table under the window. The Arab sat down without taking his eyes off Daru.

"Are you hungry?"

"Yes," the prisoner said.

Daru set the table for two. He took flour and oil, shaped a cake in a frying-pan, and lighted the little stove that functioned on bottled gas. While the cake was cooking, he went out to the shed to get cheese, eggs, dates, and condensed milk. When the cake was done he set it on the window sill to cool, heated some condensed milk diluted with water, and beat up the eggs into an omelette. In one of his motions he knocked against the revolver stuck in his right pocket. He set the bowl down, went into the classroom, and put the revolver in his desk drawer. When he came back to the room, night was falling. He put on the light and served the Arab. "Eat," he said. The Arab took a piece of the cake, lifted it eagerly to his mouth, and stopped short.

"And you?" he asked.

"After you. I'll eat too."

The thick lips opened slightly. The Arab hesitated, then bit into the cake determinedly.

The meal over, the Arab looked at the schoolmaster. "Are you the judge?"

"No, I'm simply keeping you until tomorrow."

"Why do you eat with me?"

"I'm hungry."

The Arab fell silent. Daru got up and went out. He brought back a folding bed from the shed, set it up between the table and the stove, perpendicular to his own bed. From a large suitcase which, upright in a corner, served as a shelf for papers, he took two blankets and arranged them on the camp bed. Then he stopped, felt useless, and sat down on his bed. There was nothing more to do or to get ready. He had to look at this man. He looked at him, therefore, trying to imagine his face bursting with rage. He couldn't do so. He could see nothing but the dark yet shining eyes and the animal mouth.

"Why did you kill him?" he asked in a voice whose hostile tone surprised him.

The Arab looked away.

"He ran away. I ran after him."

He raised his eyes to Daru again and they were full of a sort of woeful interrogation. "Now what will they do to me?"

"Are you afraid?"

He stiffened, turning his eyes away.

"Are you sorry?"

The Arab stared at him openmouthed. Obviously he did not understand. Daru's annoyance was growing. At the same time he felt awkward and self-conscious with his big body wedged between the two beds.

"Lie down there," he said impatiently. "That's your bed."

The Arab didn't move. He called to Daru:

"Tell me!"

The schoolmaster looked at him.

"Is the gendarme coming back tomorrow?"

"I don't know."

"Are you coming with us?"

"I don't know. Why?"

The prisoner got up and stretched out on top of the blankets, his feet toward the window. The light from the electric bulb shone straight into his eyes and he closed them at once.

"Why?" Daru repeated, standing beside the bed.

The Arab opened his eyes under the blinding light and looked at him, trying not to blink.

"Come with us," he said.

In the middle of the night, Daru was still not asleep. He had gone to bed after undressing completely; he generally slept naked. But when he suddenly realized that he had nothing on, he hesitated.

He felt vulnerable and the temptation came to him to put his clothes back on. Then he shrugged his shoulders; after all, he wasn't a child and, if need be, he could break his adversary in two. From his bed he could observe him, lying on his back, still motionless with his eyes closed under the harsh light. When Daru turned out the light, the darkness seemed to coagulate all of a sudden. Little by little, the night came back to life in the window where the starless sky was stirring gently. The schoolmaster soon made out the body lying at his feet. The Arab still did not move, but his eyes seemed open. A faint wind was prowling around the schoolhouse. Perhaps it would drive away the clouds and the sun would reappear.

During the night the wind increased. The hens fluttered a little and then were silent. The Arab turned over on his side with his back to Daru, who thought he heard him moan. Then he listened for his guest's breathing, become heavier and more regular. He listened to that breath so close to him and mused without being able to go to sleep. In this room where he had been sleeping alone for a year, this presence bothered him. But it bothered him also by imposing on him a sort of brotherhood he knew well but refused to accept in the present circumstances. Men who share the same rooms, soldiers or prisoners, develop a strange alliance as if, having cast off their armor with their clothing, they fraternized every evening, over and above their differences, in the ancient community of dream and fatigue. But Daru shook himself; he didn't like such musings, and it was essential to sleep.

A little later, however, when the Arab stirred slightly, the school-master was still not asleep. When the prisoner made a second move, he stiffened, on the alert. The Arab was lifting himself slowly on his arms with almost the motion of a sleepwalker. Seated upright in bed, he waited motionless without turning his head toward Daru, as if he were listening attentively. Daru did not stir; it had just occurred to him that the revolver was still in the drawer of his desk. It was better to act at once. Yet he continued to observe the prisoner, who, with the same slithery motion, put his feet on the ground, waited again, then began to stand up slowly. Daru was about to call out to him when the Arab began to walk, in a quite natural but extraordinarily silent way. He was heading toward the door at the end of the room that opened into the shed. He lifted the latch with precaution and went out, pushing the door behind him but without shutting it.

Daru had not stirred. "He is running away," he merely thought. "Good riddance!" Yet he listened attentively. The hens were not fluttering; the guest must be on the plateau. A faint sound of water reached him, and he didn't know what it was until the Arab again stood framed in the doorway, closed the door carefully, and came back to bed without a sound. Then Daru turned his back on him and fell asleep. Still later he seemed, from the depths of his sleep, to hear furtive steps around the schoolhouse. "I'm dreaming! I'm dreaming!" he repeated to himself. And he went on sleeping.

When he awoke, the sky was clear; the loose window let in a cold, pure air. The Arab was asleep, hunched up under the blankets now, his mouth open, utterly relaxed. But when Daru shook him, he started dreadfully, staring at Daru with wild eyes as if he had never seen him and such a frightened expression that the schoolmaster stepped back. "Don't be afraid. It's me. You must eat." The Arab nodded his head and said yes. Calm had returned to his face, but his expression was vacant and listless.

The coffee was ready. They drank it seated together on the folding bed as they munched their pieces of the cake. Then Daru led the Arab under the shed and showed him the faucet where he washed. He went back into the room, folded the blankets and the bed, made his own bed and put the room in order. Then he went through the classroom and out onto the terrace. The sun was already rising in the blue sky; a soft, bright light was bathing the deserted plateau. On the ridge the snow was melting in spots. The stones were about to reappear. Crouched on the edge of the plateau, the schoolmaster looked at the deserted expanse. He thought of Balducci. He had hurt him, for he had sent him off in a way as if he didn't want to be associated with him. He could still hear the gendarme's farewell and, without knowing why, he felt strangely empty and vulnerable. At that moment, from the other side of the schoolhouse, the prisoner coughed. Daru listened to him almost despite himself and then, furious, threw a pebble that whistled through the air before sinking into the snow. That man's stupid crime revolted him, but to hand him over was contrary to honor. Merely thinking of it made him smart with humiliation. And he cursed at one and the same time his own people who had sent him this Arab and the Arab too who had dared to kill and not managed to get away. Daru got up, walked in a circle on the terrace, waited motionless, and then went back into the schoolhouse.

The Arab, leaning over the cement floor of the shed, was washing his teeth with two fingers. Daru looked at him and said: "Come." He went back into the room ahead of the prisoner. He slipped a hunting-jacket on over his sweater and put on walking-shoes. Standing, he waited until the Arab had put on his *chèche* and sandals. They went into the classroom and the schoolmaster pointed to the exit, saying: "Go ahead." The fellow didn't budge. "I'm coming," said Daru. The Arab went out. Daru went back into the room and made a package of pieces of rusk, dates, and sugar. In the classroom, before going out, he hesitated a second in front of his desk, then crossed the threshold and locked the door. "That's the way," he said. He started toward the east, followed by the prisoner. But, a short distance from the schoolhouse, he thought he heard a slight sound behind them. He retraced his steps and examined the surroundings of the house; there was no one there. The Arab watched him without seeming to understand. "Come on," said Daru.

They walked for an hour and rested beside a sharp peak of limestone. The snow was melting faster and faster and the sun was drinking up the puddles at once, rapidly cleaning the plateau, which gradually dried and vibrated like the air itself. When they resumed walking, the ground rang under their feet. From time to time a bird rent the space in front of them with a joyful cry. Daru breathed in deeply the fresh morning light. He felt a sort of rapture before the vast familiar expanse, now almost entirely yellow under its dome of blue sky. They walked an hour more, descending toward the south. They reached a level height made up of crumbly rocks. From there on, the plateau sloped down, eastward, toward a low plain where there were a few spindly trees and, to the south, toward outcroppings of rock that gave the landscape a chaotic look.

Daru surveyed the two directions. There was nothing but the sky on the horizon. Not a man could be seen. He turned toward the Arab, who was looking at him blankly. Daru held out the package to him. "Take it," he said. "There are dates, bread, and sugar. You can hold out for two days. Here are a thousand francs too." The Arab took the package and the money but kept his full hands at chest level as if he didn't know what to do with what was being given him. "Now look," the schoolmaster said as he pointed in the direction of the east, "there's the way to Tinguit. You have a two-hour walk. At Tinguit you'll find the administration and the police. They are expecting you." The Arab looked toward the east, still holding the package and the money against his chest. Daru took his elbow and turned him rather roughly toward the south. At the foot of the height on which they stood could be seen a faint path. "That's the trail across the plateau. In a day's walk from here you'll find pasture-lands and the first nomads. They'll take you in and shelter you according to their law." The Arab had now turned toward Daru and a sort of panic was visible in his expression. "Listen," he said. Daru shook his head: "No, be quiet. Now I'm leaving you." He turned his back on him, took two long steps in the direction of the school, looked hesitantly at the motionless Arab, and started off again. For a few minutes he heard nothing but his own step resounding on the cold ground and did not turn his head. A moment later, however, he turned around. The Arab was still there on the edge of the hill, his arms hanging now, and he was looking at the schoolmaster. Daru felt something rise in his throat. But he swore with impatience, waved vaguely, and started off again. He had already gone some dis-tance when he again stopped and looked. There was no longer any-one on the hill.

Daru hesitated. The sun was now rather high in the sky and was beginning to beat down on his head. The schoolmaster retraced his steps, at first somewhat uncertainly, then with decision. When he reached the little hill, he was bathed in sweat. He climbed it as fast as he could and stopped, out of breath, at the top. The rock-fields to the south stood out sharply against the blue sky, but on the plain to the east a steamy heat was already rising. And in that slight haze, Daru, with heavy heart, made out the Arab walking slowly on the road to prison.

A little later, standing before the window of the classroom, the schoolmaster was watching the clear light bathing the whole surface of the plateau, but he hardly saw it. Behind him on the blackboard, among the winding French rivers, sprawled the clumsily chalked-up words he had just read: "You handed over our brother. You will pay for this." Daru looked at the sky, the plateau, and, beyond, the invisible lands stretching all the way to the sea. In this vast landscape he had loved so much, he was alone.

Questions for discussion

1. W. Somerset Maugham said that a short story "must sparkle, excite, or impress; and it must have unity of effect or impression." Do you find the unified impression in "The Guest" to be one of these: optimism about progress toward brotherhood, pessimism about such progress, stark irony in sincere decisions in crises, aloneness—a confrontation with reality in human experience, or the agony of violence and crime? Point to proof in the story to support your choice, or discuss your own impression.

2. Rarely is a setting so intensely interwoven with the other elements of a story. Describe the effect of the landscape on the characters in this sentence from page 237: "And yet, outside this desert, neither of them, Daru knew, could have really lived," and in the last two sentences of the story.

3. In this story, all the characters make decisions. What are these decisions? Did you expect the characters to make the decisions they did? Why or why not? How do you explain these decisions?

4. There is a strong prevailing serious mood throughout the story, but Camus does provide some light touches, such as Balducci withdrawing his moustache from the tea and the tea kettle "singing on the stove." What is the purpose of these light touches? Point out other instances that either accentuate the serious, sombre mood, or serve to bring out effective contrasts.

5. Keeping in mind that in European schools students complete their basic education at an earlier age than in the United States, how old do you imagine Daru to be? How old is the Arab? Balducci? Point to the clues in the story.

6. This story is set at a time when the native Arab population of Algeria was growing very belligerent toward government by a foreign power. Even the two non-Arab characters were not in agreement about suitable procedures for dealing with problems growing out of the unrest. Describe their differing attitudes.

7. The guest is an Algerian Arab. For centuries, his people had lived by the code of the desert. Some elements of the code are *hospitality*, explained in the introduction on page 230, and *vengeance* as an instrument of justice. An injured person must seek revenge. If he is unable to act, it becomes the obligation of the nearest living relative to take vengeance, on behalf of the kinsman wronged, on the offender who has inflicted harm or death. Other elements of the code are *the right of the offender* to remain free as long as he escapes his pursuers

and *the oath* that may be taken, through a mediator, to forego vengeance. Enmity may also be ended with the act of "breaking bread" together—the oath of brotherhood—by the offering, accepting, and sharing of food. How and where do all of these aspects of the desert code appear in the story?

8. How well do you get acquainted with the guest? His words are few and simple, but very revealing. His eyes are often mentioned. Cite some of these instances. What impression did Daru get when the Arab first "looked him straight in the eyes"? What change has come about in their relationship by the time the meal is finished and the guest is in bed?

9. The schoolmaster, Daru, has been appointed by the French government. Thus, other officials such as the police officer, Balducci, expect him to cooperate with them. How would *you* finish Daru's impulsive beginning, "The orders? I'm not . . ." (page 233)

10. What items would have to be included if you were going to write a character sketch of the French Algerian schoolmaster, Daru? Look at the words, actions, and thoughts revealed by Camus.

11. Policemen are sometimes accused of being brutal toward those in their custody. Does Balducci, the gendarme (zhän'därm) with the "bristling mustache," seem to be this kind of officer? Does he show awareness of the desert code? Would he have understood the reason the Arab later gave to Daru when asked the question, "Why did you kill him?" (page 238)

12. Both irony and suspense make strong contributions to the effectiveness of the plot. What clues in the story make the ending believable? The sense of irony is strongest at the ending, but as a thread, it is interwoven throughout the story. Point to instances of the use of irony other than the last paragraph.

Vocabulary growth

CONTEXT. Read the following sentences. What meaning is suggested to you for each italicized word? Check with a dictionary to clarify your understanding. Then write sentences of your own using these words.

a. "If you want to drop us, go ahead; I'll not *denounce* you. (page 235)

b. "He could still hear the gendarme's farewell and, without knowing why, he felt strangely empty and *vulnerable*." (page 240)

c. "Merely thinking of it made him smart with *humiliation*." (page 240)

For composition

1. At the end of the story the reader's mind travels forward with Daru and the Arab. What experiences might await each? Choose one character and show him in a situation which might have followed at some time in the future.
2. Assume that you are an American foreign newspaper correspondent. In Tinguit you learn that a young Arab has surrendered himself to the French authorities under most unusual circumstances. One officer, fortunately, understood the code of the desert and, after much effort, succeeded in getting the Arab set free. Write your news story—headlines, too.
3. In a short essay or narrative sketch set forth some of your thinking about brotherhood.
4. Write a character sketch of one of the persons in the story.
5. In 1957 Camus won the Nobel Prize for Literature. Read the following excerpts from his speech accepting this award. Notice that some of the ideas in "The Guest"—isolation, solitude, community, and liberty—also appear in the acceptance speech. Relate the ideas in the speech to those in the story. Does a writer, like Camus, have anything in common with any of the characters in "The Guest"?

Excerpts from Camus' speech accepting the
Nobel Prize for Literature

I cannot live as a person without my art. And yet I have never set that art above everything else. It is essential to me, on the contrary, because it excludes no one and allows me to live, just as I am, on a footing with all. To me art is not a solitary delight. It is a means of stirring the greatest number of men by providing them with a privileged image of our common joys and woes. Hence it forces the artist not to isolate himself; it subjects him to the humblest and most universal truth. And the man who, as often happens, chose the path of art because he was aware of his difference soon learns that he can nourish his art, and his difference, solely by admitting his resemblance to all. The artist fashions himself in that ceaseless oscillation from himself to others, midway between the beauty he can not do without and the community from which he can not tear himself. This is why true artists scorn nothing. They force themselves to understand instead of judging . . .

. . . the writer's function is not without arduous duties. By definition, he cannot serve today those who make history; he must serve those who are subject to it. Otherwise he is alone and deprived of his art. All the armies of tyranny with their millions of men cannot people his solitude— even, and especially, if he is willing to fall into step with him. But the silence of an unknown prisoner subjected to humiliations at the other end of the world is enough to tear the writer from exile, at least whenever he manages, amid the privileges of freedom, not to forget that silence but give it voice by means of art.

No one of us is great enough for such a vocation. Yet in all the circumstances of his life, unknown or momentarily famous, bound by tyranny or temporarily free to express himself, the writer can recapture the feeling of a living community that will justify him. But only if he accepts as completely as possible the two trusts that constitute the nobility of his calling: the service of truth and the service of freedom. Because his vocation is to unite the greatest possible number of men, it cannot countenance falsehood and slavery, which breed solitudes wherever they prevail. Whatever our personal frailties may be, the nobility of our calling will always be rooted in two commitments difficult to observe: refusal to lie about what we know and resistance to oppression . . .

Probably every generation sees itself as charged with remaking the world. Mine, however, knows that it will not remake the world. But its task is even greater, for is consists in keeping the world from destroying itself . . .

Truth is mysterious, elusive, ever to be won anew. Liberty is dangerous, as hard to get along with as it is exciting. We must progress toward those two objectives, painfully but resolutely, sure in advance that we shall weaken and flinch on such a long road . . .

. . . I have never been able to forget the sunlight, the delight in life, the freedom in which I grew up. But although that nostalgia explains many of my mistakes and shortcomings, it doubtless helped me to understand my calling, and it helps me to stand implicitly beside all those silent men who, throughout the world, endure the life that has been made for them only because they remember or fleetingly re-experience free moments of happiness.

Reduced in this way to what I am in reality, to my limits and to my liabilities, as well as to my difficult faith, I feel freer to show you in conclusion the extent and generosity of the distinction you have just granted me, freer likewise to tell you that I should like to receive it as a tribute paid to all those who, sharing the same fight, have received no reward, but on the contrary have known only woe and persecution. It remains for me then to thank you from the bottom of my heart and to make you publicly, as a personal token of gratitude, the same age-old promise of allegiance that every true artist, every day, makes to himself in silence.

About the Authors

Isaac Asimov (1920–   ) combines the career of scientist with that of writer. He is a professor of biochemistry at Boston University's Medical School, as well as one of today's leading writers of science fiction. His interest in this type of literature developed at an early age. Later, he was able to pay his way through Columbia University on the proceeds from his own science-fiction writings. He has written more than forty books, half of which are science books for the layman, and the rest science fiction.

Stephen Vincent Benét (1898–1943) began writing in his youth and had already published a volume of verse before he entered Yale. He is equally celebrated as a short story writer and as a poet. His great poem of the Civil War, *John Brown's Body*, won for him a Pulitzer Prize. "The Devil and Daniel Webster" ranks among the all-time favorite American short stories, and has been made into a motion picture, a one-act play, and an opera. In his final years, Benét wrote radio plays on patriotic themes to rally support for America's cause in World War II.

Morley Callaghan (1903–   ) was born in Toronto, Ontario, attended St. Michael's College at the University of Toronto, and was graduated from the Osgood Law School. Between college and law school he worked as a newspaper reporter for the *Toronto Star*. He later visited France at the invitation of Ernest Hemingway, who introduced him to the American writers then living abroad. His first stories were published in Ezra Pound's magazine *The Exile* and *Scribner's Magazine*. Though he continues to devote some of his time to law practice, Mr. Callaghan works steadily at writing stories. He has the distinction of having had his stories published for nine consecutive years in the annual anthology *The Best Short Stories*. His best work to date is the novel *They Shall Inherit the Earth* (1935). He is generally considered one of Canada's best writers of fiction.

Albert Camus (1919–1960) was born in Mondovi, Algeria. The family was very poor, but Camus won a scholarship to secondary school and worked at a variety of jobs to finance his university education. During these years, he played soccer with great enthusiasm He was an actor and playwright, a journalist, essayist, and novelist. Camus was awarded the Nobel Prize for Literature at the age of 44, the second youngest writer ever to have received this honor. (Rudyard Kipling was 43.) His writings reflect his deep concerns about freedom and justice in relation to the daily lives of human beings. He died in an automobile accident.

Anton Chekhov (1860–1904) was born in south Russia, the son of a freed serf. Though he was educated at the University of Moscow to be a physician, he never practiced his profession. He turned instead to writing, and won for himself the reputation of being Russia's foremost writer of short stories. Aside from his great achievement as a writer of short stories, he was also a master dramatist. Among his memorable plays are *The Cherry Orchard, The Sea Gull, Three Sisters,* and *Uncle Vanya.* In recent years, there have been excellent revivals of his plays on Broadway and off-Broadway.

Borden Deal (1922–   ) was born in Mississippi. His first published short story, "Exodus," was reprinted in *The Best American Short Stories 1949* while he was still in college. Since then he has published over a hundred short stories. His novels include, *The Spangled Road, Dragon's Wine, The Insolent Breed, Dunbar's Cove,* and *Walk Through the Valley.* Mr. Deal has been awarded a Guggenheim Fellowship, among other honors. His books have been translated into more than a dozen languages. His work has been adapted for movies, television, radio, and the Broadway stage.

Guy de Maupassant (1850–1893) is the most famous French short-story writer and one of the great short-story writers of all time. Throughout his childhood in Normandy, his short army career, and ten years as a government clerk, he observed closely many types of people, all of whom found a place in his stories. He has an objective way of presenting characters as though he himself were not involved with them. He never passes judgment on them, but lets them reveal themselves through how they act and what they say.

Walter Edmonds (1903–   ), born on a farm near Utica, New York, has used his native state and its early history as the setting for many of his short stories and novels. While studying chemical engineering at Harvard, he began to write stories about the Erie Canal and the Mohawk River region. When one of these stories was published in *Scribner's Magazine*, he decided to make writing his life's work. His first successful novel, *Rome Haul*, deals with the early days of the Erie Canal. It was subsequently dramatized for the stage by Marc Connolly as *The Farmer Takes a Wife*. Edmonds' best known novel is *Drums Along the Mohawk*. His children's book, *The Matchlock Gun*, was awarded the Newberry Medal as the most distinguished contribution to American literature for children in 1942.

Arthur Gordon (1912–   ) is a free-lance writer of both fiction and nonfiction. His books include *Fighters Up* (1945), the story of American fighter pilots in World War II; *Reprisal* (1950), a novel about tragedy at Morgan's Creek; *Norman Vincent Peale, Minister to Millions,* a biography of New York's dynamic preacher; and *Countdown for Decision* (1960), the story of the United States' missile program, which he wrote for Maj. Gen. John B. Medaris.

Shirley Jackson (1919–1965) was one of America's most promising authors before her untimely death at the age of forty-five. A native of California, she lived in Vermont for most of her adult life with her husband and their four children. As a writer, she first drew widespread attention with the publication of "The Lottery" in 1947, and with a collection of her highly imaginative tales in the following year. Subsequently, she published several novels, most notably *The Haunting of Hill House* (1959) and *We Have Always Lived in the Castle* (1962), which were characterized by their skillful fusion of reality and the eerie world of nightmare. In addition to these spine-tinglers, Ms. Jackson also wrote two autobiographical works, in a lighter key.

In *Life Among the Savages* (1953) and *Raising Demons* (1957), she amusingly described life in her own hectic household.

William Melvin Kelley (1937–   ) was born in New York City. He was graduated from Harvard University. Among his numerous awards are the Dana Reed Prize; the Richard and Hinda Rosenthal Award of the National Institute of Arts and Letters; fellowships to the New York Writers' Conference, the Breadloaf Writers' Conference; and a grant from the John Hay Whitney Foundation. His stories and articles have appeared in *The Saturday Evening Post, Esquire, The Negro Digest, The Dial, Mademoiselle,* and other national magazines. His first novel, *A Different Drummer,* has won wide acclaim. He feels that a writer "should depict people, not symbols or ideas disguised as people."

Jim Kjelgaard (1910–1959) grew up on a farm in Tioga County in the Pennsylvania mountain region. It was a wonderful place for a boy because of the abundance of fish and game in the region. Here Kjelgaard acquired his great love of the outdoor life. Many of his books reflect this love of hunting, trapping, and forest lore. It was almost a process of elimination that brought Kjelgaard to writing. Earlier, he had tried his hand as a laborer, a teamster, a factory worker, a plumber's apprentice, and as a surveyor's assistant. Among his books are *Big Red, Red Siege,* and *Forest Patrol.*

John MacDonald (1916–   ) received the Ben Franklin Award in 1955 for the best American story of the year, "The Bear Trap." He has numerous cinema and television credits and has been published widely in major periodicals. He also continues to write novels.

Liam O'Flaherty (1896–   ) was born on the Aran Islands of Ireland. He originally planned to study for the priesthood, but having a change of heart, he entered University College, Dublin. At this time, World War I was in progress, and O'Flaherty decided to leave school and join the Irish Guards. He spent six months on the Western Front, seeing for himself the tragedy of war. At its conclusion,

O'Flaherty embarked on a trip around the world, making his way as a stoker, a deckhand, a beachcomber, and a lumberjack. O'Flaherty writes with a special compassion for the common man, but he is also able to write keen psychological studies of troubled individuals. His great novel, *The Informer*, a highly charged adventure story of Ireland's struggle for independence, has become a film classic.

Edgar Allan Poe (1809–1849) was the first American writer of mystery and adventure tales. He also wrote stories which were solved by clever deduction and which may be considered the first modern detective stories. His poems, like his tales, are about men tortured by nameless fears and longings. Although he is acclaimed today as one of America's great writers, he knew little but failure in his own unhappy lifetime. He parents died when he was a boy. His health was never strong, and he was haunted by deep emotional problems. His love for his young and beautiful wife was the one bright part of his life. But even she died before her time, leaving Poe lonely and helpless. He himself died several years later.

William Saroyan (1908–   ) was born into an Armenian family in California. The people in his family and in the Armenian community in which he grew up are presented in his stories with pride, humor, and sympathy. But while he portrays the distinctive qualities of these Armenian folk, he also writes of the lives and problems of all men. Saroyan began writing at the age of thirteen, and poured out quantities of materials before winning publication. His short story "The Daring Young Man on the Flying Trapeze" brought him fame in 1934. His short stories and novels, particularly *The Human Comedy*, have won him a place in the front rank of American writers. He has written several short plays and full-length dramas. *The Time of Your Life* won the Pulitzer Prize in 1940.

John Steinbeck (1902–   ) sets many of his stories in California, where he was born. During the depression of the 1930's he earned his living at a variety of odd jobs. Packing fruit, carrying a hod, working as a painter and as a reporter, Steinbeck gathered impressions and insights into people that were later to appear throughout his stories and novels. *The Grapes of Wrath*, dealing with migratory workers and their pitiful struggle for survival in the depression years, won the Pulitzer Prize. Many of his emotion-packed stories have been turned into highly successful films and plays.

Jesse Stuart (1907–   ) was born and brought up in the hills of Kentucky. In *The Thread That Runs So True*, he tells of his boyhood and his early days of teaching in the schools of Kentucky and Ohio. Mr. Stuart no longer teaches but spends much of his time in writing stories, poetry, and biography.

James Thurber (1894–1961) was one of America's best known and most loved humorists. In 1927, after working as a journalist in this country and abroad, he joined the staff of *The New Yorker*, a magazine of contemporary wit, humor, and fiction. His first book, written in collaboration with another staff member of the magazine, E. B. White, was a satire on Thurber's favorite subject: the war between the sexes. Illustrated with Thurber's own distinctive drawings, the book was an enormous success. It was quickly followed by a number of articles, essays, short stories, and anthologies, which were at all times permeated by his good humor and his down-to-earth humanism.

Jessamyn West (1907–   ) began writing stories when an attack of tuberculosis confined her to bed for a long period of time. She writes often of Indiana, where she was born, and of California, where she is now living. She knows the Quakers well, and her first book, *The Friendly Persuasion*, consisted of gently humorous sketches of a Quaker family living in Indiana at the time of the Civil War. She has written a number of stories with humor and understanding about Cress Delahanty, portraying the often bewildering experiences of a high school girl.

Glossary of Literary Terms

action: what takes place during the course of a short story.

falling action: See *denouement.*

rising action: the series of incidents that grow out of the problem to be solved and that build up to the climax.

antagonist: the force (usually a person) that opposes the main character (the protagonist) in his attempt to solve a problem and thus to resolve the conflict in which he is involved.

anticlimax: an outcome of a situation of series of events that, by contrast to what was anticipated, is ludicrous or disappointing. The anticlimax can often create a humorous effect.

atmosphere: the over-all feeling of a story, conveyed in large part by the setting and the mood.

character: a person in a work of fiction; sometimes an animal or object.

consistent character: a character whose actions, decisions, attitudes, etc., are in keeping with what the author has led the reader to expect.

dynamic character: a character who changes or develops during the course of a work of fiction.

static character: a character who does *not* change or develop during the course of a work of fiction.

characterization: the portrayal in a story of an imaginary person by what he says or does, by what others say about him or how they react to him, and by what the author reveals directly or through a narrator.

cliché: an expression so often used that it has lost its freshness and effectiveness.

climax: the point of highest interest or dramatic intensity. Usually it marks a turning point in the action, since the reader is no longer in doubt about the outcome.

coincidence: the chance occurrence of two events which take place at the same time.

conflict: the struggle between two opposing forces, ideas, or beliefs which form the basis of the plot. The conflict is resolved when one force—

253

usually the protagonist—succeeds or fails in overcoming the opposing force or gives up trying.

external conflict: a struggle between the protagonist and some outside force.

internal conflict: a struggle between conflicting forces within the heart and mind of the protagonist.

connotation: the implied or suggested meaning of a word or expression.

contrast: the bringing together of ideas, images, or characters to show how they differ.

denotation: the precise, literal meaning of a word or expression.

denouement: the unraveling of the plot, following the climax, in which the writer explains how and why everything turned out as it did. See also *resolution*.

dialect: the speech that is characteristic of a particular region or of a class or group of people.

episode: a related group of incidents, or a major event, that comprises all or part of the main plot or, in a long work, is related to the main plot.

fantasy: a tale involving such unreal characters and improbable events that the reader is not expected to believe it. Some fantasies are intended merely to entertain; others have a serious purpose as well; namely, to poke fun at outmoded customs or at the stupidity of certain people or groups of people.

flashback: a device by which a writer interrupts the main action of a story to recreate a situation or incident of an earlier time as though it were occurring in the present.

foreshadowing: the dropping of important hints by the author to prepare the reader for what is to come and to help him to anticipate the outcome.

idiom: the language or manner of speaking that is typical of a particular region or group of people.

image: a general term for any representation of a particular thing with its attendant and evocative detail. It may be a metaphor, a simile, or a straightforward description. An image may also have a symbolic meaning.

incident: one of the events (usually minor) that make up the total action or plot of a work of fiction.

initial incident: the event in a story that introduces the conflict.

irony: a mode of expression in which the author says one thing and means the opposite. The term also applies to a situation, or to the outcome of an event (or series of events), that is the opposite of what might be expected or considered appropriate.

locale: the particular place in which the action in a work of fiction occurs.

metaphor: a figure of speech in which two things are compared without the use of *like* or *as;* for example, "The fog was a gray veil through which I viewed the city."

mood: the frame of mind or state of feeling created by a piece of writing; for example, the *eerie* mood of a story by Poe.

moral: the lesson taught by a literary work.

narration: an account or story of an event, or series of events, whether true or imaginary.

paradox: a statement which seems on the surface to be contradictory; yet if interpreted figuratively, it involves an element of truth; for example: "The country mobilized for peace."

pathos: that quality in prose that evokes in the reader a feeling of pity and compassion.

plot: the series of events or episodes that make up the action in a work of fiction.

point of view: the method used by the short story writer to tell his story; the position, psychological as well as physical, from which he presents what happens and the characters involved in it.

first-person point of view: the narration of a story by the main character or, possibly, a minor character. As the narrator, he uses the pronoun *I* in referring to himself.

omniscient point of view: the narration of a story as though by an all-knowing observer, who can be in several places at the same time and can see into the hearts and minds of all characters.

omniscient third-person point of view: the narration of a story by an all-knowing observer but limited primarily to what one of the characters (usually the main character) can see, know, hear, or experience.

protagonist: usually the main character, who faces a problem and, in his attempt to solve it, becomes involved in a conflict with an opposing force.

realism: the faithful portrayal of people, scenes, and events as they are, not as the writer would like them to be.

resolution: the events following the climax in a work of fiction; sometimes called the *falling action*.

satire: a piece of writing that criticizes manners, individuals, or political and social institutions by holding them up to ridicule.

sentimentality: a superabundance of emotion in a story.

setting: the time and place in which the events in a work of fiction occur.

simile: a figure of speech in which a comparison is made between two objects essentially unlike but resembling each other in one or more respects. This comparison is always introduced by *like* or *as*; for example, "The moon shone like a silver dollar."

stereotype: a character in a story who is presented according to certain widely accepted ideas of how such a person should look, think, or act; for example, a "good" student wears glasses and is poor at sports.

style: the distinctive manner in which the writer uses language; his choice and arrangement of words.

suspense: a feeling of excitement, curiosity, or expectation about the outcome of a work of fiction.

symbol: an object that stands for, or represents, an idea, belief, superstition, social or political institution, etc.; for example, a pair of scales is often used as a symbol for justice.

theme: the idea, general truth, or commentary on life or people brought out through a story.

tone: the feeling conveyed by the author's attitude toward his subject and the particular way in which he writes about it.

unity: an arrangement of parts or material that will produce a single, harmonious design or effect in a literary work.